Cinema and Its Discontent

ALSO BY ZACHARIAH RUSH

Beyond the Screenplay: A Dialectical Approach to Dramaturgy (McFarland, 2012)

Cinema and Its Discontents

The Dialectical Nature of Character

ZACHARIAH RUSH

McFarland & Company, Inc., Publishers
Jefferson, North Carolina

ISBN (print) 978-0-7864-7538-4
ISBN (ebook) 978-1-4766-2506-5

British Library cataloguing data are available

© 2016 Zachariah Rush. All rights reserved

No part of this book may be reproduced or transmitted in any form or by any means, electronic or mechanical, including photocopying or recording, or by any information storage and retrieval system, without permission in writing from the publisher.

Front cover image of Johnny Depp in *Edward Scissorhands*, 1990 (Twentieth Century Fox/Photofest)

Printed in the United States of America

McFarland & Company, Inc., Publishers
  Box 611, Jefferson, North Carolina 28640
     www.mcfarlandpub.com

To my brown-eyed girls

Anyone who can achieve a unified vision is dialectical and anyone who can't isn't.

—Plato

He exists and understands his human existence only as the dialectical unity of all these opposites. ... this unity of opposites is, and is man's ontological definition and status. Existentially, this unity of opposites is lived as conflict; dialectic is the logical, which is, the universal and necessary, formulation of the truth of human existence in the world.

—Gustav E. Mueller

It is the living and dialectical unity of so many opposites.

—Jean-Paul Sartre

Dialectics, in one form or another, has existed for as long as there have been human beings on this planet. This is because our lives have always involved important elements of change and interaction.

—Bertell Ollman

Table of Contents

Acknowledgments — ix
Preface — 1
Introduction — 3

Part One: The Dialectic 9

1.1 An Abbreviated History of Dialectic — 11
1.2 Dialectic *in principio* — 18
1.3 Speculative Dialectic — 24
1.4 Platonic Dialectic — 34
1.5 Early Christian Dialectic — 40
1.6 Gnostic Dialectic — 44
1.7 Patristic Dialectic — 48
1.8 Augustinian Dialectic — 55
1.9 Cartesian Dialectic — 59
1.10 Pascalian Dialectic — 62
1.11 Kantian Dialectic — 65
1.12 Hegelian Dialectic — 67
1.13 Marxian/Engelian Dialectic — 71
1.14 Nietzschean Dialectic — 75
1.15 Freudian Dialectic — 77
1.16 Twentieth Century Dialectic — 80

Part Two: Of Character 87

2.1 Introduction to Character: The Dialectic of Ethos — 89
2.2 Gypsies, Tramps; Tramps and Thieves — 95

Table of Contents

2.3 Aristos, Scholars and Swans   101
2.4 Freaks, Tycoons and Contenders   109
2.5 Vaudevilleans, Hollywoodians and Magicians   120
2.6 April Lovers, Chanteuses and Writers   129
2.7 Ascetics, Asses and Alters   137
2.8 Politicos, Cabbies and Jedis   146
2.9 Arias and Angels   154
2.10 Edward and Max   160
2.11 Lions, Lightyears and Llamas   165
2.12 Male Models, Machinists and Matrimony   173

Conclusion: Towards a Cinema of Agony   180
Filmography   185
Chapter Notes   189
Bibliography   195
Index   197

Acknowledgments

I would like to thank everybody who made it possible to write and complete this book under the varying circumstances, some of which were not always favorable. Thank you especially to my long-suffering wife who has always supported me and has never doubted my vision even when I doubted myself. Lastly I offer thanks to my daughter who is both beautiful in form and name, and although not yet aware, she was a source of great inspiration as I held her with my left hand and wrote most of this manuscript with my right.

Preface

This book is about *dramatic beings*—or Characters—but it is also a book about *human beings* in the sense that dramatic beings are traditionally considered to be the imitation (sometimes the invention) of human beings. If tragedy is an imitation of human action, as Aristotle posits, then Character must be an imitation—mimesis—of the human. Even a fabulous ass is not portrayed for the sake of being a fabulous ass—*l'âne pour l'âne*—but is anthropomorphized, or endowed with humanity, being the mimesis of the human, for the sake the human.[1]

Our claim is that Characters are dialectical because human beings are dialectical and human beings are, in turn, products of a universe that is dialectical. The best way to understand dramatic characters is to understand dialectic.

An innumerable amount of books have been written offering the mystical keys to great writing, in fact, an entire economy exists on selling the idea of *How to Write This* and *How to Write That* all espousing a particular theory or paradigm, from revealing a hero's "tragic flaw" at "plot point two" to "saving cats" in scene one so as to be more sympathetic; and yet almost all authors express the same idea in their own peculiar way without specifically saying so. For example, Blake Snyder writes, "The perfect hero is the one who offers the most conflict,"[2] and Linda Seger writes, "There is a conflict between the characters that threatens to pull them apart and that provides much of the drama."[3] Both authors without knowing so avow the dialectical nature of Character. And they are not the only authors that do so. The sole purpose of this work is to demonstrate that the essential nature of dramatic characters is dialectical. Therefore we request our readers forget everything they have previously read or heard regarding characters and all that has been taught and published in works of purported theory. If one can purge from one's mind such peculiar notions as "Fake-Opponent Ally" and

Preface

"Threshold Guardians," as well as the often flagrant flirtation with Jungian archetypes then we believe we can offer a simple and sound theory of Character. We believe two things are necessary: Dialectic and Character. Thus the bipartite structure of this book mirrors its twofold purpose.

(1) We set forth an abbreviated history of dialectic to acquaint the unfamiliar reader with the many guises worn by dialectic over time. We aim to establish beyond any reasonable doubt that the nature of the world and the universe is dialectical and to trace the origin of dialectic in Western philosophy, from its emergence in antiquity with the ancients Greeks—where Western dramaturgy also had its birth—through to the twenty-first century.

(2) We will apply dialectical analyses to a number of cinematic characters from a wide variety of narratives: short films, foreign language films, avant-garde films, as well as numerous narratives produced in the Hollywood studio system. Our aim is to demonstrate that the essential nature of *all* dramatic characters is dialectical. In the most engaging characters, as in real life experience, we find the "inexorable entanglement of joy and sorrow, celebration and despair, Eros and Thanatos."[4]

Introduction

In the seventeenth century the English clerical poet John Donne began the last of his *Holy Sonnets* with the following quatrain:

> *Oh, to vex me, contraryes meete in one:*
> *Inconstancy vnnaturally hath begott*
> *A constant habit; that when I would not*
> *I change in vowes, and in devotione.*[1]

Couched within this metaphysical conceit is a serious truth. And although this truth is hued by Donnesque wit it is nevertheless perturbing. The universal nature of this truth and its particular importance to dramatic Character is the subject of this work. What is this truth; and why is it so perturbing?

Simply put it is the vexatious nature of existence. It is consciousness of conflict; it is cognizance of life as a series of struggles: it is the awareness that we often act contrary to how we would like to act. This truth disturbs the speaker of Donne's poem because he finds himself conflicted. He is caught between contrary impulses. In modern parlance we would say that Donne's speaker is stressed out or anxious because he wants to act one way but behaves in a way that is contrary. Such conflict is perturbing because it is inescapable. The "contraryes" mentioned by Donne's speaker are opposite impulses, desires, and courses of action. The speaker in the poem expresses his desire to be faithful or "constant" but at the same time the speaker acknowledges deep within himself the desire to be unfaithful or "inconstant" to his "vowes." When these contraries "meete in one,"—that is to say, when these opposite desires are united in one mind, one heart, one consciousness—as they are with the speaker of the poem—the resulting conflict of opposites is profound vexation. We have entered the arena of dialectic.

The writings of so many poets testify to the vexatious nature of existence. From Homer to Harold Pinter human existence has been depicted as opposite wills, ideologies, desires and values united in perpetual conflict.

Introduction

From Hector battling Achilles to the tense homecoming of Teddy and his wife, Ruth—vexation reigns. That this is true is not as disturbing as its ineluctability. Consider again Donne's speaker. United within the being of the speaker are "constancy" and "inconstancy," or, in modern speech, fidelity and infidelity. One would like to think that this person's desire to be faithful is genuine but in spite of the genuineness of the desire to be faithful Donne's speaker must contend with infidelity in one form or another. The man who swears perforce "I did not have sexual relations with that woman" has already proven unfaithful to his wife. The woman who says "I could never lie to my husband" has already done so countless times. Such is human nature.

We have all experienced such conflict within ourselves and continue to experience it just as we witness it in others. Whenever such opposites as constancy / inconstancy, faithfulness / unfaithfulness, happiness / unhappiness, fulfilled / unfulfilled, etc., are united and engage in an interplay of conflict we call this *dialectic*. When such opposites are grounded in the everyday experience of life and the varied conflicts of *human beings* we can rightly call it an *existential dialectic*. When such opposites are grounded in the experience of drama and the fictional conflict of *dramatic beings* then we can rightly call it a *dramatic dialectic*. For the purpose of this work we set forth this definition: *dialectic is the unity of opposites in conflict*.

Literature is replete with examples of dialectical characters, that is to say, characters which find themselves conflicted between one course of action and another, consciously pushing in one direction while simultaneously being pulled in another, either by external or internal factors. Whether we are considering mythical Mesopotamians like Gilgamesh and Enkidu, Job or Jonah in the Bible, Arjuna in the Bhagavad Gita, the Olympic gods of the Homeric works, the Attic tragedies, the Dialogues of Plato, the poetic works of the anonymous troubadours and Arthurian Romances, Mediaeval "Miracle Plays," the Nordic Sagas, the first modern novels of Cervantes and Daniel Defoe, the plays of Shakespeare, Modernist works by James Joyce and Virginia Woolf, or the latest novel by Thomas Pynchon, we find a mighty host of characters manifesting dialectic—characters in which opposite wills and desires are united in conflict.

William Shakespeare more than any other dramatist in the English language presented us with an array of characters that were written with unparalleled insight into the psychology of conflict. As a brief example we might consider a few lines from Shakespeare's *King Richard II*, lines uttered

Introduction

by King Richard himself in Act III, Scene 3. King Richard is aware of Bolingbroke's designs on his throne and is fully aware that he will not remain as king for much longer. Richard asks himself a series of rhetorical questions:

> What *must* the king do now? *must* he submit?
> The king shall do it: *must* he be deposed?
> The king shall be contented: *must* he lose
> The name of a king? o' God's name let it go.[2]

In this outcry of Richard (emphasis added) one can sense the agony and the conflict—the momentous dialectic—that is, the profound dialectic of the moment. A king such as Richard in the Middle Ages was believed to wield absolute power on earth, as kings believed that they possessed their authority by "divine right," that their throne was ordained by Providence. John Neville Figgis writing of the historical Richard II says that this divine right was "the definite theory of kingship held by King Richard II,"[3] and yet Shakespeare's Richard, under threat of being deposed by Bolingbroke, a mere man, finds himself subject to the most imperative of words—*must*. King Richard *must* and *must not*—opposites united in conflict.

This work does not concern itself with literature and its manifold expressions of dialectical characters; rather we concern ourselves only with the cinema and those characters that belong to the cinematic tradition. To expose the soul of Character and expose its agony, to peer into the conflict that rends in opposite directions a single being is the ultimate aim of drama. This is the type of conflict we are concerned with. In the very best characters of cinema we find this is to be true. And when such characters come to realize the "irreconcilable antagonism" within them their discontent is manifest.[4]

In this work we have chosen a modest cross-section from a vast array of cinematic characters in which we find dialectical conflict, that is to say, dramatic beings that manifest discontent by being torn between opposite desires, goals, moralities, and wills, etc., whose unity of being is perpetually threatened by disunity. This work is confined to the investigation and analysis of characters taken from the world of cinema, from the embryonic days of early twentieth century cinema and silent films to the furthest reaches of twenty-first century world cinema. Some of our discontents are famous, some infamous, and some not so famous, but all are dialectical in nature.

Cinematic characters are legion. In order to reduce this number to a

Introduction

reasonable and manageable degree we have chosen to eliminate any cinematic adaptations of Shakespeare or key characters from his oeuvre. Our focus is on the characters that have arisen both from and for the cinematic art, and so for the remainder of this work we request the reader forgive us the conspicuous absence of Hamlet, Falstaff, Lear, Mr. and Mrs. Macbeth and their beloved companions. The same consideration was made for characters whose names are so well known, studied, and documented from the sphere of classic literature. Such characters as Huckleberry Finn or Tom Sawyer, for example, who have found some species of representation in the cinema, have been omitted. Such internationally renowned characters as Robinson Crusoe, Don Quixote, Sherlock Holmes, Dr. Jekyll and his alter ego Mr. Hyde in any of their various cinematic incarnations are also absent. Other names of fame and familiarity as Sinbad, Tarzan, Count Dracula, Dr. Frankenstein and his monstrous creation have an existence that transcends their literary origins and will always exist as something much more than any cinematic representation can offer—these too are omitted.

Lastly we eliminated all cinematic representations of characters based on, half-based on, or only inspired by real persons. Examples of such films include Waldo Salt and Norman Wexler's *Serpico* (1973), John Riley's *Ghandi* (1982), Jean-Claude Carrière's *Danton* (1983), Jean-Luc Godard's *Je vous salue, Marie* (1985), Susannah Grant's *Erin Brockovich* (2000), John Brownlow's *Sylvia* (2003), Marc Abdelnour and Martin Provost's *Séraphine* (2008), Bruno Dumont's *Camille Claudel* (2013), to name only a few of the many biographical or biopic films that exist. The simple reason for this is that such works adulterate fiction with facts. To dilute the imagination with too much truth would only obfuscate such an inquiry as ours.

It was our purpose to analyze characters written specifically for the cinema, whose first and last breath began and ended with the scenarist and the screenplay. However, doing so was not always easy. A simple survey will reveal that over ninety percent of cinema produced in the English speaking world—primarily the pre-sold franchises of the Hollywood studio system—is based on pre-existing texts such as novels, stories, and stage plays (a more recent trend is the cinematization of graphic novels and comic books). Where we have resorted to the analysis of cinematic characters that *are* derived from a pre-existing text we have erred on the side of unfamiliarity choosing them from the literature of the non-Western canon and the seldom read so as to be as free as possible from prior analytical or critical bias. If

Introduction

such characters are known at all, they are certainly not as familiar as Hamlet, Huck, or Holmes.

The character of Hamlet has over three hundred years of critical writing and analysis devoted to him. Huckleberry Finn has much less. But the characters written for and belonging to the cinema are still being discovered. The oldest character written for the cinema cannot be much more than a century old. It is the aim of this work to shine a little glimmer of light on these as-yet-undiscovered beings, to analyze and explore their driving force—that dialectic is the essential nature of Character.

Part One

The Dialectic

Everything around us can be regarded an example of dialectic.
—Hegel

Dialectical thought is always in the process of extracting from each phenomenon a truth which goes beyond it, waking at each moment our astonishment at the world and at history.
—Maurice Merleau-Ponty

1.1

An Abbreviated History of Dialectic

Dialectic is not a philosophy it is a process. Therefore what follows is not an historical survey of philosophy *per se*, even though much of what we cover is philosophical in nature, rather our aim is to introduce dialectic as a distinct historical process.

It will become evident that dialectic is manifest everywhere: from the microscopic existence of bacteria to the macroscopic scale of planets orbiting within the cosmos, and everything in between; all things can be viewed dialectically as Hegel proclaimed in our epigraph. As a process dialectic has been manifest mostly under the umbrella of philosophy. In fact it was the ancient Greek philosopher Plato that gave dialectic its name. This is not to say that every philosophy is dialectical or every philosopher a dialectician, but every philosopher (poet and playwright also) has at some point in expressing their philosophy had recourse to dialectic. From Anaximander to Žižek dialectic is always at work and this book like everything else is no exception. We do not consider this work to be philosophical in the sense that a treatise might be considered philosophical, this book is first and foremost about dramatic being, or Character; but it does concern itself with a process that is grounded in philosophy and much that lies ahead will rely on what philosophy has to offer.

It seems only prudent to begin with a brief history of dialectic which will transport us back in time almost three millennia to the ancient Greeks. What we propose to do by way of introduction is to survey the prevalence of dialectic from the beginning of philosophy in the Western tradition up to the philosophies of the twentieth and twenty-first centuries. As we have said dialectical discourse is most commonly found among philosophy, but is not exclusive to philosophy, and so throughout we will bring to bear examples from life, history, drama, and literature in order to elucidate and concretize the often obscure and abstract nature of philosophical writing (anyone who has tried reading Hegel or Heidegger for the first time knows how obscure and abstract philosophy can be). The purpose is to set a solid and unshakeable foundation on which we construct our character analyses. Plato said of dialectic: "We have placed dialectic at the top of the other subjects like a coping stone and that no other subject can rightly be placed above it."[1] Like Plato before us we begin now the work of setting our coping stone.

Dialectic can be likened to a thread woven through the length of the Western philosophical tradition. It is incumbent upon to us point out that Eastern philosophical and religious traditions are not without dialectic. For example the *Bhagavad Gita* is a dialectical masterpiece comparable to Plato's great *Dialogues*. Other ancient Sanskrit texts such as the Brahmanical *Upaniṣads* embrace a dialectical conception of the cosmos, often manifest as the soul and body in opposition—the immaterial and the material. The Taoist text *Tao Te Ching* attributed to Lao Tzu is another masterpiece of philosophical poetry that embraces the truth of contradiction. Buddhist sutras juxtapose seemingly contradictory statement as matters for meditational koans. We could also mention the religion of Persian prophet Zoroaster, the heretical Manichaeans, the mystical Sufis, Hindus and Sikhs, as well as many others but to do so would be to write a different book than the one we set out to write. With the exception of a few citations we must confine our history to that of the Western tradition, not only because of consideration of space but because the aesthetic origin of our cinema, as we shall see, belongs to the West.[2]

Dialectic as Anecdote

Without Ariadne's thread the mythological Theseus would have been condemned to wander the labyrinth pursued by the Minotaur; likewise the thread of dialectic has assisted many a philosophical Theseus weave their way through the labyrinth of wonder. One such philosophical Theseus was Plato. In the fourth book of Plato's *Republic* Socrates is in conversation with Glaucon, one of Plato's brothers. During a discussion of appetite and the soul Glaucon relates a curious anecdote about a man named Leontius. The story is very short—only a paragraph—and is sufficiently curious and telling of human nature, both ancient and modern, that we will quote directly from Plato.

1.1 An Abbreviated History of Dialectic

> Leontius, the son of Aglaion, was going up from the Piraeus along the outside of the North Wall when he saw some corpses lying at the executioner's feet. He had an appetite to look at them but at the same time he was disgusted and turned away. For a time he struggled with himself and covered his face, but, finally, overpowered by the appetite, he pushed his eyes wide open and rushed toward the corpses, saying, "Look for yourselves, you evil wretches, take your fill of the beautiful sight!"[3]

Why cite this anecdote? Firstly, if we are to draw any benefit we must assume that Leontius is not insane, that he is as emotionally stable as Socrates or Plato and not the recipient of the god's divine mania—psychosis as we postmoderns are apt to call it. Assuming as we do that Leontius is emotionally sound we are told that Leontius is walking outside the northern wall of Athens where he sees a number of corpses lying at the feet of the executioner. Leontius *wants* to look at the corpses, or as Plato writes, he had an "appetite" or an urge to look at the corpses, but at the same time he was disgusted by the sight, he *does not want* to see such carnage and so he turns away. Leontius is conflicted. Anyone who has driven slowly along the freeway as the blue and red emergency lights bounce off car windshields while paramedics attend to crash victims can relate to Leontius' circumstance: the simultaneous appetite or urge to *look at* and *look away*, *wanting* and *not wanting* to see the mangled bodies. Leontius agonizes with himself—he experiences an internal struggle or "civil war" as Plato calls it.[4] He covers his face to avoid looking at the corpses. This is the dialectic of conscience. Such a gesture is an active suppression of appetite; it is the physical self in conflict with the metaphysical self. In the end what happens? As the story goes Leontius is so overwhelmed by his "appetite" to see the executioner's victims that he forces his eyes to open wider than is natural and rushes bug-eyed toward to corpses.

This is more than just an interesting anecdote: it exemplifies the idea behind this book—it exemplifies dialectic. Leontius' actions, his gestures and psychological tumult, all of which we deduce from the text itself, are an obvious manifestation of dialectic—the unity of opposites in conflict—wanting and not wanting, appetite and suppression of appetite and the resulting agony. Leontius was a *dramatic being* created by Plato and drawn in such a way as to portray something pertaining to *human beings*—some kind of human truth. If a dramatic being like Leontius is dialectical and we accept that dramatic beings are *created by* and are *imitations of* human beings, then surely it follows that human beings too are dialectical? Plato certainly thought so. And if this is so, Leontius can be taken as a *type* of human nature—a kind of everyman—then the "Leontine" dialectic can be viewed as an *existential dialectic*.

All of us experience conflict in one way or another. The art of the artist is conflict. The dance of the dancer is conflict. The drama of the dramatist is conflict. The characters created by the dramatist are by necessity conflicted. This is the primary appeal of narrative. Everyone likes a happy ending, but a happy ending is only satisfactory if it follows conflict. Charles Perrault's Cinderella does not marry her prince until losing her glass slipper and suffering the abuse of her stepsisters. Hans Christian Andersen's Swan is not acknowledged as beautiful until it has been castigated as a loathsome and ugly duckling. In the Grimm story *The Magic Mirror* Snow White is not returned to her original status as princess until she is poisoned and experiences a species of death—safe in the arms of thanatos. Conflict is a necessary step on the road to happiness. Such conflict is an expression of dialectic.

Leontius *wants-to-see* and *wants-not-to-see* the corpses. Leontius *wants opposite* things. Such a unity of opposites in conflict is the essence of dialectic. The inner struggle that pulls Leontius one way and at the same time another continues back-and-forth like a tug-'o'-war until something gives. He is simultaneously repulsed and attracted, he experiences desire and revulsion, both appetite and nausea. To an uninformed observer Leontius might appear sick or even insane. But once we peer beneath the surface—the veneer of normality requisite for civilization to function—what appears at first glance to be an irrational act becomes comprehensible when seen from the viewpoint of dialectic. Once we comprehend the dialectical nature of existence we readily find the complimentary in the contradictory, the point of counterpoint; the sense in nonsense.

The dramatic character Medea from Ovid's *Metamorphoses* provides another dialectical anecdote from antiquity. Ovid completed his version of the myth around A.D. 8, but the story of Medea goes back many centuries prior to the ancient Greeks. Medea's character was well known in antiquity for displaying maternal malfeasance in one particularly brutal act. In Ovid's retelling Medea finds herself in state of conflict. Medea loves her husband, Jason, the famous leader of the Argonauts, but she also hates him because he was unfaithful to her. Naturally Medea wants revenge and avenges herself in the most heinous manner: she murders her own children, annihilating Jason's progeny. The following soliloquy by the Ovidian Medea is translated by seventeenth century Irish poet Nahum Tate.

1.1 An Abbreviated History of Dialectic

> But love, resistless love, my soul invades;
> Discretion this, affection that perswades.
> I see the right, and I approve it too,
> Condemn the wrong—and yet the wrong pursue.[5]

Here Medea is torn between opposite courses of action, the "right" and the "wrong." She is pulled "this" way by "discretion" and "that" way by "affection." She does not want to murder her children for the sake of murdering her children but she does want to hurt Jason. The fact that persuasion is involved implies contrary arguments and deliberation within Medea. Only killing their children will achieve the synthesis sought by Medea. It is by means of destroying that dialectic creates. Of course the particular situation of Medea is vastly different from that of Leontius mentioned above, but the emotional conflict and struggle of being pulled in opposite directions is identical. In a more modern translation of Ovid by Horace Gregory the same passage is translated as follows:

> O if I could, I would,
> But now against my will an unknown power
> Has made me weak: heat sways me one way,
> And my mind another: I see the wiser,
> Yet I take the wrong.[6]

Under the influence of this "unknown power" Medea considers both the right and the wrong course of action. Vacillating between opposites drives the inner conflict pushing Medea further into a state of emotional agony. What happens in the end? Even though Medea is honest with herself in condemning the wrong course of action it is the path of wrongdoing that she pursues. She knows killing her children is wrong but she does it anyway. Approval and disapproval, right and wrong, this way and that: the unity of these opposites within Medea's character creates the dramatic crisis and what follows is the *mythos* or mythological tale. Everything that takes place is the outworking of this "unknown power." Yet, this "unknown power" is perfectly knowable. It is dialectic.

Dialectic is a part of human nature. Dialectic *as* human nature has been replicated, imitated, subjected to artistic mimesis, explored in myth, theatre, fiction, poetry, and with the beginning of the late nineteenth and early twentieth century dialectic has been explored in cinema. Just as Leontius was both repulsed by and attracted to the disgusting beauty of the corpses we find the same conflict of opposites within characters, our friends, even ourselves. Whether we choose the word soul, psyche, ego, self, mind, heart, consciousness, or being, this "entity" that we are is constantly facing conflict, torn between opposite forces, choices, wills, feelings, beliefs, desires, appetites, moralities and so on—this is dialectic.

John Donne whom we cited in our introduction was not the only man of faith to express his spiritual struggle dialectically. The first century Christian evangelizer, Paul of Tarsus, who famously converted from Jewish Pharisaism to Christianity on the road to Damascus, also made public declaration of his own conflict, what he referred to as the "wretchedness" of his condition—the famous "thorn in his side." We read in Paul's letter to the Christians in Rome: "For we know that the law is spiritual: but I am carnal, sold under sin.... O wretched man that I am! ...with the mind I myself serve the law of God; but with the flesh the law of sin."[7]

The unity of opposites is manifest. The juxtaposition of spirit and flesh, the will to practice God's law but the reality of practicing what opposes God's law. Paul confesses to a struggle between opposite forces, the transcendent heavenly rewards of the spiritual man against the immanent earthly pleasures of the carnal or fleshly man. Just like Leontius who was conflicted between looking at and not looking at the corpses and Medea who was conflicted between pursuing right and wrong, Paul too is conflicted. Jesus of Nazareth on the night of his betrayal and execution acknowledged to his sleepy disciples the same dialectical reality: "The spirit indeed *is* willing," he told them, "but the flesh *is* weak."[8] Young Hamlet torn by his love for his murdered father and hatred of his mother cannot decide if he wants to live or die. His most famous phrase is perhaps the most often articulated expression of dialectic in all of Shakespeare: "To be, or not to be."[9] Hamlet simultaneously seeks both life and death but cannot choose and so is incapacitated by agony. Two thousand years after Paul and three hundred years after Hamlet, Sigmund Freud would reiterate the same dialectical nature of man. In the late work *Civilization and Its Discontents*, Freud expresses the universal dialectic of existence as the "irreconcilable antagonism of the primal drives, Eros and death."[10] Again the dialectical unity of opposites is manifest in conflict. Freud's "irreconcilable antagonism," for psychoanalysis at least, proved to be at the core of human behavior, civilization and the general discontent of mankind. The perpetual struggle between opposites is the essence of dialectic and is universal.

Dialectic, like everything else under the sun, is nothing new. It has been expressed in the earliest writings of civilization, in the earliest creation

1.1 An Abbreviated History of Dialectic

myths, in the earliest philosophies, in the earliest poetry, and in the earliest religious texts. Dialectic has continued to be made manifest throughout history and continues to be expressed today. Let us like Theseus follow the thread of dialectic from the very beginning thus firmly setting in place our coping stone like Plato before us.

1.2

Dialectic *in principio*

In principio creavit Deus cælum et terram is the opening line of the Genesis account in St. Jerome's Latin Vulgate. More familiar to most is the English rendering, "In the beginning God made the heaven and the earth." What this opening phrase accomplishes for both theology and cosmogony in the Western tradition is establish a God that created the universe and everything in it at the very beginning of time. But if we look at these words from a dialectical point of view we find the opening line of universal history also sets up a unity of opposites that continue in opposition until now.

The dialectic that we find in the opening words of the Genesis is that of *heaven* (*cælum*) and *earth* (*terram*). Both heaven and earth are as opposed now as they were then, a conclusion that needs no great metaphysical leaps of understanding to achieve; it is rather obvious to everybody. According to Genesis the two realms were established simultaneously—"in the beginning," thus both heaven and earth share a species of unity despite difference. In the great cosmic event that saw heaven and earth derive from God's being out came opposites and to this day heaven and earth remain united in opposition. Heaven is invisible, intangible, ethereal, airy, the spiritual realm where immaterial beings dwell in eternity. The earth, on the contrary, is visible, tangible, solid, gravid, a material realm, a space for flesh and blood beings whose existence is finite—clearly opposite spheres of existence. In one of the most famous opening sentences from one of world's most famous books we find testimony to the process and existence of dialectic. *In the beginning was dialectic…*

The Mosaic account of creation is not the only creation account that manifests dialectic. In the period that saw the rise of Higher Civilizations, like the Sumerians on the plains of Mesopotamia, creation accounts and epics were recorded in hieroglyphs and in cuneiform script in which we find expressions of dialectic. Such civilizations, as best as scholars can

1.2 Dialectic in principio

adduce, conceived of existence as a unity of forces in opposition. One such grand unity of opposites was that of the Cosmos and the Individual, that is, the whole universe or the macrocosm and the individual ego or microcosm. The sacred meeting place for two such states of opposition—the macrocosm and the microcosm—was the *mesocosm* or middle world, and the most sacred place for such early civilizations to witness the meeting of two opposites was the summit of the sacred ziggurat.[1]

What began as a simple raised platform developed into the prototype of the pyramids that still stand today in some parts of Central America, China and Egypt. This sacred point of contact between the earthly and the heavenly was a point of synthesis, a place of union between the universal forces in opposition and, as Joseph Campbell suggests, was the place where the ultimate union of physical opposites took place between a king and his queen-consort—copulation between the sexes.[2] In that sacred moment man merges with woman, woman merges with man, until there is no longer male and female, there is no longer differentiation between self and other; and yet, despite being opposites neither the self nor the other are entirely negated or cancelled out. They are *sublated* and only One Being remains, a higher form of being—a synthesis.[3] In many early societies the most sacred unity of opposites was male and female, and the most sacred act of all was copulation. By means of this rite the cosmos was regenerated, man and the universe were reconciled, and in the minds of these early agricultural societies the gods were appeased and another bountiful harvest was assured.

The copulative dialectic emerged in many ancient civilizations as the sustaining power of the universe and is prevalent in many creation stories from around the world. In fact there is scarcely a creation myth we have studied that does not in some way manifest some form of dialectic. We do not have the space to examine myth and the dialectic of myth but what emerges almost universally is the conflict of opposite elements that at some later stage are synthesized into a unity somewhat higher or greater than the initial divided elements.

In *Creation Myths of the World*, a compendium of various creation myths, David A. Leemings writes:

> In our post–Freudian age few people would suggest that dreams are simply untrue stories unworthy of examination.... If we see myths as cultural dreams, we naturally take them seriously as sources of information about the inner workings—the collective psyche—of the culture in question and, by extension and comparison, about the psyche of the human species as a whole.[4]

Part One. The Dialectic

The prevalence of dialectic—the unity of opposites—in ancient legends and creation myths necessarily leads to the question of dialectic and what its influence has been on the "psyche of the human species" or what Carl Gustav Jung called "the collective unconscious"—the rich storehouse of wisdom and symbolism that transcends human consciousness but which all human consciousnesses can tap into—like downloading data from cloud storage. For Jung the collective unconscious contained the countless ideas that have been "stamped on the human brain for aeons" and which "lie ready to hand in the unconscious of everyman."[5] If we can accept that a myth is a "cultural dream" and can accept that these myths or "cultural dreams" are subject to, and part of, the dialectical process then it is no mere syllogism to conclude that dialectic is an essential part of our *cultural processes* (Karl Marx and Vladimir Lenin were convinced that dialectic was a cultural and historical process). If we can accept that cultural processes are dialectical then we must accept that certain creative spheres of culture such as art, the artist, and such artistic concepts such as Character, Plot, Narrative, etc., must also be dialectical.

In the introduction to *Before Philosophy: The Intellectual Adventure of Ancient Man*, H. and H. A. Frankfort, along with their contributors, unconsciously allude to dialectic as the fundament for understanding ancient myth and its invention.

> In telling such a myth, the ancients did not intend to provide entertainment. Neither did they seek, in a detached way and without ulterior motives, for intelligible explanations of the natural phenomena. They were recounting events in which they were involved to the extent of their very existence. They experienced, directly, a conflict of powers, one hostile to the harvest upon which they depended, the other frightening but beneficial: the thunderstorm reprieved them in the nick of time by defeating and utterly destroying the drought.[6]

The purpose of *mythos* for the ancients was not to supply material for fables or stories for moralistic or entertainment purposes, rather *mythos* developed as a way of coming to terms with the dialectical nature of the world, it was a groping for understanding when faced with the ferocity and felicitousness of Mother Nature. The same sun withers that which it does not nurture. In the human sphere we find the relationship between the individual and everything but the individual becomes dialectical, what Frankfort, et al., refer to as the "I-and-Thou" dialectic.[7] The self is dialectically related to everything that is not-the-self, just as we are related to everything that we are not. In the same way a cat is related to every other cat in the world by

1.2 *Dialectic* in principio

being the cat it is and not being every other cat in the world. This is a dialectical relation. In terms of myth, when we are confronted by the conflict between the primitive "I" and the "Thou," the Self and Other, a cultural hero and natural forces such as lightning and tempest, Hercules and the Hydra, this mythological conflict is dialectical—*the unity of opposites*—and it remains central to dramatic narratives to this day. To speak of man-versus-nature or man-versus-man in terms of plot is to speak of dialectic.

In ancient Egyptian theories of cosmogony—of which there are numerous and contradictory versions depending upon the dominant religious center (there was an opposition between Upper and Lower Egypt)—we find similar unities of opposites. That which is most common is often what is most pertinent; and what is most pertinent is dialectic. For the ancient Egyptian the sun god dies with each sunset and is reborn with each dawn or sunrise. The sun as a personified deity lives by day passing through the arch of the sky and after falling below the horizon at sunset spends each night in the underworld waters of Nun.[8] It is a simple and poetic picture of natural processes and again we see the inexorable unity of life and death each giving way to the other at the appointed time. Death without life is as inconceivable as life without death. The living sun above is unified with the dead sun below; that which is light enters into darkness and that which is dark contains that which is light (the similarity to the Taoist yin-yang dialectic is noteworthy). These opposites are unified in Egyptian cosmogony and principal mythologies. Egyptian existence was understood dialectically even if the concept of dialectic not fully available to them.

Similarly on the plains of Mesopotamia where the great Babylonian Empire arose we find one of the oldest creation myths—the *Enuma elish*, an account that antedates Moses' writing of Genesis by a thousand years. The very beginning of the *Enuma elish* begins with a unity of opposites—the *salt waters* of Tiamat combine with the *fresh waters* of Apsu and the union of these opposites brings forth the twin sibling gods Lahmu and Lahamu. The identity and function of the twins Lahmu and Lahamu are not altogether clear but their incestuous union of opposites—the copulative dialectic of brother and sister—brought forth the sibling gods Anshar and Kishar. Anshar and Kishar's incestuous dialectic brought into being the all important Anu, the supreme Mesopotamian sky god.[9] In the beginning we have dialectic: the opposites of freshwater commingling with saltwater then the union of male and female deities and after two generations of Caunian union we reach a final synthesis—the supreme deity of the Mesopotamian pantheon.

The same Babylonian creation myth also tells us that the great mother goddess Tiamat, after giving birth to Marduk and creating an army of demons, changed herself into a serpentine monster or dragon. Marduk, the son, rebelled against his mother and slew the dragon goddess. We read in the *Enuma elish* that Marduk cuts his mother Tiamat into two pieces, like a bivalve shellfish, one part he threw into the air which became heaven, the other half he used to form the earth.[10] Here we have the same unity of opposites that began the Mosaic account—*In the beginning God made the heavens and the earth.* The creation of heaven and earth, the upper and lower, the spiritual and material, derives from an initial state of unity that is sundered by violence in the Babylonian epic; and these opposites remain united in a state of irreconcilable conflict. Unity brings forth separation: separation brings forth unity—this is the key to understanding dialectic.

The ancient Akkadian poem *Epic of Gilgamesh*, also from Mesopotamia, begins with the principal character Gilgamesh who meets his opposite self or alter ego, Enkidu. The two men represent opposite states of being. Gilgamesh is from the civilized city of Uruk where he is a leader of men while Enkidu is an uncultivated Chewbacca creature grazing on grass and galloping with gazelles. Enkidu is innocent of sensual pleasures, whereas Gilgamesh is a brutish rapist. In time the two opponents are brought together in violence but neither Gilgamesh nor Enkidu are destroyed, they are sublated (as opposed to being negated), and become united in loyal friendship. Also, further on in the *Gilgamesh* epic, on the tenth tablet we get a glimpse of "the great gods" known as the Anunnaki. There is no indication as to how many gods belong to the Anunnaki but the poem is clear that they are the ones responsible for establishing "both Death and Life," two of the most intractable and united opposites.[11]

We have by no means exhausted the vast library of creation myths that have been collected by anthropologists nor was it our intention to do so, rather our intention was to examine some of the more accessible myths in order to demonstrate the dialectical nature of primitive beliefs and to highlight the prevalence of dialectic at a time when dialectic had not yet been consciously conceived *as dialectic* but was still recognized in natural phenomena as opposites united in conflict.

Gravity has always exerted its influence. It was only brought into con-

1.2 *Dialectic* in principio

sciousness when Sir Isaac Newton gave it its name. When Icarus first fell from the sky his descent was attributed to folly and hubris—his waxen wings flying too close to the sun—but it was only after the science of Newton that we understood Icarus had fallen prey to gravity. Similarly dialectic has been exerting its influence from time immemorial. The early poets of myth in trying to comprehend the opposition of natural phenomena did not have recourse to the concept of dialectic just as they did not have recourse to the concept of gravity, but the effects of both have been observed and recounted in cosmogonies and mythologies the world over. In the second part of this work our aim is to demonstrate dialectic as something approaching narrative gravity.

Before closing this section on mythology it is worth noting the etymology of the word "mythology" because the word itself conceals in plain sight an etymological dialectic. The Greek word *mythos* or *muthos* (μυθος) can mean several things including "tale," "story," "fiction," "plot," etc., and as such is opposed to the Greek *logos* (λογος) which can mean among numerous things "reasoned account," "serious study," even "truth" or "word." Such is the opposition between *mythos* (μυθος) and *logos* (λογος), between fictions and non-fictions, and yet despite this fundamental opposition neither *mythos* (μυθος) nor *logos* (λογος) are negated but the two are unified into a synthesis (μυθος / λογος)—the study or discipline of mythology—the truth of fiction and the fiction of truth. True falsehoods and false truths are brought together in the primitive mind to make sense of the world. Mythology bears witness to itself as a unity of opposites, to its own dialectical nature. Mythology is dialectical.

Dialectic, like everything else under the sun, is nothing new. It has always existed but it required a certain comprehension to bring it out of the primitive mythopoeic consciousness and into the rational consciousness of the proto-scientific mind. This new type of comprehension first appears with the speculative thought of the earliest Greek philosophers, commonly referred to as the presocratic philosophers. It is to philosophy that we now turn.

1.3

Speculative Dialectic

The advent of speculative thought saw rapid development in the Ionian city of Miletus, Asia Minor (part of modern day Turkey) with the emergence of the presocratic philosophers (so-called because they flourished before Socrates, or pre–Socrates, 470/469–399 BC). Three preeminent philosophers were Thales who achieved stardom for predicting an eclipse and cornering the market in olive oil production; Anaxagoras who brought philosophy to the city of Athens and identified the Milky Way as a concentration of stars; and Anaximander who was the first cartographer of the Mediterranean and an early proponent of evolution conjecturing that early humans were gestated inside fish and spat out on the beach when born.

All three thinkers challenged the established mythos, particularly by questioning the two pillars of Hellenic mythos—Homer and Hesiod—by seeking a more scientific explanation for the wide variety of natural phenomena rather than believe in tales of gods and goddesses. To the Presocratics the idea of deities seemed less rational, less subject to empirical investigation; so too did the chaos cosmogonies in the poetry of Hesiod and Homer: although, at the time in which they lived, to deny outright the ruling hand of the gods could result in exile or death. Anaxagoras was, in fact, exiled for impiety late in his life. The gods may not be real but it was best not to offend them. Thales is often quoted as saying, "All things are full of gods," while Pythagoras (after whom the theorem is named) considered himself to be a god when he wasn't living underground, but it was Socrates who would pay the highest price in 399 BC when sentenced to death by an Athenian court on charges of impiety.

What set the presocratics apart from their predecessors was their curiosity and willingness to look beneath the surface of phenomena for first causes and principles in nature itself and not in deities. John Burnet in *Early Greek Philosophy* writes:

1.3 Speculative Dialectic

> The earliest cosmologists could find no satisfaction in the view of the world as a perpetual contest between opposites. They felt that these must somehow have a common ground, from which they had issued and to which they must return once more. They were in search of something more primary than the opposites, something which persisted through all change, and ceased to exist in one form only to reappear in another.[1]

This common ground or *unity* is what Hegel later termed the *Absolute* in his philosophy. It is the state of *synthesis* in which opposed elements of *thesis* and *antithesis* exist in an elevated state of being. The presocratics like the early mythopoeics—the Sumerian or Akkadian mythmakers, for example—acknowledged the unity of opposite forces in nature, but rather than attribute such forces to the jealousies of Hera and cantankerousness of Zeus, the presocratics sought the very origin of the opposites, the initial state from which the opposites emerged. It was in the search for the ultimate and absolute unity that the cosmogonies and mythopoeic works subsided and the first scientists and physicists emerged who would also be the first group to be identified as philosophers.

First among these early speculative philosophers is Thales of Miletus (c. 624–546 BC). Thales achieved notoriety even in antiquity for predicting a solar eclipse that took place in 585/584 BC. Owing to descriptions of him in doxographers like Diogenes Lærtius; Thales appears as the archetype of the absent-minded professor. One amusing anecdote relates how Thales fell into a well while staring at the stars only to be chastised by a child for having his head in the heavens but not watching where his feet were going. The story is charming although it is almost certainly apocryphal. Burnet states in the citation above that these early philosophers were searching for "something more primary than the opposites," and for Thales that primary thing or first principle—in Greek, *arche* ($\alpha\rho\chi\eta$)—was water. Water was the ultimate and *permanent* stuff from which all other *impermanent* stuff derives. In searching for this first principle Thales was searching for a unity, something that was capable of containing and producing all things, both *existent* and *inexistent*; those things that *actually* exist and those things that had the *potential* to exist.

All we know about Thales is reported to us by ancient writers such as Herodotus, Aristotle and other doxographers who, like Diogenes Lærtius mentioned above, compiled and quoted ancient sources either for the purpose of refutation or preservation. Thales no doubt saw that land sat on top of the oceans and it was known to him that fossils of sea creatures had been discovered upon mountain tops which might have, quite naturally, led him to the conclusion that water had at one time flooded the earth—flood and deluge myths are widespread and almost universal among ancient cultures—or perhaps he agreed with Hesiod that the original state of the earth was a swathing mass of water in the timeless past. Certainly his cosmology was influenced by his travels in Egypt where he witnessed the seasonal inundation of the River Nile, without which life along its banks would be impossible to sustain. Even Aristotle noted that most living things seem to contain some moisture, thus he speculated that Thales before him had arrived at a similar conclusion, "water is the origin of the nature of moist things."[2]

But the idea of water is not so absurd. After all if we consider tidal motion: the ebb and flow of tides, the back and forth motion of the seas and oceans, flux this way and that. These are movements that unify opposites. Water evaporates and precipitates—what goes up to form clouds must come down as rain—this is also dialectical. Thales' aquatic philosophy ultimately sets water as *that-which-causes* therefore whatever is *not water* must be *that-which-is-caused*—the effect: unity of opposites. Thales never developed his dialectic beyond a qualitative series of changes but we can ascertain a proto-dialectic—an early groping for unity in opposites and in this Thales took the first step toward dialectical philosophy.

The first recognizably dialectical philosophy was developed by another Milesian, Anaximander (c. 610–546 BC). Anaximander was the first Western thinker with whom dialectic "clearly appears" as we might recognize it today.[3] Anaximander went beyond the aquatic theory of Thales. He observed that soft things like feathers and grass are opposed to hard things like rocks and tree trunks and that hot substances like fire had opposites such as cold water. Clearly Anaximander was not the first person to notice the soft properties of feathers but he was the first philosopher—certainly in the Western philosophical tradition—to build a theory of existence based on mutual opposition, and as Anaximander's theory developed he progressed from feathers and rocks to speculating about the properties of stars and the visible planets, the cosmos and everything contained within it.

Anaximander put forward the idea of the *apeiron* ($\tau o\ \alpha \pi \varepsilon \iota \rho o \nu$) usually translated as the "boundless," "unlimited," or "infinite." Anaximander's *apeiron* contains within it all that *comes to be* and all that *ceases to be*. The *apeiron* is the absolute unity of all possible opposites, it contains *all that is* and *all that is not*: life and death, material and immaterial, time and timelessness,

1.3 Speculative Dialectic

space and spacelessness, being and nothingness—all things and their negations. All possible existences and all possible inexistences belongs somewhere within Anaximander's *apeiron*.

Thales sought for first principles in water, Anaximander conceived of the boundless *apeiron*, but another Milesian, Anaximenes (c. 585–528 BC) considered air, in Greek *aera* (αερα), to be the first principle. Like Anaximander's *apeiron* Anaximenes' *aera* is an infinite and absolute substance containing and unifying all opposites. By means of *aera* all things undergo qualitative change either by condensation or rarefaction (opposite processes such as the cooling of water (into ice) and the heating of water (into steam) for example). For Anaximenes, *aera* when condensed becomes solid forming the earth and when *aera* is rarefied it is far less dense becoming fire—a substance lacking solidity. As an experiment we may pass our hand through a flame but not through a rock, and yet both the rock and fire are substantively identical, sharing substance with the *aera*. Because the *aera* undergoes degrees of qualitative change—a key dialectical process—substances such as rock and flames are manifest as opposites. Condensation and rarefaction of the same substance are processes that produce opposites or different states of the same substance. For Anaximenes these qualitative changes of *aera* bring all things into being, from the smallest grain of sand to the largest stellar body.

Xenophanes (c. 570–475 BC) was a philosopher poet from the city of Colophon. Xenophanes was something of an atheist who considered the anthropomorphic gods of Homer and Hesiod an affront to mankind. Because the gods are pernicious and vicious in nature Xenophanes concluded that they were almost certainly made in man's image because man himself is pernicious and steeped in vice. Homer's Zeus resembled men and behaved like men because he was created by men. To prove his point Xenophanes famously stated that if cows were idolatrous and had hands their gods they would be shaped like cows and behave like cows—bovinely divine.

But Xenophanes' dialectical approach to knowledge is of far more importance than his Momusesque antitheism. Xenophanes concerned himself as most skeptics do with the question of knowledge: what can truly and irrefutably be known? Of what can we be absolutely certain? In terms of dialectic, what is *known* is opposed or contrary to what is *not-known*. The known is knowledge that we have in possession, the not-known is knowledge that exists that we do not possess. Known knowledge is opposed to unknown knowledge—*gnosis* is opposed to *agnosis*. The opposites share a relation, a unity of separation. This dialectic is the sphere of skepticism. Xenophanes died before he could reconcile knowledge but his dialectical epistemology raised important questions that were taken up by Plato and Immanuel Kant two thousand years later.

Zeno of Elea (c. 490–c. 430 BC) is renowned for his dialectical paradoxes. Aristotle summarizes them in a long passage in the *Physics* in which he argues against the fallacious logic of Zeno. The passage is well worth reading but will not be quoted here.[4] Zeno's paradoxes demonstrate that one thing can, at the same time, be considered its opposite. For example, whatever is considered *motion* can at the same time be considered rest, non-motion or *immotion*; that whatever can be considered *infinite* when looked at dialectically can be viewed as it opposite *finite*. As illogical as it sounds whatever is *up* can also be considered *down* and vice versa.

Zeno's most famous paradox is the foot race between Achilles and a tortoise. Because the tortoise is a small cold-blooded reptile it is given the advantage of a head start. The race begins and the tortoise sets off. Achilles patiently waits for his turn to start. Because Achilles is the "swift-footed" demigod it takes very little time before he halves the distance between himself and the tortoise, but in the short time it take Achilles to halve the distance between himself and the tortoise the tortoise has made slow and steady progress. Achilles still running in pursuit halves the distance between himself and the tortoise again, but in the intervening period the tortoise has made a little more progress. "Swift-footed" Achilles continues running and again halves the distance between himself and the tortoise but once more the tortoise has made just a little more progress. And so each time Achilles halves the distance between himself and the tortoise the tortoise has progressed just that little bit extra forcing Achilles to play catch-up indefinitely. Theoretically, in a race that never ends, "swift-footed" Achilles will always be chasing the tortoise. Even though the distance between the tortoise and Achilles is finite, Achilles must traverse an infinite number of finite steps, thus Achilles will never catch the tortoise. It sounds illogical but Zeno's point is dialectical. A finite distance can be understood as an infinite number of smaller distances—in dialectical terms *that which is finite* is also *that which is infinite*.

Another equally famous paradox is sometimes called the Paradox of Motion and has direct links to early Zoetropes and Kinematescopes—the origin of motion pictures and the cinema. Zeno says an archer shoots an arrow at a target. The arrow is in flight heading towards the target. Zeno then points out, and correctly, that at any point during the arrow's flight the arrow must occupy some space in time, this is necessary given the laws of physics. Zeno then raises an intriguing question: If an arrow is occupying a specific place at a specific time then it must be at rest, but if the arrow is at rest then how can the same arrow be in flight? Rest and motion are opposites, so how can this be? Further, the arrow eventually hits the target so we must conclude that the arrow has been in motion, but we must also acknowledge that the arrow has occupied some point in space and time along its flight. It must follow then that movement consists of points of rest. But this appears to be an absurdity, an irreconcilable antagonism. Not according to Zeno, because Zeno understands *motion as immotion, immotion as motion*: motion can only be understood as a contradiction. Motion is dialectical—a unity of opposites.

Around the same time there appeared from the thriving metropolis of Ephesus the most dialectic of presocratic thinkers: his name was Heraclitus (c. 535–475 BC). We are fortunate in that some of what Heraclitus wrote still survives, albeit in fragmentary form, but the essence of his thought and his dialectical worldview are very much in evidence. Although Aristotle gave Zeno of Elea the credit of being the first dialectician, it is almost certain that Heraclitus can be considered the first in a long line of dialecticians. Heraclitus is renowned for his contradictory aphorisms and was much admired by Friedrich Nietzsche who ranked Heraclitus among the class of "royal and magnificent hermits."

Heraclitus' aphorisms are patently dialectical. He frequently unifies contraries in seemingly paradoxical and insoluble riddles. One of Heraclitus' most famous aphorisms states: "You cannot step into the same river twice."[5] Common sense is at first indignant at such a statement retorting, "Of course we can, we can step into a river twice. I have done it with the Thames, the Seine, and the Mississippi and these same rivers remain." But Heraclitus' point was that all things are in flux, forever changing. Consider the water molecules that belong to any given river. They are interrupted when we step into it—they are here now passing over one's foot and then gone forever: it is an unrepeatable experience. The next time we step into the *same* river the water molecules will be *different*. Fresh water continues to flow and once flown over our foot is gone: hence the same river is *not* the same river.

Part One. The Dialectic

Many other aphorisms of Heraclitus are preserved in Aristotle, Sextus Empiricus, Hippolytus, Diogenes Lærtius, and Stobæus, et al. The few examples below ought to demonstrate sufficiently the dialectical nature of Heraclitus' thought and the frequent juxtaposition of opposites in unity:

(a) *Fire is want and surfeit.*
(b) *Fire lives the death of air, and air lives the death of fire; water lives the death of earth, earth that of water.*
(c) *God is day and night, winter and summer, war and peace, surfeit and hunger;*
(d) *Cold things become warm, and what is warm cools; what is wet dries, and the parched is moistened.*
(e) *You cannot step twice into the same rivers; for fresh waters are ever flowing in upon you.*
(f) *It is the opposite which is good for us.*
(g) *Good and ill are one.*
(h) *Mortals are immortals and immortals are mortals, the one living the others' death and dying the others' life.*[6]

Heraclitus took note of the world around him and observed the constant conflict of opposites, some of which are mundane like cold and hot water, others of which were supramundane like the celestial bodies, all of which consisted of conflicting opposites necessary for the creation and existence of the universe. Heraclitus' fragmentary philosophy is clearly an expression of existence as dialectical. Although Heraclitus, like the philosophers before him, did not have recourse to the word dialectic he knew the reality of phenomena as it appears; a reality of contraries and opposites in unity. Heraclitus thoroughly understood dialectic.

Another glowing figure from the presocratic age is the infamous Empedocles (c. 490–430 BC). According to legend Empedocles sought to prove his immortality by jumping into the volcanic mouth of Mount Etna. Empedocles never appeared again, as he said he would, but one of his sandals was said to have been spat out.

Like Heraclitus, who posited that opposites in unity created and maintained balance in the cosmos, Empedocles conceived of two creating and sustaining principles: Love or *Philotes* (Φιλοτες) and Strife or *Neikos* (Νεικος). Empedocles saw the cosmos as the perpetual battleground between Love and Strife, one pulls apart and the other brings together, one

1.3 Speculative Dialectic

is the solution of all things the other the dissolution of all things. Empedocles' dialectic will find a twentieth century correlative in the later works of Sigmund Freud whose opposites, Eros and Death—the promoter of life and the destroyer of life—are the fundamental opposites underlying human civilization. Like many of the presocratics some of what Empedocles wrote still survives and these extant fragments provide us with a glimpse into Empedocles' personal expression of dialectic the fundamental principle of which is warring opposites; each taking their moment of dominance before subsiding and becoming subservient.

One of the most significant fragments is preserved by Simplicius. It is noteworthy how many pairs of opposites Empedocles strings together as he constructs his cosmology:

> A double tale I will tell: at one time it grew to be one only from many, at another it divided again to be many from one, fire and water and earth and the vast height of air, dread Strife too, apart from these, everywhere equally balanced, and Love in their midst, equal in length and breadth... there are these things alone, and running through one another they become now this and now that and yet remain as ever as they are.[7]

One and many, earth and air, fire and water the basic elemental opposites all under the governorship of Love. Love rules until Strife takes over and then at the appointed time Strife ceases to rule as Love takes over once more. Kirk and Raven summarize Empedocles' dialectical conception of the cosmos: "Two polar stages represented by the rule of Love and the rule of Strife, and two transitional stages, one from the rule of Love towards the rule of Strife, and the other back again from the rule of Strife towards the rule of Love."[8]

Heraclitus had previously claimed that all things are in flux. Likewise the universe in Empedocles' dialectic is always in flux between Love and Strife, but this movement is what keeps the cosmos alive, the tension is what energizes the *coming to be*, and only an act of *ceasing to be* can provide the momentum for another's coming. Empedocles thoroughly embraced dialectic. The images used by Empedocles resemble a cosmological drama played out on a universal stage with two great characters embraced in a struggle for life.

Another philosophical movement, and the last we will briefly present here, bridges the Presocratic thinkers with the lifetime of Socrates. This philosophical worldview arose around two philosophers, Leucippus (fl. 5th

Part One. The Dialectic

Century BC) and Democritus (c. 460–370 BC). The philosophy of these two philosopher was later called atomism from the belief held by Democritus and Leucippus that all things were made of tiny particles they called atoms (from the Greek ατομος, *atomos*, "indivisible," "not cuttable," "uncuttable,") Leucippus, who was possibly a Milesian by birth, and Democritus who derived from Abdera, considered the whole universe to be divided into opposite states of being. One half of all that exists in the universe is made of atoms or stuff, and the other half is nothing but void, or non-atoms. Aristotle summarized the philosophy of the Atomists in a manner that ought to be recognizable as dialectical:

> Leucippus and his associate Democritus say that *full* and the *empty* are the elements, calling the one *being* and the other *non-being*—the *full* and the solid being *being*, the *empty non-being* (whence they say *being* no more is than *non-being*, because *solid* no more is than *empty*) [italics added].[9]

Leucippus and Democritus viewed all things in the universe as being made up of opposites. Aristotle strings several of these opposite elements together in his critique: the *full*, the *solid*, the *being* (*atoms*) and the *non-being* (*void*). The dialectical nature of existence is made up of these two elements—*atom* and *void*—and both are as necessary as the other. The unity of opposites is similar in expression to Heraclitus and Empedocles as we have seen. While Leucippus and Democritus' theory sounds much more scientific and plausible to a post-quantum theory civilization than the mystical forces of Love and Strife, the ancient theory of atoms was little different to the competing cosmologies of their predecessor in that they reduced all existence to a dialectal unity of opposites. The force remains only the names change.

In his book *God and the Atom*, author Victor J. Stenger attempts to link the proto-atomic theory of Leucippus and Democritus with Quantum theory that emerged at the beginning of the twentieth century. Stenger's book is somewhat tendentious but reveals that even today the structure of the universe—at least as far as particle physicists are concerned—"atoms and void is all there is."[10] This is the same dialectical construct of opposites that the early Greek atomists suggested over two thousand years ago. With advancements in technology physicists have manage to *cut* the *uncuttable* atom and have revealed that within the atom itself is a juxtaposition of subatomic particles arranged into opposites—the negatively charged electron and the positively charged proton (as well as opposite particles: the negative proton or "antiproton" and the positive electron or "anti-electron," better known as positron). Whether we are viewing the world through the eyes of Democritus or Erwin Schrödinger the universe and everything in it appears to be a unity of opposite elements—early atomism is as dialectical as quantum theory.

Thus far we have witnessed the emergence of science and philosophy from primitive religious belief and various attendant mythologies and yet we traced the thread of dialectic running through both. The rational philosopher and the mythopoeic religionist are both conscious on some level of a unity of opposites that lies at the source of all existence. It is clear from what we have read that the concept of dialectic existed for the presocratic thinkers even if the word itself was not yet utilized in discourse. But now we have arrived at a time in Greek philosophy that represents its acme and the mind of one particular philosopher who produced the ultimate synthesis of ancient thought into a dialectic that would go on to influence the rest of Western philosophy for the next two thousand years. This dialectical mind belonged to Plato.

1.4

Platonic Dialectic

Over a period of two centuries presocratic philosophers made attempts at understanding the cosmos from a more scientific aspect. From Anaximenes' *apeiron* and Heraclitus' world in flux, to the constant conflict of Empedocles' Love and Strife and the Atomists' atom and void, the structure and sustaining activity of the cosmos appeared to be governed by opposite elements in conflict. Into this intellectual milieu, and under the mentorship of Socrates (notwithstanding a few mystical influences), appeared the broad mind of Plato (427–347 BC).

This section is not a treatise on Plato or Platonic dialectic which would require a book length treatment of its own. Rather, in the following section our aim is to examine a handful of extracts taken from a selection of Plato's most famous texts with the purpose of highlighting dialectic, dialectic that will be of use later in this work and which we hope to bring to bear on our analyses of Character. The sole purpose of this abbreviated history is to give the reader as firm a footing as possible on the sometimes stable sometimes friable ground of dialectic.

We quoted Plato earlier concerning dialectic and its importance to his philosophy. It can do no harm to reiterate its importance to our work. "We've placed dialectic at the top of the other subjects like a coping stone and that no other subject can rightly be placed above it."[1] A coping stone is a structural necessity. It is indispensable if the bridging arms of an arch are to remain in place and if it is to support any planned construction above. It serves like a foundation. Without a foundation one may as well build on a sandy ground. For Plato dialectic was as necessary as it was indispensable. Likewise, our survey of cinematic characters finds dialectic equally indispensable and necessary. What follows are several examples of dialectic in the dialogues of Plato. Sometimes dialectic is used as an illustration, other times it is a pattern of discourse used by Socrates, still other examples are explicit references to dialectic as a process. Plato's work is suffused with dialectic and has been written on at great length by much abler minds than ours. Because ours is an abbreviated history we must confine ourselves to a handful of instances from three of the more popular dialogues: *Phaedo, Sophist,* and *Symposium.*

Dialectic in the Phaedo

The *Phaedo* dramatizes the final hours of Socrates in jail before his sentence of death is enforced and is famous for the conspicuous absence of Plato due to illness: "Plato, I believe, was ill,"[2] says Phaedo who narrates the events of the eponymous dialogue. The majority of the dialogue is Phaedo's report of what Socrates discussed with his companions from his prison cell. Among the topics discussed is a memorable and influential discussion on the immortality of the soul. But the obvious dialectic of soul and body is not the focus here, what we want to focus on is something quite different uttered by Socrates.

Phaedo reports that Socrates sat up and began to discuss a pain in his leg and remarked how astonishing it is that pain is accompanied by pleasure. "What a strange thing that which men call pleasure," Socrates says to his friends, "how astonishing the relation it has with what is thought to be its opposite, namely pain!"[3] Socrates' remark seems insignificant but is pregnant with dialectical possibility. Socrates is unifying two opposites—pain and pleasure—sensations that are experienced in everyday human existence. Aristotle also affirmed the unity of these opposites, "Where there is sensation, there is also pleasure and pain." We pursue one and flee from the other but the one from which we flee is in close pursuit. Even today the notion of pleasure and pain being one and the same thing is not uncommon—sadomasochism being an obvious instance. What begins with pleasure often ends with pain and that which is painful produces pleasure. It is a contradiction. Like Zeno's arrow that is both in motion and at rest simultaneously. Pain is the opposite of pleasure and pleasure the opposite of pain and yet the two are inextricably united so much so that one can be confused with the other. The unity of pain and pleasure is an expression of dialectic. It is contradictory and all too human. It is not a strange and mystical experience shared by a privileged few; the pleasure of pain and the pain of pleasure is common to all—it is universal as is dialectic.

Part One. The Dialectic

A reliable barometer of common experience is the popular song. A simple search of song titles reveals the universal prevalence of the pleasure / pain dialectic in modern and popular consciousness. Titles that readily come to mind are "Pain Is So Close to Pleasure," by Queen; "Pain and Pleasure," by Judas Priest; "Pleasure and the Pain," by The Damned; "Pleasure and Pain" by the Chameleons; "Pleasure & Pain" by the Divinyls; and the somberly narrated "Pain and Pleasure" by The Residents are just a few examples of this sort. This is by no means an exhaustive list but serves to demonstrate the prevalence of the pleasure / pain dialectic in current consciousness. If we were to add the work of the world's poets—from Anacreon to Zukofsky—we would be compiling infinitely, but that is not purpose of this work.

Still referring to pleasure and pain Socrates tells his friends, "A man cannot have both at the same time. Yet if he catches the one, he is almost always bound to catch the other, like two creatures with one head."[4] Pleasure brings pain into being and pain pleasure. The religious ascetic, the Stylites for example, is an instance of this. He denies himself pleasure enduring physical pain so as to be pleasing to the Lord—paining the flesh to pleasure the spirit. In fact any moment of sacrifice is a moment of dialectic. He that loseth his life will find it.

Dialectic in the Sophist

Sophists in ancient Athens were teachers of rhetoric and oratory who were paid by rich young men who wanted to learn how to win arguments even if those arguments were patently fallacious. Sophistry was the "art" of the sophist and received much opprobrium from Plato; and Plato in his early dialogues went to great lengths to prove that Socrates was not a sophist. The dialogue *Sophist* is ostensibly a discussion regarding the nature of the sophist and his art, and Plato presents the sophist as being inferior in all aspects and abilities when compared to philosophers in general, and certainly inferior to the philosopher *par excellence*—Socrates. But as is often true of Plato much more lurks beneath the surface of his criticism.

In the *Sophist* an Eleatic visitor (inspired by Zeno of Elea mentioned above), discusses the various methods employed by sophists. Around the middle section of the dialogue the Eleatic finds himself entangled in an ontological discussion with Theaetetus. The topic shifts to the nature of

1.4 Platonic Dialectic

being and *non-being* (note the unity of opposites) in a discussion that anticipates the spirit of Hegel. It does not take long before the Eleatic admits his confusion:

> VISITOR: Then we've now given a complete statement of our confusion. But there's now hope, precisely because both *that which is* and *that which is not* are involved in equal confusion. That is in so far as one of them is clarified, either brightly or dimly, the other will be too. And if we can't see them either of them, then anyway we'll push our account of both of them as far as we can.[5]

The Eleatic is confused but he reasons that if he can comprehend *that-which-is* (*being*) then its opposite *that-which-is-not* (*non-being*) will become comprehensible. One will illuminate the other. In a similar way biologists hope to understand death by studying life. This is the hope of the Eleatic. But the discussion becomes more perplexing when a further set of opposites, *the same* and *the different*, are brought to bear on the conversation. So now the Eleatic is discussing *that-which-is* (*being*), *that-which-is-not* (*non-being*), *the same* and *the different*—the latter also being expressed as *identity* and *non-identity*.

This section of the dialogue is explicitly dialectical as it proceeds with opposites in unity. It is not necessary to know what *that-which-is* literally means or represents; it is an abstract expression for the purpose of thought. It is necessary, however, to recognize that *that-which-is* has an opposite *that-which-is-not*. It might be illustrated this way, using a couple of cinematic analogies. In *Jaws* (1975) *that-which-is-Chief Brody* is opposed to *that-which-is-not-Chief Brody*, which is the shark. Or take *Jurassic Park* (1993), *that-which-is-Dr. Sattler* has her opposite, *that-which-is-not-Dr. Sattler*. The most important being the dinosaurs. The dialectic of being and non-being in the *Sophist* is only one particular example of dialectic, like the Empedoclean dialectic of Love and Strife we introduced earlier. When dialectic is applied to the analysis of cinema dialectic takes on another particular aspect. These two notions: *that-which-is* and *that-which-is-not* is dialectical—a unity of opposites in direct conflict. Dialectic, as we have stressed from the beginning of this work, is the unity of opposites in conflict and in the *Sophist being* is in conflict with *non-being*.

That which exists has a dialectical relation to that which does not exist. Everything has its opposite. Even nothingness has its opposite. Consider negative numbers. We can easily picture 1 apple, but it is not so easy to picture -1 apple, yet both share a dialectical relation: one is the negation of the other. When we think of *life*, we also contemplate *death*, so that we are able to think in terms of wholes and universals, not just particulars. So when we reach the point in the dialogue when the Eleatic says he must "insist by brute force both *that which is not* somehow is, and then again that *that which is* somehow is not," we are no longer perplexed.⁶ The Eleatic has discovered the great dialectical truth: *What does not exist does exist and what does exist does not exist.* Opposites unified by conflict because they appear to be contradictory—*what is* is not and *what is not* is. Reading Plato's *Sophist* is a lesson in how to think dialectically. Dialectical cognition is a way of thinking that takes account of the whole, even if parts of the whole are contrary or even inexistent. Dialectical cognition is the genius of the greatest dramatists.

Dialectic in the Symposium

Our third and final example is taken from Plato's poetic and dramatic masterpiece. The *Symposium* (from the Greek συμπόσιον "symposion" meaning "drinking party" or "banquet") is one of the most famous and widely read of Plato's dialogues. It is also the text from which the concept of "platonic love" is derived. But our focus remains platonic dialectic. In the following passage the topic for discussion is the god of love—*Eros*. Each banqueter takes their turn speaking in praise of love while the others drink. When it is the turn of comic poet Aristophanes—the same Aristophanes who depicted Socrates with his head in the clouds—he offers a curious origin of the sexes and the search for love:

> First you must learn what Human Nature was in the beginning and what has happened to it since, because long ago our nature was not what it is now, but very different. There were three kinds of human beings, that's my first point—not two as there are now, male and female. In addition to these, there was a third, a combination of those two; its name survives, though the kind itself has vanished. At that time, you see, the word "androgynous" really meant something: a form made up of male and female elements, though now there's nothing but the word, and that's used as an insult.... Now, since their natural form had been cut in two, each one longed for its own other half, and so they would throw their arms about each other, weaving themselves together, wanting to grow together. In that condition they would die from hunger and general idleness, because they would not do anything apart from each other. Whenever one of the halves died and one was left, the one that was left still sought another and wove itself together with that. Sometimes the half he met came from a woman, as we'd call her now, sometimes it came from a man; either way, they kept on dying.⁷

1.4 Platonic Dialectic

In Aristophanes' conception of Love we are all separate parts of a whole and the process of searching for a "soul-mate" and falling in love is to bring into being a unity of opposites, to bring sameness or *identity* to difference, or *non-identity*; to unify that which has been divided into a state of synthesis—the perfect balance of opposites. And so Aristophanes offers a very early version of the sexual dialectic. This dialectic is deployed in almost every Hollywood romance, from *An Affair to Remember* (1957), and *Breakfast at Tiffany's* (1961), to *You've Got Mail* (1998) and *Ziegfeld Girl* (1941). Aristophanes concludes his great speech by summarizing desire in general:

> Everyone would think he'd found out at last what he had always wanted: to come together and melt together with the one he loves, so that one person emerged from two. Why should this be so? It's because, as I said, we used to be complete wholes in our original nature, and now "Love" is the name for our pursuit of wholeness, for our desire to be complete.[8]

For Aristophanes we are all *incomplete* searching for *completion*. Our individual self is searching for the self of the other so as to be complete. Our search for the other is the search for that which is opposite. In dialectical terms *Love is the self is searching for the not-self*. Only when the self has finally found its not-self can it declare "I am in love!"

"Opposites attract" is a common, almost proverbial, expression today but few comprehend the dialectical implications or its origin in the *Symposium*. The dialectic of eros is the fundament of every love story ever composed, and to engage with such a narrative is to involve oneself in the sublime process. Cary Grant, Audrey Hepburn, Humphrey Bogart, Lauren Bacall, Tom Hanks and Meg Ryan are all avatars of Aristophanic love in Hollywood.

The three dialogues of Plato considered above offer numerous instances of dialectic in a variety of guises. Socrates remarks about the pleasure / pain dialectic in the *Phaedo*, the ontological conundrum of being and not-being is discussed in the *Sophist*, and Aristophanes offers the origins of romantic love in the *Symposium*. What we find is that dialectic itself is both the same and different (just as dialectic should be). The above examples of dialectic all have in common a unity of opposites that are conflicting or contradictory, yet the subject matter differs greatly from physical pain to metaphysical abstractions. Is it any wonder Plato is considered the founder of philosophy *as* dialectic?

1.5

Early Christian Dialectic

Between Plato and the first Christians there were countless philosophers and variants of philosophy. Diogenes the Cynic (404–323 BC) took cynical philosophy to ascetic extremes by living in a barrel. Aristotle (384–322 BC) founded the Lyceum and virtually all branches of science. Epicurus (341–270 BC) founded a garden where atheism was accepted. Zeno of Citium (334–262 CC) founded Stoicism, named from the stoa or porch from which he taught. Marcus Tullius Cicero (106–43 BC), under the influence of Stoicism, took oratory and rhetoric to new heights and was the greatest Latin prose stylist in antiquity. Stoicism was also popularized by Lucius Annæus Seneca (4 BC—AD 65) and later by the Roman Emperor Marcus Aurelius (121–180), a true philosopher king. All the above thinkers, and countless more besides, in some way touched on or utilized dialectic in their writings but did not pursue dialectic in a systematic way, with the exception of Aristotle. With the rise of Christianity in the first century, however, a new dialectic was emerging—the apostolic dialectic of Paul.

The epistles of the converted evangelizer Paul (c. 5–67), formerly the Pharisee Saul of Tarsus, form half of the New Testament canon and almost all of early Christian doctrine. What is constantly stressed by Paul throughout his epistles is the perpetual tension between the spiritual man and the fleshly man. There is a constant conflict between the will of God and the will of self that manifests itself in tribulations. Paul constantly uses analogies of combat and warfare to bolster his belief in a battle between the spirit world and the world of fallen man. The Pauline epistles view existence as warfare. Many times throughout his letters he refers to a battle between such opposed forces as light and dark, good and bad, angelic and demonic. The spiritual man submits to God's will and the fleshly man submits to the will of the self, physical pleasures, lust and so forth. His first explication of this spiritual dialectic and perhaps his most famous is written to the Christians in Rome.

1.5 Early Christian Dialectic

> For we know that the law is spiritual: but I am carnal, sold under sin. For that which I do I allow not: for what I would, that do I not; but what I hate, that do I. If then I do that which I would not, I consent unto the law that *it is* good. Now then it is no more I that do it, but sin that dwelleth in me. For I know that in me (that is, in my flesh,) dwelleth no good thing: for to will is present with me; but *how* to perform that which is good I find not. For the good that I would I do not: but the evil which I would not, that I do. Now if I do that I would not, it is no more I that do it, but sin that dwelleth in me. I find then a law, that, when I would do good, evil is present with me. For I delight in the law of God after the inward man: But I see another law in my members, warring against the law of my mind, and bringing me into captivity to the law of sin which is in my members. O wretched man that I am! Who shall deliver me from the body of this death?[1]

A Christian must choose the spiritual path over the fleshly path, to seek God's Kingdom first and not pursue worldly fame and prominence, but as Paul points out it is easier said than done. The Christian is torn one way and then another in a constant struggle (like Medea above) and the resulting strife feels like undergoing death. The Christian wants to do what is right but does the opposite. The Christian is conflicted. Every choice is conflict. Every day is a sortie into spiritual warfare. The good that the Christian would do he cannot perform and the evil he would not do is what he practices. The only "deliverance" for the Christian is "death," a death that equates to life because the death of every Christian is already negated by the death of Christ.

Using similar expressions Paul wrote to the Christians in Galatia exhorting them to be spiritual persons, not secular: "For the flesh lusteth against the Spirit, and the Spirit against the flesh: and these are contrary the one to the other: so that ye cannot do the things that ye would."[2] Again the line is drawn between Spirit and Flesh between God and Man. The biblical commentator Matthew Henry writes concerning the above verse:

> That there is in every one a struggle between the flesh and the spirit (Gal. 5:17): *The flesh* (the corrupt and carnal part of us) *lusts* (strives and struggles with strength and vigor) *against the spirit*: it opposes all the motions of the Spirit, and resists everything that is spiritual. On the other hand, *the spirit* (the renewed part of us) strives *against the flesh*, and opposes the will and desire of it: and hence it comes to pass *that we cannot do the things that we would*. As the principle of grace in us will not suffer us to do all the evil which our corrupt nature would prompt us to, so neither can we do all the good that we would, by reason of the oppositions we meet with from that corrupt and carnal principle. Even as in a natural man there is something of this struggle (the convictions of his conscience and the corruption of his own heart strive with one another; his convictions would suppress his corruptions, and his corruptions silence his convictions), so in a renewed man, where there is something of a good principle, there is a struggle between the old nature and the new nature, the remainders of sin and the beginnings of grace; and this Christians must expect will be their exercise as long as they continue in this world.[3]

Part One. The Dialectic

Henry's explication of this verse is also a vivid use of dialectical language. Henry makes mention of struggles, resistance, and oppositions, of the kind we have been encountering from the beginning of this work. Henry juxtaposes—that is to say he brings into unity—a number of binary oppositions: flesh / spirit; carnal / spiritual; good / evil; grace / sin; old nature / new nature. These are all expression of dialectic that he derives from a single Pauline verse—a dialectical explication of dialectic.

Paul emphasized throughout his letters that the early Christians must contend with opposing factors, whether it is persecution from Imperial Rome, persecution from Jews or their own sinful nature. The Christian life is nothing if it is not dialectical. The Pauline cosmos is a unity of opposites in conflict. All of creation is subject to dialectic including the heavenly and the earthly. The sinless and the sinful are united in warfare between submission to God or submitting to the fleshly self. It is a life of constant contraries, like John Donne who was "vexed" by "contraryes" the Christian through Paul cries out, "O wretched man that I am," because flesh is pitted against spirit, and spirit against flesh; for Paul wretchedness is the human condition, the spiritual dialectic.

Paul's remaining writings are replete with dialectic. A further example is found in his second letter to the Corinthians: "Though we walk in the flesh, we do not war after the flesh (For the weapons of our warfare are not carnal)."[4] In another passage to the Christians in Rome Paul sends the stern reminder, "For to be carnally minded *is* death; but to be spiritually minded *is* life and peace." And as a way of emphasizing the need to takes sides he confirms "The carnal mind *is* enmity against God."[5] For a Christian to lose his spiritual focus is to succumb to the fleshly desires; to pursue such a course renders one at enmity with, or opposed to, God. Just to ponder on fleshly desires is to take up a position of hostility toward God. Paul concludes with this passage:

> And if Christ *be* in you, the body *is* dead because of sin; but the Spirit *is* life because of righteousness. But if the Spirit of him that raised up Jesus from the dead dwell in you, he that raised up Christ from the dead shall also quicken your mortal bodies by his Spirit that dwelleth in you. Therefore, brethren, we are debtors, not to the flesh, to live after the flesh. For if ye live after the flesh, ye shall die: but if ye through the Spirit do mortify the deeds of the body, ye shall live. For as many as are led by the Spirit of God, they are the sons of God. For ye have not received the spirit of bondage again to fear; but ye have received the Spirit of adoption, whereby we cry, Abba, Father. The Spirit itself beareth witness with our spirit, that we are the children of God.[6]

1.5 Early Christian Dialectic

Life is death unless one acknowledges Christ, just as death is life if one submits to being a child of God. To be a spiritual man is to be a child of God, and the opposite is necessarily true. To be a man of flesh is to be a son of the Devil. Paul was not the only apostle who adopted dialectic as a means of preaching the Gospel. We also find the same dialectical language in the apostle Peter. In his first letter to the scattered Christians he writes of the Christ: "He might bring us to God, being put to death in the flesh, but quickened by the Spirit."[7] And in the same letter a he writes of the faithful dead that "they might be judged according to men in the flesh, but live according to God in the spirit."[8] Peter uses the same fleshly / spiritual dialectic as used by Paul. Life is death without God and death is life with God. For as long as the Christian remains in this world his life must consist of conflict. This is the wretchedness of the Christian condition: this is the Pauline dialectic.

1.6

Gnostic Dialectic

In the years following the death of the original apostles Christianity took on various shades as the foretold apostasy became rampant, and dissenting Christian sects began appropriating pagan philosophies and mystical belief systems in an attempt to makes sense of its existence. More importantly, to bolster its numbers the "catholic" or universal Church began assimilating pagans and there was no greater pagan in the fourth century than Constantine, emperor of Rome. Foremost of these post-apostolic sects were the mystical group called Gnostics who flourished in the second century. Gnostics (from the Greek γνοσις "gnosis"meaning "knowledge") believed that knowledge was the way to salvation. To know was to be saved. But gnostic knowledge or *gnosis* was not an intellectual or rational knowledge, rather is was a knowledge that one experienced in the heart as opposed to the intellect and only by attaining this secret experiential knowledge could one escape the realm of flesh and become one with the spirit. The Gnostic Gospel of Philip strings together a series of inseparable opposites that reads like the lost gospel of Heraclitus: "The light and the darkness, life and death, the right and the left, are brothers one to another. It is not possible to separate them one from another. Because of this, neither are the good good, nor the evil evil, nor is life a life, nor death a death."[1]

These three sentences confront us with an inextricable unity of opposites—all at variance with each other, seemingly contradictory, and yet inseparable. Such is the basis of gnostic knowledge. For the devout Gnostic, to know that one does not know is to know—it is reminiscent of the apocryphal dictum of Socrates, "All that I know is that I know nothing." Ignorance of one's ignorance is slavery but knowledge of one's ignorance is freedom. By knowing one's not-knowing the Gnostic passes from the quantitative state of slavery into freedom.

One general belief of Gnosticism was the conflict between the True

1.6 Gnostic Dialectic

God and the Demiurge. The Gnostic of the second century admitted two creators: God created the good, the spiritual, and the perfect while the Demiurge created the evil, the material, and the imperfect. This dialectic shaped the Gnostic's entire *weltanschauung*. The goal of the individual Gnostic was to attain to the knowledge that allows one freedom from the physical realm of the Demiurge so they might enter into the perfect spiritual world of God eventually becoming one with The One—*at-one-ment* or atonement. The ignorant lacking the saving grace of gnostic knowledge were condemned to material imperfection—the physical body. The flesh is corrupt but the spirit is incorruptible. Knowledge is salvation ignorance is damnation: this was the gnostic dialectic.

The historian of freemasonry Albert G. Mackey writes within his work *The Symbolism of Freemasonry*, a passage worth quoting at length because it provides a brief but lucid summary of many of the Gnostic and heretical cults prevalent in the first couple of centuries. The passage offers enough information to make plain the dialectical philosophies of the various groups. Some of these groups are well known others are more obscure and recondite, but all manifest dialectic as the fundament of their beliefs. Like the presocratics centuries prior many of these Gnostic sects saw the cosmos as composed of opposite forces united in conflict.

> Light was venerated because it was an emanation from the sun, and, in the materialism of the ancient faith, light and darkness were both personified as positive existences, the one being the enemy of the other. Two principles were thus supposed to reign over the world, antagonistic to each other, and each alternately presiding over the destinies of mankind.
> The contests between the good and evil principle, symbolized by light and darkness, composed a very large part of the ancient mythology in all countries.
> Among the Egyptians, Osiris was light, or the sun; and his arch-enemy, Typhon, who ultimately destroyed him, was the representative of darkness.
> Zoroaster, the father of the ancient Persian religion, taught the same doctrine, and called the principle of light, or good, Ormuzd, and the principle of darkness, or evil, Ahriman. The former, born of the purest light, and the latter, sprung from utter darkness, are, in this mythology, continually making war on each other.
> Manes, or Manichaeus, the founder of the sect of Manichees, in the third century, taught that there are two principles from which all things proceed; the one is a pure and subtile matter, called Light, and the other a gross and corrupt substance, called Darkness. Each of these is subject to the dominion of a superintending being, whose existence is from all eternity. The being who presides over the light is called God; he that rules over the darkness is called Hyle, or Demon. The ruler of the light is supremely happy, good, and benevolent, while the ruler over darkness is unhappy, evil, and malignant.
> Pythagoras also maintained this doctrine of two antagonistic principles. He called the one, unity, light, the right hand, equality, stability, and a straight line; the other he

named binary, darkness, the left hand, inequality, instability, and a curved line. Of the colors, he attributed white to the good principle, and black to the evil one.

The Cabalists gave a prominent place to light in their system of cosmogony. They taught that, before the creation of the world, all space was filled with what they called Aur en soph, or the Eternal Light, and that when the Divine Mind determined or willed the production of Nature, the Eternal Light withdrew to a central point, leaving around it an empty space, in which the process of creation went on by means of emanations from the central mass of light. It is unnecessary to enter into the Cabalistic account of creation; it is sufficient here to remark that all was done through the mediate influence of the *Aur en soph*, or eternal light, which produces coarse matter, but one degree above nonentity, only when it becomes so attenuated as to be lost in darkness.

The Brahminical doctrine was, that "light and darkness are esteemed the world's eternal ways; he who walketh in the former returneth not; that is to say, he goeth to eternal bliss; whilst he who walketh in the latter cometh back again upon earth," and is thus destined to pass through further transmigrations, until his soul is perfectly purified by light.

In all the ancient systems of initiation the candidate was shrouded in darkness, as a preparation for the reception of light. The duration varied in the different rites. In the Celtic Mysteries of Druidism, the period in which the aspirant was immersed in darkness was nine days and nights; among the Greeks, at Eleusis, it was three times as long; and in the still severer rites of Mithras, in Persia, fifty days of darkness, solitude, and fasting were imposed upon the adventurous neophyte, who, by these excessive trials, was at length entitled to the full communication of the light of knowledge.

Thus it will be perceived that the religious sentiment of a good and an evil principle gave to darkness, in the ancient symbolism, a place equally as prominent as that of light.[2]

Such an overview requires little commentary. However, it is worth highlighting certain themes in this passage, some of which have been discussed already while others remain to be discussed in the second part of this work. For instance Mackay describes the ancient veneration of light and its enemy darkness as "alternately presiding over the destinies of mankind." This is no different from the alternating administrations of Love and Strife in the Empedoclean dialectic (from a historiographical perspective the Dark Ages in Europe were followed by the Enlightenment, and we suspect a future time of darkness awaits, perhaps a digital dark age). The dialectic of dark and light is the same antagonistic relationship of opposite forces that plays out in the great cosmic drama. Take for instance the passage beginning, "The contests between good and evil..."; this phrase is descriptive of the same agonic relationship that exists between contesting protagonists and antagonists in all drama that is dialectical whether it is the Attic tragedy of Oedipus killing his father, the Shakespearean tragedy of Henry Bolingbroke usurping Richard II's kingship, the cinematic battle of Chief Brody and the Great White shark, or Lieutenant Ripley grappling with the Alien. The old adage states, "There are two sides to every story." Dialectic also has two sides—opposites

1.6 Gnostic Dialectic

united in conflict. The relationship between opposites in such belief systems, whether orthodox or not, testifies to the activity of dialectic as a cultural and spiritual process. We read of good and evil, light and dark, knowledge and ignorance among other contraries that are in perpetual and mutual conflict. It is clear that these various religious philosophies and world views, although different in ritual particulars and eschatologies, all share a belief in universal opposites perpetually and unitedly in conflict. The gnostic searching for truth and the mystic searching for enlightenment through initiation discovers no greater set of contraries than the light of knowledge and the darkness of ignorance. Such a unity of opposites in conflict is what we call dialectic.

Mackay also cites Pythagoras, whom we mentioned in a previous section, and who is said to have attributed good and evil to the colors white and black respectively; a chromatic topos that has prevailed throughout the millennia. From black magic and white magic, black and white witches and wizards, the melodramatic use of white hatted heroes and black hatted villains in western movies, to Gandalf the White and his arch-enemy Sauron decked in black armor in Lord of the Rings, the dualism—or dialectic—of black and white is as pervasive as dialectic itself. Take for instance the character of Luke Skywalker—whom we will discuss in a later section—who is almost always dressed in white along with his sister Princess Leia while their evil father, Darth Vader, is shrouded in black from head to foot. Luke is even tempted to join the "dark side" alongside his evil father thereby implying a correlative "light side" to which the honorable Jedi, and Luke himself, belong. It is no coincidence that the Jedi's weapon of choice is the lightsaber. Even the lions in the Lion King are colored according to their disposition. Young Simba who will become the titular lion king is the same golden (light) color as his good and upright father, but the wicked and scheming uncle Scar wears a black mane as if draped in iniquity.

What we find in Mackay's synopsis of heresy is that the cosmos of Gnosticism was a great unfurling drama where opposites battled for supremacy, each opposite in turn ascending before being displaced and plummeting into subservience, all of which maintained balance and universal harmony. In the pursuit of knowledge the gnostic of antiquity found himself a spectator seated in the ultimate arena where the archetypal agon between good and evil was perpetually fought.

1.7

Patristic Dialectic

The Patrists or Church Fathers were the Christians who took the lead in the centuries following the death of the last apostles. They were a disparate group of men from varying backgrounds. Some were converted Jews while others were Greeks. Some were raised as Christians, while others, like Augustine, were former heretics. They differed in levels of education and occupation, some were teachers or scholars while some were bishops; some were sainted like Justin Martyr and others like Origen remain unsainted. They were scattered throughout the various provinces of the Roman Empire until its eventual collapse. Among the diverse patristic writings that span many centuries we also find an undercurrent of dialectic, no different from that of gnostic and philosophic discourse, particularly in the patristic approach to Christianity and scriptural exegesis.

One of the earliest Church Fathers is Justin Martyr (c. 100–165). In Justin Martyr's writings we find a similar dialectic to that of Paul. The following passage is taken from Justin Martyr's most well-known text, the *First Apology*:

> But that it is by free choice they both walk uprightly and stumble, we thus demonstrate. We see the same man making a transition to opposite things. Now, if it had been fated that he were to be either good or bad, he could never have been capable of both the opposites, nor of so many transitions. But not even would some be good and others bad, since we thus make fate the cause of evil, and exhibit her as acting in opposition to herself; or that which has been already stated would seem to be true, that neither virtue nor vice is anything, but that things are only reckoned good or evil by opinion.[1]

For Justin Martyr there is no such thing as predestination because dialectic precludes it. If a man is predestined to be evil then he must be evil, but as we know, people can change—the proverbial leopard can change its spots. Everything is in flux, said Heraclitus, therefore a person can turn from doing bad things to doing good things: "The same man making a transition to opposite things," is the way Justin Martyr expresses it. A former criminal can put away a life of crime just as a law-abiding citizen can adopt a criminal way of life. A pharisaic Jew can become a Christian and a Manichaean heretic a bishop, because each individual has freedom of choice: freedom to choose this and freedom to choose that; freedom to pursue good and freedom to pursue its opposite. Justin Martyr himself began with Stoicism, before settling with Platonism: Plato being the great philosopher of dialectic. Choice is possible because the universe is dialectical—Martyr's universe is dialectical—it is a universe in which opposites change into their opposites, in which conflict is the engine of change. Any doctrine that denies the possibility of freedom is undialectical.

Theophilus of Antioch (fl. second century AD) was born a pagan not far from the rivers Tigris and Euphrates. After studying the Holy Scriptures, in particular the prophetic books, he embraced Christianity. His one extant work is an apologetic letter to a man named Autolycus in which Theophilus expresses a worldview that is familiarly dialectical.

> But someone will say to us, Was man made by nature mortal? Certainly not. Was he, then, immortal? Neither do we affirm this. But one will say, Was he, then, nothing? Not even this hits the mark. He was by nature neither mortal nor immortal. For if He had made him immortal from the beginning, He would have made him God. Again, if He had made him mortal, God would seem to be the cause of his death. Neither, then, immortal nor yet mortal did He make him, but, as we have said above, capable of both; so that if he should incline to the things of immortality, keeping the commandment of God, he should receive as reward from Him immortality, and should become God; but if, on the other hand, he should turn to the things of death, disobeying God, he should himself be the cause of death to himself. For God made man free, and with power over himself.[2]

A choice must be made. Like the Pauline "wretch," Theophilus agonizes over the good he would do and the bad he would rather not. And the outcome for one is immortality and the other mortality. The Christian must live his death and die his life. Living for God is dying to oneself. "He that findeth his life shall lose it: and he that loseth his life shall find it," said Christ to his disciples.[3] Theophilus' remarks are reminiscent of the dialectical thinking we encountered in Plato's *Sophist* and Zeno's arrow: "He was by nature neither mortal nor immortal," says Theophilus. But reason dictates that a man must be either mortal or immortal, surely one cannot be neither mortal nor immortal. Only dialectical thinking can rescue us from such an aporia. Man is *neither* mortal nor immortal because he *is both* mortal and immortal. He is a synthesis of mortality and immortality, a unity of opposites; a simultaneity of negation. Man for Theophilus is a mortal immortal and an immortal mortal. Recall Heraclitus' dialectical dictum, *mortals are immortals and immortals mortals*, cited above. For Theophilus who was capable of thinking dialectically the conundrum was no conundrum: Man is *actually* mortal and *potentially* immortal. If the true Christian does the will of God his *potential* immortality will become immortality *actualized*.

Clement of Alexandria (c. 150–215) was an educated pagan who later converted to Christianity. He was well versed in Greek philosophy and literature and some of his fragmentary works still extant also suggest that Clement was familiar with Jewish mysticism and Gnosticism. In the second book of his *Stromata* (written c. 198–203) Clement writes a fascinating passage:

> What, then, will they have the law to be? They will not call it evil, but just; distinguishing what is good from what is just. But the Lord, when He enjoins us to dread evil, does not exchange one evil for another, but abolishes what is opposite by its opposite. Now evil is the opposite of good, as what is just is of what is unjust. If, then, that absence of fear, which the fear of the Lord produces, is called the beginning of what is good, fear is a good thing. And the fear which proceeds from the law is not only just, but good, as it takes away evil.[4]

When Clement writes that the Lord "abolishes what is opposite by its opposite," he is describing the dialectical process of negation, in this case, as it is at the behest of God, a numinous negation. Here, as in other places, we meet with the opposites good and evil, just and unjust, and contrary fears— the one a healthy fear and the other an unhealthy fear—that are governing aspects of the spiritual life; the negation and sublation of which can only occur when such opposites are united in conflict. We will meet with negation fifteen hundred years later with Hegel, and afterward with Marx and Engels, but it is fascinating to find an aspect of the dialectical process in this early Christian text.

Among the most prominent but unsainted Church Fathers was Tertullian (c. 160–225). He was a pagan Carthaginian who converted to Christianity. Tertullian is considered to be the "father of Latin Christianity," as opposed to the Church Fathers who wrote in Koine Greek, the language of the original apostles. Tertullian wrote many treatises. In particular he wrote against the heretical sects of Gnosticism, whom we have previously encountered. It is interesting that Tertullian's explications of Scripture and his criticism of Gnosticism uses the same dialectic that we have discovered in Gnosticism (in the same way that Bible commentators use dialectical language in biblical exegesis). The following passage is worth quoting in length:

1.7 Patristic Dialectic

> Reflect on what you were before you came into existence. Nothing. For if you had been anything, you would have remembered it. You, then, who were nothing before you existed, reduced to nothing also when you cease to be, why may you not come into being again out of nothing, at the will of the same Creator whose will created you out of nothing at the first? Will it be anything new in your case? You who were not, were made; when you cease to be again, you shall be made. Explain, if you can, your original creation, and then demand to know how you shall be re-created. Indeed, it will be still easier surely to make you what you were once, when the very same creative power made you without difficulty what you never were before. There will be doubts, perhaps, as to the power of God, of Him who hung in its place this huge body of our world, made out of what had never existed, as from a death of emptiness and inanity, animated by the Spirit who quickens all living things, it's very self the unmistakable type of the resurrection, that it might be to you a witness—nay, the exact image of the resurrection. Light, every day extinguished, shines out again; and, with like alternation, darkness succeeds light's outgoing. The defunct stars re-live; the seasons, as soon as they are finished, renew their course; the fruits are brought to maturity, and then are reproduced. The seeds do not spring up with abundant produce, save as they rot and dissolve away;—all things are preserved by perishing, all things are refashioned out of death. Thou, man of nature so exalted, if thou understandest thyself, taught even by the Pythian words, lord of all these things that die and rise,—shalt thou die to perish evermore? Wherever your dissolution shall have taken place, whatever material agent has destroyed you, or swallowed you up, or swept you away, or reduced you to nothingness, it shall again restore you. Even nothingness is His who is Lord of all. You ask, Shall we then be always dying, and rising up from death? If so the Lord of all things had appointed, you would have to submit, though unwillingly, to the law of your creation. But, in fact, He has no other purpose than that of which He has informed us. The Reason which made the universe out of diverse elements, so that all things might be composed of opposite substances in unity—of void and solid, of animate and inanimate, of comprehensible and incomprehensible, of light and darkness, of life itself and death—has also disposed time into order, by fixing and distinguishing its mode, according to which this first portion of it, which we inhabit from the beginning of the world, flows down by a temporal course to a close; but the portion which succeeds, and to which we look forward continues forever.[5]

Tertullian's description of the universe is explicitly dialectical. He unifies such opposites as void and solid (similar to the presocratic atomists Democritus and Leucippus), animate and inanimate, light and darkness, life and death, and so on. All of which was produced by the "Reason," in other words God. Tertullian's God purposely produced a dialectical universe placing "opposite substances in unity" wherein comprehensible and incomprehensible unite. Further in Tertullian's writing we come across another remarkable passage which reads:

> We affirm, then, that this diversity of things visible and invisible must on this ground be attributed to the Creator, even because the whole of His work consists of diversities—of things corporeal and incorporeal; of animate and inanimate; of vocal and mute of moveable and stationary; of productive and sterile; of arid and moist; of hot and cold. Man, too, is himself similarly tempered with diversity, both in his body and in his sensation. Some of his members are strong, others weak; some comely, others

Part One. The Dialectic

> uncomely; some twofold, others unique; some like, others unlike. In like manner there is diversity also in his sensation: now joy, then anxiety; now love, then hatred; now anger, then calmness. Since this is the case, inasmuch as the whole of this creation of ours has been fashioned with a reciprocal rivalry amongst its several parts, the invisible ones are due to the visible, and not to be ascribed to any other author than Him to whom their counterparts are imputed, marking as they do diversity in the Creator Himself, who orders what He forbade, and forbids what He ordered; who also strikes and heals. Why do they take Him to be uniform in one class of things alone, as the Creator of visible things, and only them; whereas He ought to be believed to have created both the visible and the invisible, in just the same way as life and death, or as evil things and peace?[6]

The sheer volume of dialectical expressions in this short passage, which is only one among many extant texts that survive, ought to establish Tertullian's dialectical *weltanschauung*. "Corporeal and incorporeal," "visible and invisible," and "animate and inanimate," are just some opposites in unity. But Tertullian also demonstrate the dialectical process of change or transition when he writes of sensations, "now joy, then anxiety," and "now love," which passes into its opposite "hatred," and so on. These qualitative changes are a fundamental aspect of character dialectic, of which we will read more in the second section of this work.

In briefly surveying the patristic writings of one so widely read and as influential as Tertullian and whose writings placed Christianity at variance with the prevailing and developing Heresies we find the same dialectical world view of opposites unified in conflict. That the universe is dialectical is supported both in the Christian and Heathen traditions. It should not surprise us that dialectic, being so prevalent throughout theology and philosophy, heresy and mythology should also be expressed by dramatists in tragedy and comedy and that the characters peopling their dramas embody and personify dialectic.

Origen Adamantius (185–254) was from the same Alexandrian school as Clement, cited above, and was a prolific writer of textual criticism, biblical exegesis and hermeneutics. Among his voluminous writings are found many passages that are dialectical in nature. From such a plethora of examples we first turn to the *Contra Celsum*, one of Origen's most famous works, in which he even appeals to Scriptural authority for the use of dialectic: "Let us show from the Holy Scriptures that the word of God also encourages us to the practice of dialectics."[7] For Origen dialectic has divine sanction.

In the following passage from *De Principiius* Origen expresses himself in language similar to the apostle Paul:

1.7 Patristic Dialectic

> Every rational soul is possessed of free-will and volition; that it has a struggle to maintain with the devil and his angels, and opposing influences, because they strive to burden it with sins; but if we live rightly and wisely, we should endeavor to shake ourselves free of a burden of that kind. From which it follows, also, that we understand ourselves not to be subject to necessity, so as to be compelled by all means, even against our will, to do either good or evil. For if we are our own masters, some influences perhaps may impel us to sin, and others help us to salvation; we are not forced, however, by any necessity either to act rightly or wrongly, which those persons think is the case who say that the courses and movements of the stars are the cause of human actions, not only of those which take place beyond the influence of the freedom of the will, but also of those which are placed within our own power.[8]

The pattern of unified contraries is like so many passages we have read so far. Good and evil, sin and salvation, right and wrong; between such opposites we must choose because "we are our own masters," Origen tells us, very much like Justin Martyr. The difficulty of the Christian way of life, which is the fundamental message of all patristic writing, lies not in knowing the right thing to do, or in not knowing what to do; but in actively doing the right thing in the face of contrary desire. The tension between the contraries is the great source of inner conflict; a Christian's spiritual agony.

The controversial Church Father Novatian, or Novatus (c. 200–258), was a scholar, priest, theologian and an antipope, a title he held for seven years until his death. Among the extant works that Novatian wrote was a treatise on the Trinity doctrine and in the following passage he describes God in a way that is reminiscent of presocratic writings:

> He is always intent upon His own work, and pervading all things, and moving all things, and quickening all things, and beholding all things, and so linking together *discordant* materials into the *concord* of all elements, that out of these *unlike principles* one world is so established by a *conspiring union*, that it can be no force be dissolved, save when He alone who made it commands it to be dissolved, for the purpose of bestowing other and greater things upon us [emphasis added].[9]

We find in Novatian's conception of God and creation a great similarity with Empedocles' Love and Strife. There is a perpetual and unbreakable link between all things in the universe both discordant and concordant—a unity of opposites. Expressions such as "unlike principles" (or contraries) and "conspiring union" (or unity of opposites) are dialectical. Novatian, like all dialecticians, was able to peer beneath the surface, to observe the unity of opposites that underlies all things—the dialectical structure that governs existence.

Appearance obfuscates reality and face value is not true value. Only the practice of dialectic can reveals to us the depth of reality—that ultimate reality composed of unified opposites. The atom was long believed to be the smallest known particle and therefore indivisible; but with time and scientific progress the atom was discovered to be divisible and composed of smaller—oppositely charged—particles called protons and electrons. The unity of the positive protons and the negative electrons maintains the structural integrity of the atom. Atoms upon atoms, molecules upon molecules, compounds upon compounds; upon these the whole edifice of nature is built—dialectic is the coping stone.

Both Christianity and paganism—the very paganism that the patristic writers sought to refute—are grounded in dialectic and this same dialectic is the very motive force of drama just as it is the motive force of the Empedoclean or Tertullianian cosmos. Dialectic has been all-pervasive in the thoughts and conceptions of mankind, and the same minds that conceived of religious doctrines, both sacred and secular philosophy, also influenced the development of Western drama. In doing so dramaturgy became a dialectical pursuit.

1.8

Augustinian Dialectic

By the fourth century Rome was in decline and by the time of Saint Augustine's death in AD 430 Rome was only forty years from complete collapse. Christianity was emerging as the new empire and no man had greater influence on the Romish Church than Saint Augustine (354–430). Augustine was born a pagan, in youth he was a heretic, as a young man he was turned on to philosophy by Cicero, when matured he was baptized a Christian, and by the age of forty-one he was an ordained Bishop of Hippo (modern Annaba, Algeria). Augustine's writings became the most influential works in the Western hemisphere, second only to Plato, to whom Augustine owed much of his thought (and dialectic). We can, of course, only examine a small fraction of Augustine's dialectic. As stated previously, our purpose in this first section is to trace the dialectical thread woven through philosophy and the history of ideas. At this point in our abbreviated history, however, it is worth noting that a thousand years separates Augustine from Anaximander, with whom dialectic in Greece began.

Augustine's work is replete with dialectic. This is due in no small part to the influence of Plato. The great work of Saint Augustine (aside from his humorous *Confessions*) is his *De Civitate Dei* (in English *City of God*); a dialectical treatise in which the temporal and earthly city of man is set in opposition to the eternal and heavenly city of God. We only have to think back to the epistles of Paul and the dialectic of the Christian who must daily battle the carnal in order to pursue the spiritual.

We begin with a remarkable sentence taken from the eleventh book of the *Civitate*: "The beauty of the course of this world is achieved by the opposition of contraries."[1] Such a sentence would not be out of place in the works of Hegel. Here Augustine admits of the beauty that is the dialectical. The dawning and setting of the sun, admired by so many because of the beauty of the spectacle, belongs to the process of dialectic. Night is the opposite of day, and it is only at night that we see the splendor of the stars bejeweling the night sky. Wherever we find beauty in our world we find "opposition of contraries."

Just prior to Augustine's statement on dialectical beauty he touches on the dialectic of good and evil.

> For God would never have created any, I do not say angel, but even man, whose future wickedness He foreknew, unless He had equally known to what uses in behalf of the good he could turn him, thus embellishing the course of the ages, as it were an exquisite poem set off with antitheses.[2]

If God were to create anything which He foreknew would be evil He would do so only to oppose the Good that exists so that it would serve an antithetical purpose. In a dialectical universe, such as Augustine's, opposites in conflict create balance like Empedocles' Love and Strife that reign and serve in turns maintaining balance in the cosmos. Augustine's God created the possibility of evil and foresaw its actuality because evil compliments the good. Similar to the tension a literary critic searches for in a "well wrought" poem, the tension between good and evil "embellishes" this life; the unity of good and evil throughout the ages creates the "exquisite poem" of existence the author of which is God. If the Augustinian existence is an "exquisite poem" of antithesis then, because of its dialectical nature, we may consider drama to be the exquisite art of antitheses.

Augustine later considers the profound struggle of the Christian caught between two opposite courses of actions. It is the same agony expressed in the Pauline dialectic cited above. The passage is written with such clarity that it is worth citing in full:

> In fine, virtue itself, which is not among the primary objects of nature, but succeeds to them as the result of learning, though it holds the highest place among human good things, what is its occupation save to wage perpetual war with vices,—not those that are outside of us, but within; not other men's, but our own,—a war which is waged especially by that virtue which the Greeks call σωφροσυνη, and we temperance, and which bridles carnal lusts, and prevents them from winning the consent of the spirit to wicked deeds? For we must not fancy that there is no vice in us, when, as the apostle says, "The flesh lusteth against the spirit"; for to this vice there is a contrary virtue, when, as the same writer says, "The spirit lusteth against the flesh." "For these two," he says, "are contrary one to the other, so that you cannot do the things which you would." But what is it we wish to do when we seek to attain the supreme good, unless that the flesh should cease to lust against the spirit, and that there be no vice in us against which the spirit may lust? And as we cannot attain to this in the present life, however ardently we desire it, let us by God's help accomplish at least this, to preserve the soul from succumbing and yielding to the flesh that lusts against it, and to refuse our consent to the perpetration of sin. Far be it from us, then, to fancy that while we

are still engaged in this intestine war, we have already found the happiness which we seek to reach by victory. And who is there so wise that he has no conflict at all to maintain against his vices?³

Augustine refers directly to the writings of the apostle Paul, quoting the same verses that manifest the dialectic of the flesh and the spirit. Like Paul who used analogies of warfare Augustine uses the phrase "intestine war" or a civil war. There is no greater struggle for the Christian than resisting the temptations of the devil. Although five hundred years separate Paul's Christianity from Augustine's Christianity the basic struggle of all Christians is the same. But struggle is universal because dialectic is universal. Life and death, like all contraries, are intertwined ineluctably. At the end of the passage Augustine asks, "Who is so wise that he has no conflict?" Whether one is religious or not, rich or poor, male or female, young or old, no one is exempt from the beautiful agony of existence.

Our last example is found at the end of Book Nineteen. Augustine is writing about the wicked and their future punishment but what is of interest is the way Augustine expresses his ideas.

> War being contrary to peace, as misery to happiness, and life to death, it is not without reason asked what kind of war can be found in the end of the wicked answering to the peace which is declared to be the end of the righteous? The person who puts this question has only to observe what it is in war that is hurtful and destructive, and he shall see that it is nothing else than the mutual opposition and conflict of things. And can he conceive a more grievous and bitter war than that in which the will is so opposed to passion, and passion to the will, that their hostility can never be terminated by the victory of either, and in which the violence of Fain so conflicts with the nature of the body, that neither yields to the other? For in this life, when this conflict has arisen, either pain conquers and death expels the feeling of it, or nature conquers and health expels the pain.⁴

As in previous examples from Augustine and the patristic writers prior to him, we see a documented conception of the world that is viewed in terms of opposites: war and peace (synonymous now with Tolstoy's novel), misery and happiness, life and death, wickedness and righteousness, and a life on earth that knows no rest from conflict except in death, which is itself the contrary of life. For Saint Augustine existence was thoroughly dialectical. Existence "is nothing else than the mutual opposition and conflict of things." Even Augustine's private existence was no exception. In his *Confessions* he wrote, "My inner self was a house divided against itself." Like every other Christian the inner struggle between the flesh and the spirit pervades. One millennium after a pagan philosopher declared the cosmos is ruled by

Part One. The Dialectic

opposite forces a Christian bishop declares the souls of men are ruled by opposite forces. Such is the universality of dialectic.

After the fall of the Roman Empire in the fifth century Europe descended into the Dark Ages; an age that lasted almost a thousand years. But while Europe languished in darkness great technological advancements were made by Islamic scientists and the discovery and translation of the Greek philosophers by Arab scholars into Arabic saw the Islamic philosophical enlightenment take place centuries before it would in Europe. While the dark times lasted in Europe scientific progress was stifled but conflict was ever-present. Bertrand Russell writes of this period:

> During the period of darkness, from the end of the fifth century to the middle of the eleventh, the western Roman world underwent some very interesting changes. The conflict between duty to God and duty to the State, which Christianity had introduced, took the form of a conflict between Church and king.... The conflict between Church and State was not only a conflict between clergy and laity; it was also a renewal of the conflict between the Mediterranean world and the northern barbarians.[5]

Dialectic remains. Russell's synoptic description of the Middle Ages clearly demonstrates dialectic functioning as an historical process (an approach Karl Marx would take up in his economic philosophy). The Church, which for Augustine represented the City of God, and the State which is the City of Man are opposed in the same way that the spirit and the flesh are opposed in the Pauline writings. One cannot be a spiritual man and at the same time a fleshly man; in the same manner one cannot profess loyalty to God and at the same time to the State—"we ought to obey the gods rather than men," declaimed Antigone in Sophocles' tragedy; a sentiment echoed by the apostle Peter centuries later as a persecuted Christian.[6]

During this time Europe was not bereft of philosophers nor was the thread of dialectic severed by the maw of darkness, in fact the Scholastics or Schoolmen as they are sometimes called were Mediaeval philosophers who taught and practiced a species of dialectic that was highly logical and Aristotelian in nature, but their story is not ours and so we are driven by necessity into the time period we call Modern.[7]

1.9

Cartesian Dialectic

The French philosopher René Descartes (1596–1650) is considered almost unanimously as the father of modern philosophy. The emergence of Descartes along with other European figures such novelist Miguel de Cervantes (1547–1616), playwright William Shakespeare (1564–1616), and astronomer Galileo Gallilei (1564–1642) helped to overturn centuries of intellectual darkness and usher in the world's first period of modernity (not to be confused with the late nineteenth / early twentieth century aesthetic of modernism). Even if one has never picked up a book of philosophy it is almost certain that one has heard the infamous three word phrase of Descartes: *cogito ergo sum—I think therefore I am.*

There is much more to Descartes' philosophy than the *cogito*, if there weren't he would not hold such a place in the philosophic pantheon, but only what pertains to our subject of dialectic can be examined here. For reasons of space and concision we must limit ourselves to the *Meditations on First Philosophy* (1641) for our examples.

Descartes was insistent in the separate existence of the mind from the body. This belief is often referred to as the mind / body problem or mind / body *dualism*. What is referred to as the mind / body dualism is an expression of dialectic, a unity of opposites. In the *Sixth Meditation* Descartes writes, "I observe here that there is a great difference between the mind and the body, in this respect, that the body of its nature is endlessly divisible, but the mind completely indivisible."[1] The body is material, visible and tangible and on that account can be divided and separated from its parts. The mind on the contrary is immaterial. It cannot be seen, touched (although sight and touch derive from it), or in any way divided. And if the body should lose a limb or a foot is amputated that division of the body does not in any way cause a reciprocal division in the mind. "Although the whole mind appears to be united with the whole body, if the foot is cut off, or the arm, or any other part of the body, I know that nothing is therefore subtracted from the mind."[2] It was a perplexing unity of opposites, that two very distinct and separate entities, should be so connected.

The mind is the part of us that thinks, feels, where consciousness resides; it cannot be seen or touched yet it exists because, like Descartes, we are conscious that we think—*cogito*. We cannot feel it, or touch it, yet it interacts with our body which is tangible and visible. Anyone who has ever blushed with embarrassment has experienced the mind affecting the body. The head, the skull, the scalp are all very real, yet the mind that we presume exists somewhere within the structure of the skull, encased somehow intangibly in the tangible brain that squats like congealed blancmange, is filled with ideas, notions, schemes and intuitions and remains elusive. Mind and body are opposites but together they form a unity that exists: what we call the *Self*.

This unity of mind and body is dialectical. But the mind and body are not only separate entities. In the *Synopsis* to the *Meditations* Descartes writes, "their natures are recognized not only as different, but also in a sense contrary."[3] What is contrary is opposite ("contraryes meete in one," as Donne said). Descartes is knowingly using a dialectical framework in his discussion of mind and body. Thus the Cartesian Man is a unity of opposites: part mind, part body, but whole. Whenever we hear the phrase "mind over matter" we are hearing an unconscious expression of dialectic that can be traced through the centuries to the Father of Modern Philosophy.

The mind and body dialectic was not the only instance of dialectic to be found in the writings of Descartes. In the *Third Mediation* we find this passage:

> Nor should I think that I perceive the infinite not by a true idea but only by negation of the finite, as I perceive rest and darkness by the negation of motion and light; for on the contrary, I manifestly understand that there is more reality in infinite than in finite substance, and that therefore the perception of the infinite in me must be in some way prior to that of the finite.[4]

Descartes in his search for God's existence is here stringing together a series of opposites: finite and infinite, darkness and light, rest and motion, and pointing to negation of one as proof of the other; darkness being the negation of light, for example. Descartes is able to perceive rest as the negation of motion, because in dialectical terms rest is motion and motion is rest (as Zeno suggested). The inextricable unity of opposites in dialectic means

1.9 Cartesian Dialectic

that contraries become their contraries, opposites become opposites, light becomes dark and dark light. While Descartes here refused to accept the dialectical process of negation functioning on the finite and infinite his acceptance of negation of opposites such as rest and motion and light and dark his use of language is thoroughly dialectical, and as we have seen throughout this work it belongs to the common thread of ideas, spanning millennia.

Before we move on from Descartes we ought to return to the Cogito, because it is one of the most famous statements of philosophy and does reveal a dialectical nature. In the first part of *Principles of Philosophy*, Descartes writes, "That we cannot doubt our existence without existing while we doubt."[5] This was proof for Descartes that he existed, he thought therefore he was. If everything in the universe turns out to be an illusion the very fact that we can doubt our own existence is proof positive that we at least do exist. What we find in this proposition is a unity of opposites. We begin with a doubtful existence (thesis) but this logically leads to a certain existence (antithesis), this certainty negates the initial doubt; the resulting synthesis of this process is the Cogito, "I think." It was the ability to think dialectically that led Descartes to his most famous philosophical discovery.

Obviously Descartes was not the originator of this dialectic. We have seen how the opposites of materiality and immateriality, flesh and spirit, has been in existence from the beginning of history, but Descartes' expression is so important because he marks a point in history, like Augustine as the Roman Empire was crumbling, and Plato before him. Descartes was the locus of modern philosophy, thus a certain paternity was bestowed on him and his dialectic. Everything Descartes wrote was the springboard for philosophical affirmation or negation (a unity of opposites) from his time forward. A philosopher either agreed or disagreed with Descartes. And from Descartes' time period onward nothing has been more debated than the inexplicable unity of humanity's basic opposites—mind and body. To wrangle with Descartes is to participate in dialectic.

1.10

Pascalian Dialectic

Blaise Pascal (1623–1662) was born a generation after Descartes, and like Descartes he was educated by Jesuits and shared an interest in mathematics, optics and philosophy. Pascal is famous, particularly in his native France, for his philosophical / theological conception of "the Wager." Pascal's Wager essentially states that everyone, whoever they may be, must gamble with God. One must ask: does God exist or not? Pascal believes there is more to gain (eternal salvation for instance) by believing in God so one is better off hedging one's bets on God existing. If it is ever proven that God does not exist there is little loss but if it is proven that God does exist then you have made your stand with the Almighty. "If you win you win everything, if you lose you lose nothing."[1]

In Pascal's collection of notes and unfinished essays published as *Pensées* (French for "thoughts") we find many passages of interest that not only express, but embrace, a dialectical outlook. Pascal, a Jesuit, had an inherent Christian preoccupation and many passages throughout the *Pensées* read like apocryphal fragments from the Pauline epistles written in the first century. The Pascalian and the Pauline dialectic has its locus in man's spiritual and physical conflict, between the Godly man and the Worldly man, and at the same time shares the Cartesian anxiety—the certainty of uncertainty: "We desire truth and find in ourselves nothing but uncertainty. We seek happiness and find only wretchedness and death. We are incapable of not desiring truth and happiness and are incapable of either certainty or happiness."[2]

In this passage Pascal recognizes that we are caught in a struggle between opposites—we desire truth but can never obtain it. We are perpetually in search of that which we can never find. The Christian wants to be godly but can only think like a devil. This unity of opposites is the same dialectic that we have encountered, under different guises, for the entire

1.10 Pascalian Dialectic

thread of Western philosophy. Pascal further writes: "It is not man's nature always to go in one direction; it has its ups and downs."[3] In other words man's nature is contrary, it is dialectical, it is both up and down, left and right, back and forth, etc., a totality of unified opposites. The same phrase is used by English speakers today to describe the vicissitudes of life. "I've had my ups and downs," we hear someone say. Or we hear, "This year's been a bit of a rollercoaster." Sometimes life is joyous and fulfilling other times upsetting and filled with despair. The metaphorical use of a rollercoaster attests unconsciously to the existential dialectic. The very notion of experiencing an "emotional rollercoaster" attests to dialectic in the vernacular.

For Pascal (similar to Marx and Engels' materialist purview several centuries later) the entire history of mankind is a process of dialectic and manifests itself as a febrile spirituality: "Fever makes us both shiver and sweat. The chill is as good an indication of how high the fever will go as the heat itself. It is the same with human inventions from age to age, and with the good and evil in the world in general."[4]

The fevered body experiences rapid shifts in hot and cold. The sensation of heat is dominant throughout the body until it is taken over by a sudden and pervading chill that no amount of blankets can assuage. Like the Empedoclean Love that reigns over the cosmos before becoming subservient to Strife, this same pattern is identified by Pascal throughout the ages and inventions of man; even the prevailing atmosphere of good and evil in the world. Such opposites are perpetually united in conflict and make dialectic manifest.

Pascal next turns from the macrocosm to the microcosm—man, that is, human nature understood as conflict:

> Civil War in man between reason and passions. If there were only reason without passions. If there were only passions without reason. But since he has both he cannot be free from war, for he can only be at peace with the one if he is at war with the other. Thus he is always torn by inner divisions and contradictions.[5]

Again we note a similarity between the Pascalian and Pauline dialectic. A constant tug-of-war takes place between reason and passion. It appears logical to do this, yet it feels right to do that. Remember Medea, torn between this way and that way, or St. Augustine who spoke of "intestine war," the tension and conflict within the self is a manifestation of dialectic. Reason wants restraint but the passions want free reign. Man's very nature is conflict. It is for Pascal like civil war. Pascal's conclusion seems self-defeating: the only way to be at peace is to be at war, an idea that can be traced back to Heraclitus: "War is father of all."

Throughout the *Pensées* we find countless instances of dialectical thinking, argumentation, and illustrations even though the words dialectic or *dialectique* are nowhere to be found in the original French texts or any English translation—it is clear that Pascal was a dialectical thinker. For Pascal the human condition was dialectical. Perhaps there is no more explicit statement from Pascal than that which follows: "Is it not as clear as day that man's condition is dual."[6] And by *dual* we naturally understand *dialectical*.

1.11

Kantian Dialectic

German philosopher Immanuel Kant (1724–1804) in his *Critique of Pure Reason* (1787) set his sights on knowledge. His *Critique* is a philosophical investigation into what can truly and unequivocally be known—what kind of knowledge is truly ascertainable by our mind (Xenophanes raised similar questions in the fifth century BC). In the pursuit of his investigation Kant came to view knowledge as divided into two types—*that-which-can-be-known* and *that-which-cannot-be-known*—knowable knowledge and unknowable knowledge. The knowledge that can be known Kant called *phenomena* and the knowledge that cannot be know he called *nouemena*. Here we have a unity of opposites.

All Knowledge (which we shall spell with a capital K) is comprised of two contrary or opposite forms of knowledge mentioned above—knowable and unknowable (which we shall spell with a lower case k)—or in Kant's terminology, *phenomena* and *nouemena*. This is an expression of dialectic. For Kant all Knowledge is a unity of opposites. Absolute Knowledge contains knowable knowledge and unknowable knowledge, the unity of knowable knowledge or *phenomena* and unknowable knowledge or *nouemena* make up what we call reality, thus a Kantian reality is dialectical—a unity of opposite knowledges. But Kant does not stop there. Knowable knowledge is also comprised of opposites or contraries which Kant calls *a priori*—or knowledge that does not require experience, and *a posteriori*—or knowledge that is gained only through experience.

> It is, therefore, a question which requires close investigation, and is not to be answered at first sight—whether there exists a knowledge altogether independent of experience, and even all sensuous impressions? Knowledge of this kind is called *a priori*, in contradistinction to empirical knowledge, which has its sources *a posteriori*, that is, in experience.[1]

Knowable knowledge is comprised of distinct and contrary knowledges: non-experiential *a priori* and its opposite experiential, *a posteriori*.[2]

Part One. The Dialectic

Kant uses an illustration to explain what he means. If a man were to undermine the foundations of his house, he knows *a priori* that the house will fall because he already knows (the collective unconscious perhaps) that heavy things fall when supports are removed. He does not need to experience the collapse of his house to know that his house will fall down.

The above is only one small aspect of Kantian dialectic but is typical of Kant's expressions to be found throughout the *Critique*. There is however a much larger, longer, and more famous section of the *Critique*, called the *Transcendental Dialectic* which contains the famous Antinomies, the Theses and Antitheses. Considerations of space preclude the inclusion of Kant's antinomies at any length but we offer a single example so the reader unfamiliar with Kant might get a sense of the dialectical propositions he uses:

> *Thesis*
> The world has a beginning in time, and is also limited in regard to space.
> PROOF
> Granted that the world has no beginning in time; up to every given moment of time an eternity must have elapsed, and therewith passed away an infinite series of succession conditions or states of things in the world...
> *Antithesis*
> The world has no beginning, and no limits in space, but is, in relation both to time and space, infinite.
> PROOF
> For let it be granted, that it has a beginning. A beginning is an existence which is preceded by a time in which the thing does not exist.[3]

This is how the famous series of antinomies begins. Kant offers contradiction between the thesis and the antithesis. "The world has a beginning," and "The world has no beginning." Logically we know both cannot be true, either the world had a beginning or it did not; just as Zeno's arrow must be in motion and not at rest if it is to hit its target. But Kant is thinking dialectically, and dialectic brings together opposites and contraries into unity. Kant continues with further antinomies "*Thesis*: Every composite substance in the world consists of simple parts. *Antithesis*: No composite thing in the world consists of simple parts," and "*Thesis*: There exists ... an absolutely necessary being. *Antithesis*: An absolutely necessary being does not exist," etc.[4] The purpose of Kant's contradictory antinomies and the *Critique* as a whole is to unify "the contradictory nature of the general cognitions of reason."[5] All knowledge, and our knowledge of knowledge, is dialectical.

1.12

Hegelian Dialectic

Georg Wilhelm Friedrich Hegel (1770–1831) belonged to the German period of philosophy that has been called Idealism. Among his contemporaries were the aforementioned Immanuel Kant, as well as Johann Gottlieb Fichte (the originator of the tripartite formula: *thesis—antithesis—synthesis*) and Friedrich Schelling. Hegel's most famous work and one that is still the most widely discussed is the *Phenomenology of the Spirit* (1807). The *Phenomenology*, as it is fondly called, contains in its labyrinthine passages much that is dialectical. One section in particular is more famous than the rest and contains what is commonly known as the *Master / Slave dialectic*.

> They exist as two opposed shapes of consciousness; one is the independent consciousness whose essential nature is to be for itself, the other is the dependent consciousness whose essential nature is simply to live or to be for another. The former is lord, and the other is bondsman.[1]

Independent and dependent, one for self, and one for another, one is lord and the other is bondsman, opposites united. The roles of lord and bondsman are here fixed but in the Empedoclean dialectic, for example, the roles are interchangeable and alternate with Love and Strife each becoming and being lord and bondsman in turn. The *Phenomenology* is an infinite work and would require a book of equal length to treat it accordingly so we must turn to another work of Hegel, the *Logic* of the *Encyclopaedia*, in which we find the Hegelian dialectic more explicitly and comprehensibly expressed. In the *Logic*'s introductory section Hegel begins: "The insight that the very nature of thinking is the dialectic, that, as understanding, it must fall into the negative of itself, into contradictions, is an aspect of capital importance in the Logic."[2]

Thinking is dialectical. Thought is a dialectical process of positing and negating, of mutual contraries, of weighing in the balance differing approaches to the same thing.[3] If we are to understand anything regarding dialectic we must understand that our thought processes, and cognition itself, the essen-

Part One. The Dialectic

tial mechanism of thought is, is dialectical. All that takes place in consciousness is subject to dialectic; likewise all that takes place in nature is dialectical. Anyone who has been faced with a serious decision and then received encouragement from a friend to weigh up the "pros" and "cons" of a particular decision or course of action has undergone a process of dialectic (the classical set of scales is a dialectical instrument: opposite plates are united by a single balance, and as one of the plates descends the other ascends in equal measure). Hegel himself claimed no originality for inventing dialectic because, like gravity, it has been in existence for all times: "Besides, the dialectic is not a new thing in philosophy. Among the Ancients, Plato is called the inventor of the dialectic, and that is quite correct in that it is in the Platonic philosophy that dialectic first occurs in a form which is freely scientific, and hence also objective."[4]

Hegel then cites Immanuel Kant, whom we encountered above, as being the greatest dialectician since Plato:

> In modern times it has mainly been Kant who reminded people of the dialectic again and reinstated it in its place of honour; as we have already seen he did this by working out the so-called antinomies of reason, which in no way involve a simple seesawing between [opposite] grounds as a merely subjective activity, but rather exhibit how each abstract determination of the understanding, taken simply on its own terms, overturns immediately into its opposite.[5]

Hegel anticipates criticism from those who will "bristle" at hearing the word dialectic. Dialectic is not to be considered as belonging to scientific or philosophical spheres of study rather dialectic belongs to the sphere of existence; that is to say "everything":

> What is in question here is found already in all other forms of consciousness, too, and in everyone's experience. Everything around us can be regarded an example of dialectic. For we know that, instead of being fixed and ultimate, everything finite is alterable and perishable, and this is nothing but the dialectic of the finite, through which the latter, being implicitly the other of itself, is driven beyond what it immediately is and overturns into its opposite.[6]

The purpose of the first section of this work is to demonstrate that "everything around us" can be understood in terms of dialectic. From the earliest creation myths to the earliest scientific theories and philosophies dialectic is manifest. Dialectic "also asserts itself in all the particular domains and formations of the natural and spiritual world. In the motion of the heavenly bodies," says Hegel.[7] Today's astronomers know more about the stars and heavenly bodies than at any other time in history and the more they discover the more organic and living the universe is revealed to be. As children we are taught about the life cycle of stars and the inextricable link between life and death, that in the death of a star—the supernova—the seeds are sown for the birth of new stars. Even the most deathly state of a star—a black hole—is alive and vigorous in power. Dialectic asserts itself in the physiological systems of organisms such as ourselves, the psychological processes such as thought, and the sociological conditions of the societies in which we exist. We are surrounded by dialectic. We are embodiments of dialectic.

> [T]he physical elements prove themselves to be dialectical, and the meteorological process makes their dialectic apparent. The same principle is the foundation of all other natural processes, and it is just this principle by virtue of which nature is driven beyond itself. As to the occurrence of the dialectic in the spiritual world, and, more precisely, in the domain of law and ethical life, we need only to recall at this point how, as universal experience confirms, the extreme of a state or action tends to overturn into its opposite. This dialectic is therefore recognized in many proverbs. The legal proverb, for instance, says, "Summum ius summa iniuria," which means that if abstract justice is driven to the extreme, it overturns into injustice. Similarly, in politics, it is well known how prone the extremes of anarchy and despotism are to lead to one another. In the domain of individual ethics, we find the consciousness of dialectic in those universally familiar proverbs: "Pride goes before a fall," "Too much wit outwits itself," etc.—Feeling, too, both bodily and spiritual, has its dialectic. It is well known how the extremes of pain and joy pass into one another; the heart filled with joy relieves itself in tears, and the deepest melancholy tends in certain circumstances to make itself known by a smile.[8]

In previous sections we have used the terms *sublate* and *sublation*—the most common translation of the German "aufheben"—when speaking of dialectic and the process of negation. Hegel explains the meaning of the term in *The Science of Logic* as follows.

> *To sublate* and *being sublated* (the *idealized*) constitute one of the most important concepts of philosophy. It is a fundamental determination that repeatedly occurs everywhere in it, the meaning of which must be grasped with precision and especially distinguished from *nothing*.—What is sublated does not thereby turn into nothing. Nothing is the *immediate*; something sublated is on the contrary something *mediated*; it is something nonexistent but as a result that has proceeded from a being; it still *has in itself*, therefore, the *determinateness from which it derives*. The German "*aufheben*" ("to sublate" in English) has a twofold meaning in the language: it equally means "*to keep*," "to 'preserve,'" and "to cause to cease," "*to put an end to*." Even "to preserve" already includes a negative note, namely that something, in order to be retained, is removed from its immediacy and hence from an existence which is open to external influences.—That which is sublated is thus something at the same time preserved, something that has lost its immediacy but has not come to nothing for that.—These two definitions of "to sublate" can be cited as two dictionary *meanings* of the word. But it must strike one as remarkable that a language has come to use one and the same word for two opposite meanings. For speculative thought it is gratifying to find words that have in themselves a speculative meaning.[9]

Part One. The Dialectic

A.V. Miller, in his introduction to Hegel's *The Philosophical Propaedeutic*, offers a concrete illustration from the sphere of botany to depict the concept of sublation in action.

> The German verb aufheben is central to Hegel's entire philosophical system because it is the operative term of the dialectic. In the Logic each concept or set of concepts is said to be "sublated" at a higher stage of thought and conceptualization and this process is the dialectic at work. The German term has the dual and contradictory senses of "abolition" and "preservation." Thus what is "sublated" is at once negated but also reformulated at a different level. The proverbial little acorn which becomes the mighty oak tree may be said to have become negated by the oak which it becomes and yet to have been preserved in so far as the structure of the acorn is potentially what the oak has actually become. The process of development, in this case in the physical rather than the logical realm, is a series of "moments" within one fluid, dynamic whole. The acorn is thus one moment of a process which ends with the oak, it itself being a moment of the whole process of its growth, existence and death.[10]

Hegel is perhaps the most dialectical of philosophers since Plato, and certainly the most modern philosopher associated with dialectic. As we have seen, Hegel believed that the process of dialectic was evident in all spheres of existence, from astronomical phenomena to human consciousness. Everything, said Hegel, is a manifestation of dialectic. Included in this "everything" are art, tragedy, dramatic works, cinema, and the characters that belong to them, this work included. Opposites becoming opposites is a dialectical progression, and Hegel's philosophy had no greater opposite than that of Karl Marx, to whom we next turn.

1.13

Marxian/Engelian Dialectic

Karl Marx (1818–1883) was a disciple of Hegel in his younger years and belonged to a group of intellectuals that called themselves the Young Hegelians. After time, and which is the natural course of things, the disciple left the teacher. Marx began reformulating the dialectical concepts of Hegel shaping them into something new and original. Just as Aristotle took the mystical Plato and made him logical, Marx took the idealist Hegel and made him materialist. Marx took the spiritual Absolute that was the final synthesis of Hegel's dialectic and turned it away from heaven and toward man, so that it became earthbound and secular, historical and the driving force of social revolutions. Marx, along with his fellow theorist and life-long friend Friedrich Engels (1820–1895), set about materializing the dialectic of Hegel, which was too other-worldly for the practical Karl Marx. Their focus was how dialectic influenced progressive movements in history, class struggle, and revolutions toward a final synthesis of socialism. What they conceived of they called dialectical *materialism* as opposed to the dialectical *idealism* of Hegel—a unity of opposites.

Perhaps the most famous document that was penned by Marx and Engels was the *Communist Manifesto* (1848) containing one of their most famous dicta, "The history of all hitherto existing society is the history of class struggles."[1] Just as Empedocles understood the cosmos to be governed through the eternal struggle of Love and Strife, Marx understood the conflicts between opposing classes of society as the governing principle of history as it developed. "War is father of all," wrote Heraclitus. Conflict is a source of growth, in other words.

Marx and Engels then posit a series of opposites in unity that is the familiar manifestation of dialectic:

> Free man and slave, patrician and plebian, lord and serf, guild master and journeyman, in a word, oppressor and oppressed, stood in constant opposition to one another, carried on an uninterrupted, now hidden, now open fight, a fight that each time ended

> either in revolutionary reconstitution of society at large or in the common ruin of the contending classes.²

By means of the dialectical process various forms of society are brought into being. And in every form of society there are classes of people at variance, where the ease of one is at the expense of the other. The freeman lives at the expense of the slave's liberty, the lord's leisure is a product of serf's labor (like Hegel's Lord and Bondsman), and an oppressor reigns to disenfranchise the oppressed, and so on. Conflict and tension exists between opposite classes, sometimes a harbored resentment that is "hidden," and other times "open" violence and revolution synthesizing into a new form of society. This is the very language of dialectic. It is the language of conflict: "opposition," "fight," "contending." The Marxian articulation of history is an uninterrupted series of conflicts and revolutions caused by opposing classes in a given society. "The modern bourgeois society that has sprouted from the ruins of feudal society has not done away with class antagonisms. It has but established new classes, new conditions of oppression, and new forms of struggle in place of the old ones."³

The feudal society contained within it opposing forces that do not entirely negate each other in their conflict, but something new forms from the "ruins"—because the ruins themselves are still the stuff of which the edifice was made—it has not been annihilated. This third entity is the synthesis of the two opposites having undergone *aufheben* or *sublation*. From this new state oppositions arise and enter into new conflict with one another and the cycle continues, like Love dominating Strife, over and over—the reports of wins and losses are recorded as history. Such is the historical dialectic of Marx and Engels.

Friedrich Engels also wrote independently of Karl Marx and one such work was the unfinished and unpublished document *Dialectics of Nature*. In *Dialectics of Nature* Engels demonstrated that natural science and chemistry are, like everything else, governed by dialectical principles. He demonstrates in the sphere of chemistry how a qualitative change leads to a quantitative change and how opposites are forced to transform into their own opposites. Engels sets down the three basic tenets of dialectic that can be deduced from nature:

> It is, therefore, from the history of nature and human society that the laws of dialectics are abstracted. For they are nothing but the most general laws of these two aspects of historical development, as well as of thought itself. And indeed they can be reduced in the main to three:

1.13 Marxian/Engelian Dialectic

1. The law of the transformation of quantity into quality and *vice versa*;
2. The law of the interpenetration of opposites;
3. The law of the negation of the negation.[4]

For Engels dialectic is as natural as gravity or the water cycle of evaporation and precipitation. These laws of dialectic are not just natural laws, but are, we aim to prove, also dramatic laws. They can, with careful scrutiny, be observed in characters, the relationship between dramatic characters, and in the unfolding of narrative.

In a previous work we applied these three principles to dramatic characters. We demonstrated how changes of quality in a character (*qualis*) lead directly to the transformation of quantitative elements in a character (*quantus*). The example we used was Oedipus from the ancient tragedy by Sophocles. The heightened emotional state of Oedipus, that is, the change in emotions within Oedipus throughout the narrative because of the plague, the hunt for a murderer, the condemnation by the prophet Tiresias, and the realization of having had sex with his own mother ultimately results in a quantitative change—Oedipus' loss of eyes.[5]

The law of interpenetration of opposites, or as we phrase it, the unity of opposites in conflict is perhaps the most distinguishable and easily identifiable aspect of dialectic. From primitive mythology to speculative philosophy opposites unify with opposites, whether in ideas, or discourse, temperatures or gender. And from a dramatic perspective this "interpenetration" or unity of opposites in conflict is most evident in the concept of protagonist vs. antagonist that everyone is familiar with. This basic constituent of creative writing is also dialectical.

Engel's third principle—"the negation of negation"—is evident when two opposites have reached a stage in their conflict where neither can annihilate nor reduce to nothing the other. This is when synthesis occurs. The dialectical synthesis can be described as the simultaneous disappearance as appearance. As a crude example take the colors black and white. Both are opposites. We expect when they come together than one will negate the other, that black will cancel out the white, and vice versa; from a dialectical viewpoint black cannot negate white and white cannot negate black, thus this typical negation is itself negated or cancelled out—the negation of the negation means that nothing is negated or reduced to nothing—the black and white interpenetrate and appear as something new—the color grey, in which both black and white remain but are no longer evident—synthesis.

The resulting synthesis is the color grey. *Aufheben*, or *sublation*, or "negation of negation," leads to a synthesis but whatever the resulting synthesis may be will inevitably come into conflict with its own opposite and the cycle repeats again and again—this is in essence the principle of "negation of the negation."

1.14

Nietzschean Dialectic

Friedrich Nietzsche (1844–1900) first published *The Birth of Tragedy* (1872) when he was twenty-eight years old. It is a work of dramatic theory in which Nietzsche attempts to trace the birth of the ancient art of Attic tragedy as exemplified by Aeschylus and Sophocles. The foundation of the work is the dialectical opposition of two principles which Nietzsche calls the Dionysian and the Apollinian, named after the two Greek gods, Apollo and Dionysos. For Nietzsche Apollo is the god of order, sculpture, restraint and rationality. The other is Dionysos who is the god of wine, revelry, wild frenzy and passion. The two gods are opposed in temperament and mores. Nietzsche saw the conflict as dialectical. In the inevitable conflict between the Apollinian and the Dionysian neither god was negated nor destroyed but both were *sublated* and the resulting synthesis was a fusion of both Apollinian and Dionysian arts—the birth of Greek tragedy. The following passage form Nietzsche is a concise overview of his tragic philosophy:

> We shall have gained much for the science of aesthetics, once we perceive not merely by logical inference, but with the immediate certainty of vision, that the continuous development of art is bound up with the Apollinian and Dionysian duality—just as procreation depends on the duality of the sexes, involving perpetual strife with only periodically intervening reconciliations. The terms Dionysian and Apollinian we borrow from the Greeks, who disclose to the discerning mind the profound mysteries of their view of art, not, to be sure, in concepts, but in the intensely clear figures of their gods. Through Apollo and Dionysus, the two art deities of the Greeks, we come to recognize that in the Greek world there existed a tremendous opposition, in origin and aims, between the Apollinian art of sculpture, and the nonimagistic, Dionysian art of music. These two different tendencies run parallel to each other, for the most part openly at variance; and they continually incite each other to new and more powerful births, which perpetuate an antagonism, only superficially reconciled by the common term "art"; till eventually, by a metaphysical miracle of the Hellenic "will," they appear coupled with each other, and through this coupling ultimately generate an equally Dionysian and Apollinian form of art—Attic tragedy.[1]

What Nietzsche discovered was the foundation of modern dramatic structure. He never used the specific terms protagonist and antagonist—

Part One. The Dialectic

but as a philologists and student of Greek tragedy he was fully aware of them—but by staging the conflict between these two opposed natures embodied in the gods Apollo and Dionysos he was essentially describing these well known roles. Nietzsche's dialectical construct creates and sustains the dramatic enterprise. The same mutual opposition functions in dramatic works today. We do not meet with Apollo and Dionysos, but we are familiar with Sherlock Holmes and Professor Moriarty, Batman and the Joker, Superman and Lex Luther etc. This is dialectic. This is conflict. And it can be traced back beyond the theatres of Greece, beyond the advent of speculative philosophy, right back to the beginning of time.

1.15

Freudian Dialectic

Sigmund Freud (1856–1939) ushers our abbreviated history of dialectic into the twentieth century. The twentieth century is also the century of the cinema. Both Sigmund Freud and his theories are now an irredeemable aspect of Western consciousness. Who has not heard of a Freudian slip, or the Oedipus complex?

The science for which Freud is perhaps best known—and which is now such an integral part of popular culture that is has become a stereotype—is psychoanalysis. In Freud's early lectures he sets down the foundation for his practice, but what is of interest to us and this work is that it soon becomes evident that psychoanalysis itself is predicated on dialectic—the interpenetrative relationship between opposites—the conscious mind and the unconscious mind. In the first Clark lecture delivered in 1909 Sigmund Freud reveals how his use of hypnosis in treating a young woman for hysteria helped him discover the unconscious part of the mind:

> Through the study of hypnotic phenomena, the conception, strange though it was at first, has become familiar, that in one and the same individual several mental groupings are possible, which may remain relatively independent of each other, and which may cause a splitting of consciousness along lines which they lay down. Cases of such a sort, known as "double personality" ("*double conscience*"), occasionally appear spontaneously. If in such a division of personality consciousness remains constantly bound up with one of the two states, this is called the *conscious* mental state, and the other the *unconscious*.[1]

In offering a complex and dynamic theory of personality Freud exposes the dialectical nature of personality by dividing the mental process into contraries, that is, a conscious mode of being and its opposite, an unconscious mode of being. The conflict that arises between the two ontological modes manifests itself as neuroses in the patient. Thus the foundation of psychoanalysis is based on the dialectic of consciousness. Further, in the second lecture delivered to Clark University, Freud continued to emphasize the dialectic at the core of his patients' disorders. "We explain it dynamically by the conflict of opposing mental forces; we recognize in it the result of an active striving of each mental complex against the other."[2] Again we see the universal dichotomy of opposites in conflict, which is nothing more than the outworking of the dialectical process. What Freud describes as taking place within the single mind of an individual would not look out of place in any book devoted to dramatic theory. The "conflict of opposing mental forces," like the Empedoclean Love and Strife, the Pauline Spirit and Flesh, and the Nietzschean Apollo and Dionysos well describes the battle waged between any well-known protagonist and antagonist.

In the fifth and final lecture delivered to Clark University Freud discusses the difference between neurotics and people who struggle with the same problems as neurotics but who do not succumb to neurosis: "It depends on quantitative relationships, on the relations of the forces wrestling with each other, whether the struggle leads to health, to a neurosis, or to compensatory overfunctioning."[3] We all face similar difficulties, experience similar complexes associated with infancy and development, the daily struggle of life in trying to pay the bills and put food on the table. Then there is the wrestling within us between the unconscious drives, which are poorly understood, and the conscious mind and all that it must contend with. The outcome of the conflict is determined by the strength of each force. Whichever force is the stronger and can endure beyond the conflict is the one that will win. The neurotic is no different than the non-neurotic in Freud's theory. The difference that does matter is the strength of force in the psychic conflict.

In one of Freud's later works, *Civilization and its Discontents* (1930), Freud elaborates on two human drives or instincts—Eros and Death—that are interminably opposed or as Freud phrased it, the "irreconcilable antagonism of the primal drives, Eros and death." In everyday speech it is common to hear sex and death mentioned together, this dialectic of sex / death can be traced back to Freud's work, but it can be found in texts antedating Freud by centuries such as Shakespeare, the Marquis de Sade, and others; although such a unity of opposites goes back before recorded history. We do not have the space here to explore this work in any depth, but Freud suggests that life and civilization are born and develop out of an eternal struggle between these two interpersonal forces of love and hate (recall Empedocles' Love and Strife). This is dialectical.

It is not in the *Civilization* but in *Beyond the Pleasure Principle* (1920),

1.15 Freudian Dialectic

written a decade earlier, that we find one of Freud's most widely quoted sayings regarding the "death instinct," and one that is as contradictory and paradoxical and any Heraclitean aphorism. "The aim of all life is death."[4] On the face of it such a statement seems contradictory. Nothing that is conscious of itself being alive wants to die, but taken dialectically, which means acknowledging the interplay of opposites such as life and death, we can make sense of Freud's paradox. Freud used the terms Eros and death, and throughout this work we are in a sense following Freud—in the same way that Freud was following Nietzsche, who followed Hegel, who followed Empedocles and Heraclitus—in reducing the dialectic of character to a primal or fundamental dialectic.

We have only touched on a few of Freud's works here but we have found within his highly influential and still controversial theory of psychoanalysis a dialectical unity of opposites—the conflict between the conscious self and the unconscious self. And in *Beyond the Pleasure Principle* and *Civilization and Its Discontents* we find the unified opposition of Eros and Death—the will to life and the will to death locked in "irreconcilable antagonism." We find in Freud, as we have with every thinker prior to him, a sense of the world, existence, and the individual in conflict, and whose theories and conclusions are no more paradoxical than the presocratic dialectician Heraclitus who wrote two thousand five hundred years ago and are still perpetuated into the twentieth century.

1.16

Twentieth Century Dialectic

The twentieth century was a century of "isms." From modernism to postmodernism, from ascriptivism to Zionism, if it has been felt, thought, or considered there is a corresponding "ism" to label and compartmentalize it. The first decades of the twentieth century saw the horrors of the First World War, and in the Great War's wake Surrealism and Dadaism emerged. After the unparalleled bloodshed of the Second World War existentialism and absurdism emerged in Europe to grapple with the seeming meaninglessness of life and in Eastern Europe Communism was at its strongest. In America the disenfranchised Negro expressed their freedom with the sound of jazz, Feminism took on the Patriarchy, and abstract expressionism challenged the staid aesthetic of baby boomers in the suburbs. As the 1960s progressed disillusionment was felt on the campuses of universities as students protested against the injustice of the Vietnam War. Uprisings and revolutions led to former European colonies gaining independence and entering into an age of post-colonialism. The liberalism of counter-culture in American youths during the swinging sixties was informed by new kind of Orientalism that saw swamis and gurus imported to America which effect can still be felt in the mass consumption of yoghurt and yoga. And even the academic study of all prior history and literature saw a host of philosophical and critical "isms" generated among the universities on the Continent, from structuralism and deconstructionism to post-structuralism and multi-culturalism—each one a thesis meeting with its antithesis—dialectic continued to work as a cultural and ideological process in each and every movement. History unfolds as a dialectical process. The purpose of the following few examples is to quickly demonstrate that the same dialectical thought process continued throughout the last century. Examples here are few and brief because in reality they are at length and legion.

Sigmund Freud's most famous disciple, Carl Gustav Jung (1875–1961)

1.16 Twentieth Century Dialectic

went on to formulate his own theories, a tad more mystical and esoteric in nature than Freud, but which have become as much a part of modern cultural consciousness as the Freudian "slip" or the Oedipus complex. To Jung we owe the concept of archetypes, the collective unconscious, and the dialectical personality types—*introvert* and *extravert*. Jung's work is replete with dialectic. In his work *Aion: Researches into the Phenomenology of the Self* (1951), Jung considered the dialectical concept of *anima / animus*, the first being the feminine or "mother" principle and the second being the masculine of "father" principle. For Jung the masculine principle contains a little of the feminine and the feminine principle contains a little of the masculine (like the Yin / Yang dialectic), so that both genders become united although one remains the dominant force and the other subservient (like the Hegelian master / slave) or "unconscious." Jung writes: "For just as the man is compensated by a feminine element, so woman is compensated by a masculine one."[1] Jung then makes direct reference to the presocratic philosopher Empedocles, who by now should be familiar. "This situation is grounded on instinct and must remain as it is to ensure that the Empedoclean game of hate and love of the elements shall continue for all eternity."[2] Two thousand five hundred years separate Empedocles and Carl Gustav Jung and dialectic has yoked the two together—opposites in unity.

Another influential expression of dialectic emerged early in the twentieth century with the lectures of Swiss linguist and philologist Ferdinand de Saussure (1857–1913). Saussure gave a series of lectures in Geneva, Switzerland, the notes of which were compiled by Saussure's students and published posthumously as *Cours de linguistique générale* (*The Course in General Linguistics*) in 1916, and it is this work on which Saussure's fame rests and which has influenced much linguistic and literary theory. Saussure developed the concept of the *sign*, which can be understood as a unity of opposites. Saussure said that his concept of the *sign* was comprised of what he called the *signifier* and the *signified*. Saussure writes:

> I propose to retain the word *sign* [*signe*] to designate the whole and to replace *concept* and *sound-image* respectively by *signified* [*signifié*] and *signifier* [*signifiant*]; the last two terms have the advantage of indicating the opposition that separates them from each other and form the whole of which they are parts.[3]

Saussure may not mention the word dialectic but the use of terms such as "opposition" and "separation" with regard to a concept of forming "wholeness" from "parts"—a unity of opposites—is the language of dialectic. We have encountered this type of language many times before. The language of dialectic is itself a manifestation of dialectic. The sign is a synthesis, within which we find the signifier (thesis) and the signified (antithesis) locked in a tension. Saussure's synthetic unit of the "sign" became the constituent unit of language in Saussurean linguistics, a highly influential discipline which was instrumental in the development of Structuralism, in particular that of Claude Levi-Strauss, which in turn participated in a tension with Structuralism's antithetical critique, Deconstruction, the chief proponent of which was Jacques Derrida—unity of opposites—dialectic as theoretical process.

In the opening sentence of *The Ethics of Ambiguity* (1948) French philosopher Simone de Beauvoir (1908–1986) quotes from Michel de Montaigne, "The continuous work of our life is to build death." This is a paradoxical even fatalistic attitude towards life that anticipates Freud's famous statement, "The aim of all life is death." Beauvoir then cites Montaigne's citation of Roman philosopher Seneca and poet Marcus Manilius. The former writes, "Prima, quae vitam dedit, hora corpsit"—*the first hour of life is that which brings death*; and the latter, "Nascentes morimur."—*we die by being born*.[4] Each statement brings life and death into a unity that is dialectical. Life is the opposite of death and yet the two are inseparable. It is the irrevocable unity of eros and thanatos that both generates and maintains the cosmos by means of conflict. Whether we comprehend this in terms of Empedoclean Love conflicting with Strife, Freud's irreconcilable antagonism, or twenty-first century science of quarks and quantum mechanics—dialectic is traceable and in evidence everywhere. But Beauvoir does more than not cite the dialectical notions of others, she announces dialectic in the ambiguous nature of existence:

> A doctrine that rests on the liberation of man can not rest on a contempt for the individual; but it can propose to him no other salvation than his subordination to the collectivity. The finite is nothing if it is not its transition to the infinite; the death of an individual is not a failure if it is integrated into a project which surpasses the limits of life.[5]

We have the universal "man" and the "individual," the "finite" and the "infinite" and the ever present "life" and "death." On the following page Beauvoir writes, "the dialectic of struggle can never be stopped: the future that it envisages is not the perpetual peace of Kant but an indefinite state of war."[6] Conflict and struggle reign under dialectic. As we recall the dialectical dictum of Heraclitus, "War is father of all."

1.16 Twentieth Century Dialectic

In her most famous work, *La Deuxième Sexe* (1949), Beauvoir describes the relations between man and woman as being dialectical. "The relation between the two sexes is then a relation of struggle,"[7] she writes. Struggle is conflict; struggle is war: and in Beauvoir's conception man is warring with woman. This is the sexual dialectic. Beauvoir continues to demonstrate the transforming process of dialectic, "The same dialectic makes the erotic object into a wielder of black magic, the servant into a traitress, Cinderella into an ogress, and changes all women into enemies."[8] Opposites become opposites. As part of the ongoing struggle of the sexes the object of man's desire is transformed into a witch, or the fairy tale success of the delightful Cinderella becomes a female ogre—the beautiful becomes ugly, the desired becomes undesirable.

Two further and famous examples of twentieth century dialectic include the book-length existential essay *Being and Nothingness* (1943) by Jean-Paul Sartre, and a work influenced by Sartre, the anti-psychiatric work *Self and Others* (1961) by psychiatrist R.D. Laing. Both works present a dialectical unity of opposites in the title as well as being dialectical in content. Other works include Theodor Adorno's *Negative Dialectic* (1966), Maurice Merleau-Ponty's *Adventures of the Dialectic* (1973), Hans-Georg Gadamer's *Hegel's Dialectic* (1976), Scott Warren's *The Emergence of Dialectical Theory* (1984), Roy Baskhar's *Dialectic: The Pulse of Freedom* (2008), and Fredric Jameson's *Valences of the Dialectic* (2009), among others.

Of all the centuries since Heraclitus first told us we cannot step twice in the same river, the most explicitly dialectical century has been the twentieth. Among all the philosophical works and political speeches there are thousands of dialectical examples, both conscious and unconscious, in the theatre and from poetry, in popular songs and novels and so on, the conflict of opposites is perpetually manifest. Perhaps a book will be written that can contain the dialecticality of the twentieth century, but we are drawing close to the end of this chapter and so we will end with a few comments by thinkers who are avowedly dialectical so the reader may continue with the rest of this work as convinced of dialectic as ourselves. In the introduction to *Dialectics for the New Century*, a recent anthology of dialectical essays, we read:

> Dialectics is a way of thinking and a set of related categories that captures; neither misses nor distorts the real changes and interaction that go on in the world or any part of it. It is also, therefore, a characterization of the world, including society, in so far as

Part One. The Dialectic

it possesses these qualities. It also offers a method for investigating a reality so conceived, and of presenting our findings to others, most of whom do not think dialectically.[9]

Richard Levins in an article titled "Dialectics and Systems Theory" writes: "I found it gratifying to see science, grudgingly and haltingly and inconsistently but nevertheless inexorably, becoming more dialectical."[10] In an essay entitled *Dialectics of Emergence*, Lucien Seve begins by writing "The basis of dialectics is the unity of opposites, a unity that encompasses their concrete identity, which is to say, includes their differences."[11] Seve then elaborates on dialectic in terms of a whole and its dialectical relationship with its parts:

> When it is conceived dialectically, however, the relation of the whole to the parts remains haunted by the abstract understanding; it still seems to be an external relation in which the diversity of the parts and the unity of the whole are to a certain extent alien to each other. If the pieces of a building set, for example, have shapes that seem to prescribe how the set should be assembled, they still don't predetermine the whole that one can construct with them.[12]

Anyone who has spent time playing with Lego can relate to the illustration given by Seve. A complete Lego fire station for example is a *whole* composed of it opposite—*parts*. The parts are of various and diverse kinds, all of which parts share an *identity* as parts, although they are *different* in shape and size. Still the *unity* of these *opposites* comprises a *whole*, which is in this case a fire station. But again the *whole* of which these *parts* comprise is not always the fire station, because one can always build something other than the fire station, a house for instance. Wholes and parts, identity and difference—the unity of opposites. Lego has never been so interesting.

In the long section of this work we have attempted to record a concise history of dialectic, from the earliest creation myths to recent trends in dialectical writing. But for what purpose? To demonstrate that dialectic is universal, that dialectic is all pervasive, that all spheres of existence are somehow governed by and manifest dialectic—including the cinema and it many characters. We have demonstrated that dialectic is all-pervasive, from primitive mythologies and creation stories of pre-antiquity, it emerges in the speculative philosophy that sought out a more measurable and observable understanding of phenomena, or what we would now call science. Dialectic is as relevant to the religious man as the atheist, as important to the philosopher as the poet and is indispensible to the dramatist. And even with the latest finding in the latest scientific theories dealing with quantum

1.16 Twentieth Century Dialectic

particles, dialectic exists in the concept of the atom and void. Dialectic is very much alive in discourse as we have seen from the many quotations and passages written by theorists in the past decade, even this work is a part of the ongoing dialectical discourse that will find its opposite or contrary theory published and which itself is a part of the dialectical process. It seems to us as we draw close to ending this chapter that we can affirm three things: Consciousness is dialectical. Existence is dialectical. Cinema and its characters are dialectical. The ultimate goal of this work is to establish the dialectical nature of character, but in doing so we felt it important to lay a solid foundation on which the remainder of this book rests. We hope this opening chapter has served its purpose in demonstrating the universality of dialectic and acquainting those previously unfamiliar with dialectic with sufficient examples and explanation of the dialectical process.

Part Two
Of Character

Free will does not mean one will, but many wills conflicting in one man.
—Flannery O'Connor

To understand man, we must understand the unity of his contradictions.
—Gustave E. Mueller

2.1

Introduction to Character: The Dialectic of Ethos

A character is a *dramatic being*. Defined as such a *dramatic being* or *character* can be understood in terms of *three dimensions*. These three dimensions: *physiology, psychology* and *sociology* are aspects of a character's being—the parts that form the whole. Take any character from any dramatic work, whether it is Hamlet or Humbert Humbert, and we can approach them by means of these three distinctive, but by no means exclusive, aspects of being. This type of character analysis can be considered *ontological*, that is, it pertains to *ontology*—the study and analysis of a character's *being*.

Character is necessary to narrative. In fact the representation of the human by means of character is the supreme value of narrative. Whether a character is found embodied in fabulous animals like Apuleius' Ass, or Perrault's Puss, or is epitomized in cities like Dickensian London, or Robert Guédiguian's Marseilles, it is Character that brings Plot into being; it is Character that is the "be all and end all" of narrative. Aristotle—along with his many modern and postmodern adherents—gave primacy to the Plot or *mythos* (μυθος) over and above Character or *ethos* (ηθος). Aristotle several times speaks of a tragedy being "impossible without action" and insisted that character (*ethos*) was subordinate to plot (*mythos*). He writes in a very famous passage:

> Character gives us qualities, but it is in our actions—what we do—that we are happy or the reverse. In a play accordingly they do not act in order to portray the Characters; they include the Characters for the sake of the action. So that it is the action in it, that is its Fable or Plot, that is the end and purpose of the tragedy; and the end is everywhere the chief thing. Besides this, a tragedy is impossible without action, but there may be one without Character.[1]

Aristotle tells us that a tragedy can exist without character as long as it has a plot or *mythos*, because a character provides only "qualities," not the "action" or "what we do." To take Aristotle's comments at face value is to misrepresent him, but let us for a moment take Aristotle's statement and analyze it in light of our discussion of dialectic. Aristotle says that "Character gives us qualities." This is absolutely true if we are describing such qualities as love, jealousy, ambition, desire, fear, joy, hatred and any number of other qualities that can be possessed or manifest by a given character. This is the qualitative element belonging to a character's psychological dimension that is always in flux in dramatic beings, it is the *qualis* of character, enigmatic as it is, that transforms from one intense emotion into another such as love into hate.[2]

The dialectical nature of Character ensures that qualities are always changing, ever-flowing like Heraclitus' river, surpassing and being surpassed, overthrowing and overthrown like Empedocles dialectic of Love and Strife; hidden one moment and exposed the next: growing from timidity into its opposite bravery or developing from love into hate, loneliness into companionship, lost and then found, etc. Aristotle was correct in saying "actions" bring about the ending, but Aristotle was wrong in dismissing character, and he was wrong in attributing primacy to the *mythos* or Plot. It is Character to which the action belongs and it is Character that brings Plot, or *mythos*, into being, because Character is Plot. Characters engage in conflict and conflict is the essence of all dramatic action. Drama does not exist unless there is agony (from the Greek "agon") and the most engaging drama—that is, it is committed to by both dramatist and audience—involves conflict as fierce as that between life and death—eros and thanatos. Dialectical conflict arises from Character itself. Conflict is not inherent in plot, action, or mythos, regardless of how the narrative is structured. Plot is not in itself dramatic: Character is. It is Character from which all drama grows.

Character is dramatic being. Dramatic being is a result of a complex becoming and ceasing to be—the interplay of essential opposites that belongs to dialectic. The grand sum of these three dimensions: *physiology*, *psychology* and *sociology* are what we call Character or *ethos* ($ηθος$). All dramatic characters possess a unique *self*, a personal history that shapes and gives form to their ideas, identities, and idiosyncrasies. We are informed by science that no snowflake is identical nor is a human fingerprint. Nor should such a complex notion as a personality be identical to another notional personality. It seems reasonable then that the creation of a fictional personality—a character—should strive for a similar dissimilarity.

2.1 Introduction to Character

The English word character derives from the Greek χαρακτηρ "*kharakter*," that refers to a tool which marks or stamps, a concept rapidly becoming obsolete in our digital age, but it was, and is, the origin of the word characteristic—that which carries the mark or stamp of something or which serves to identify as typical or of a type. We still use characters today especially when we *type*. Even a modern laptop has a Character Map which hosts all sorts of exotic looking characters, ᴜ, ⱷ, foreign letters with diacritical marks, Ç, Ÿ, and symbols, ♀, ●, and so on with the proliferation of emoticons. But in dramatic terms, and for the remainder of this work, our use of the word Character does not derive from the etymology just mentioned, rather its meaning is derived from another Greek word ηθος or "*ethos*," which was used by Aristotle to describe characters in the tragedies of Sophocles and Euripides in his *Poetics*.

Every character is a unity of opposites. Every character is dialectical. One way to demonstrate this is to analyze the so-called "character arc" espoused in a multitude of books concerning characters and how to write them successfully. The basic definition of the character arc is this: "the hero should undergo a gradual transformation toward satisfying [a] need, which is induced by the plot, structure, and other characters. Such a change is called character arc."[3] This "gradual transformation" that is the "character arc" is nothing more than qualitative flux belonging to dialectic. The gradual transformation is the step-by-step transition from opposite into opposite: love becoming hate, sorrow becoming joy, innocence becoming wisdom, selfishness becoming self-sacrifice etc. The very structure of an arc is dialectical, whereby two opposite points are united by a single curve, and the purpose of an arc is to allow passage from one opposite to the other. The notion of a character arc and its praxis is dialectical. It allows the character to pass from one state (e.g., poverty) into another (riches). Following the above definition our author tells us that "without a character arc, a story could seem stagnant and devoid of purpose,"[4] that is to say, "Without dialectic a story would stagnate, etc." Characters are necessarily in flux, constantly changing, incessantly flowing, like Heraclitus' river in which one can only step once. The very nature of Character is change, and without change, without transition, without flux, Character like water becomes lifeless.

Many writers, especially whose work involves Character, have been influenced by Joseph Campbell's book *The Hero With a Thousand Faces* (1949), in which Campbell draws on mythology to outline the basic heroic plot or "the standard path of the mythological adventure of the hero," what he called the *monomyth*, (a coinage taken from *Finnegan's Wake* by James Joyce).[5] A study of Campbell reveals, as with everything else, that dialectic is the essence of myth. A full analysis of Campbell cannot be included here, and a complete work analyzing the hero's journey from the purview of dialectic has yet to be written, but a couple of examples ought to suffice when demonstrating the dialectic of the monomyth; that the hero's journey is the dialectic of Character.

For example Campbell names the first stage of the hero's journey or monomyth as the "Call to Adventure." Campbell cites the Grimm Brothers' fable *The Frog King*, in which a young princess is bored and goes down from her castle to a pond where she plays catch with a golden ball. But the princess "blunders" when throwing her golden ball because she drops it and the ball rolls into a deep dark pond and is gone. This "blunder" opens the door to adventure because a talking frog appears who retrieves the golden ball for the princess.[6]

According to Campbell this is one way in which the adventure can begin. "A blunder—apparently the merest chance—reveals an unsuspected world, and the individual is drawn into a relationship with forces that are not rightly understood." Then Campbell makes a direct reference to Freud's work *Psychopathology of Everyday Life* (1904), in which Freud posits that accidents do not just happen, that everyday mishaps like forgetting people's names, calling your wife by your mother's name, or dropping golden balls near a dark ponds, occur because of psychic conflict between the conscious and unconscious self. What this means from a dialectical standpoint is that the tension between conscious and unconscious desires results or synthesizes in action that promotes adventure. Campbell acknowledged the conflict between conscious and unconscious yet he did not recognize it as dialectic. We are correct in saying then that the princess did not drop the ball by accident—she dropped the ball accidentally on purpose.

The bored princess wanted to break the monotony of her life. She was looking for an adventure; simultaneously excited and afraid of the idea. An inner conflict motivated the princess to play by the water's edge because playing by the water would increase the chances of adventure. She could have played with the ball indoors. That would have been a safer option, considering the fact that the ball is made of gold, but the princess wanted risk; because risk rewards one with adventure. At the same time playing by

2.1 Introduction to Character

the water would aid in concealing her unconscious motives by providing a convenient explanation for the loss of the golden ball should her father demand its whereabouts.

The princess does not want to lose her golden ball. She weeps when it disappeared into the water, but at the same time she wanted to lose her ball so she could enter into adventure. She both wanted and did not want what happened like Leontius whom we encountered earlier who wanted and did not want to see the corpses. Our princess being "called to adventure" was in fact the dialectic of consciousness motivating her; an inner impulse thrusting her toward adventure—an unconscious will to adventure. The princess is a dramatic being and her actions and choices reveal much about her. Her character is dialectical and her toying with a golden ball near a dark pond is further proof that her narrative universe is dialectical.

Further in Campbell's work we find this bold statement: "The great deed of the supreme hero is to come to the knowledge of this unity in multiplicity and then make it known."[7] The ultimate purpose of Campbell's hero embarking on the hero's journey—the ultimate purpose of the monomyth—or any narrative, is a seeking, a coming to know "the unity in multiplicity." What we have here is a unity of opposites—dialectic. That one is many, that same is different; that the I and the Thou are just as interpenetrable as life and death, *eros* and *thanatos*, this is the sacred secret discovered by every hero. The hero then must not withhold such oracular knowledge but must return to disseminate the profoundest truths. We, like the other heroes of dialectic, who have come to know the sacred secret thus make it known.

Lastly, a word on why we selected the following characters. Our aim has been to cast a wide net, to incorporate cinema from the very early silent days through to films released in the new millennium. We also wished to represent characters from world cinema and independent film as well as the juggernaut assembly line in Hollywood. Some characters such as Charlie Chaplin's Tramp, Terry Malloy and Travis Bickle are now iconic figures and are often quoted whereas other characters such as Pontus, Damiel and Vogler are obscure at best. There is no particular attention given to the grouping of certain films except for chronology, beginning with the earliest and ending with the latest. Some groupings share similarity in themes, for instance the three films by Evgeni Bauer are grouped together, and the three animated films *The Lion King*, *Toy Story*, and *The Emperor's New Groove*, are placed together, although chronology played a greater role in placement than any other consideration. We have no grand kabalistic framework as others have used. Really the placement could be haphazard and arbitrary as characters are singular beings who stand alone in the context of their own narrative, but cinematic chronology mirrors nicely the dialectical chronology in Part One. No matter what era or country, whether the films were shot in black and white or full Technicolor, whether live action, animated, or a mixture of the two media, all characters share one thing—a dialectical nature. To understand dialectic is to know the science of storytelling.

2.2

Gypsies, Tramps; Tramps and Thieves

The Tramp
(from *The Vagabond*, USA, 1916)

> Vladimir: I felt lonely.—Beckett

A lonely little Tramp sets up to busk with his violin outside a saloon. It is not long before a loud Brass Band starts playing outside the same saloon, drowning out the Tramp's violin. Both the Tramp and Brass Band must compete for the finite attention and pennies of the saloon patrons, and inevitably the Tramp and the Brass Band come to blows— two parties, one source of money—but the little Tramp deftly extricates himself from the situation using his clown-craft. Having saved himself from the wrath of the saloon the Tramp stumbles upon a young Gypsy Girl—who is not actually a gypsy but a slave girl in bondage to a cruel and domineering Gypsy Chief. The Tramp, not knowing the Gypsy Girl is not a Gypsy Girl, plays his violin for her expecting payment, but of course, she cannot pay. When the Gypsy Chief returns he assaults the Tramp but once more the Tramp uses his cunning and clown-craft to escape with the Gypsy Girl, who is not a Gypsy Girl. Cupid works fast. The Tramp quickly falls in love with the Gypsy Girl who is not a Gypsy Girl and his being smitten is obvious to her. One morning the Tramp is making breakfast so he sends the Gypsy Girl who is not a Gypsy Girl out with a pail to get milk. As she is wandering about the countryside she stumbles upon an Artist who is frustrated and uninspired. As soon as the Artist sees the Gypsy Girl who is not a Gypsy Girl his absent muse returns with inspiration and he sets to painting a portrait of her which

Part Two. Of Character

he calls The Living Shamrock. Cupid again works fast. The Gypsy Girl who is not a Gypsy Girl is besotted with the Artist and invites him back to breakfast much to the chagrin of the little Tramp. The Artist returns to the city where his painting The Living Shamrock is displayed in an exhibition much to the admiration of the critics. A Wealthy Lady in attendance at the gallery recognizes the girl in the portrait as her missing daughter who was kidnapped by Gypsies years before. When the Artist is informed of the likeness between the portrait and the model he leads the Wealthy Lady to the place in the country where he last saw the Gypsy Girl who is not a Gypsy Girl. They find the Gypsy Girl who is not a Gypsy Girl still living with the Tramp but she is quite obviously feeling forlorn, mourning the absence of the Artist. The Lady and her Daughter are finally reunited after years of separation. To thank the little Tramp for rescuing her daughter from the clutches of bewitching gypsies the Lady offers him money but the Tramp chivalrously refuses—although he is in dire need of money. The Artist, the Lady, and the Girl—who was previously the Gypsy Girl who is not a Gypsy Girl—leave for the city. The Tramp is left behind, alone once more, and heartbroken. After travelling someway Cupid wakes up and the young Girl realizes that she really loves the Tramp and calls for the car to be turned around. The Girl returns to the little Tramp and he is delighted. He gladly accepts the Girl's invitation to drive back to the city.

The Vagabond contains a wealth of opposites in conflict and at the center of every conflict is the little Tramp. At the outset the vagabond violinist is set in direct opposition with a group of musicians playing brass instruments. The Tramp is one and they are many; the Tramp plays the soft violin, they the loud harsh brass instruments. As if this conflict were not obvious the title card emblazoned across the screen announces the dialectic: "The Opposition." Both the Tramp and the Band are competing for the same patrons' paltry monies—after all, the patrons of the saloon only have enough money for beer and a finite number of performances. The Tramp and the Band are opposites locked in a competitive—conflictive—unity that quickly turns violent, as it always does with Chaplin. The conflict between the characters creates the drama. But this conflict at the beginning is not the substance of the narrative it is a springboard that launches the Tramp into the narrative proper and further dramatic moments—Chaplin in his early work

2.2 Gypsies, Tramps; Tramps and Thieves

cannot produce sustained drama, only dramatic moments. The tramp has no further dealings with the Brass Band, and his altercation with them has no direct repercussions. The saloon fight is a starting point; a tension between opposites that will thrust the Tramp into the next stage of the story.

Having escaped to the countryside the Tramp meets a Gypsy Girl, who is not really a Gypsy Girl but a prisoner and slave of a Gypsy Chief—a standard trope at the beginning of the twentieth century and quite politically incorrect these days, we are sure. It is the relationship between the Tramp and the "Gypsy" girl that is the narrative proper, the uniting of opposite sexes, that is the underlying dialectic. The Tramp quickly falls in love with the Girl, then the girl falls in love with the Artist, then the Girl realizes that she loves the Tramp. This kind of helical love is common to cinematic narrative as opposites work out the differences between them toward a final synthesis. We discover later that the "Gypsy" Girl is actually an heiress, daughter of a very wealthy lady who has been missing for some time having been kidnapped by gypsies. An heiress (thesis) and a vagabond (antithesis) are on opposite ends of the social stratum. Yet they do end up together in the end, which is the point of the short film—opposites united by means of conflict. Such a happy ending is a synthesis.

The entire narrative is a direct result of the dialectical process working itself out through the character of the little Tramp. Another dialectical aspect of the Tramp is the quantitative nature of his character. His loneness, or singleness, at the outset is contrasted with the group of brass players, and it is the direct and violent conflict between these two parties—the individual in conflict with the collective—that sets in motion the rest of the narrative. If the solo Tramp had not come into conflict with his opposite he would not have had to escape from the saloon, he would never have found himself in the countryside rescuing a young girl from the clutches of vicious gypsies, and he would not have found companionship with the girl, ending his loneliness. What is most remarkable about the Tramp's character is revealed at the end when he demonstrates his willingness to return to loneliness. He is willing to sacrifice the Girl to her mother by letting her return: to negate his short-lived sense of togetherness with her. But sacrifice—which is always a moment of dialectic—is rewarded: "For whosoever will save his life shall lose it: and whosoever will lose his life for my sake shall find it."[1] Short-lived togetherness becomes singleness through sacrifice but singleness soon becomes togetherness when the Girl returns to her savior

Part Two. Of Character

Tramp. The tramp is overjoyed and the two, united as one, ride off into the city. Such a willingness to sacrifice is a qualitative transition within the character of the tramp. The Tramp's first encounter with the Girl was disappointment at not being paid but by the end of the narrative the Tramp has grown so much that he is willing to try life in the city and forfeit his own vagabondage. In the crucible of conflict the pauper is processed into a prince.

The Tramp
(from *The Floorwalker*, USA, 1916)

> And I was ta'en for him, and he for me,
> And thereupon these errors are arose.
> —Shakespeare

The Floorwalker patrols the department store keeping an eye on the employees. He is summoned by the Manager to his office. Both the Manager and the Floorwalker are stealing large sums of money but are being pursued by detectives. They decide to take the loot and disappear. Downstairs a hapless Tramp enters, tinkering with everything he can touch. The Tramp is such a distraction to the store staff that thieves (colloquially known as "bargain seekers") help themselves to the merchandise, leaving nothing but the display rack behind. When the innocent Tramp tries to buy the rack for a nickel the Tramp gets his collar felt by one of the two detectives in the store but the Tramp temporarily evades the detective using his clown-craft. Meanwhile, in the upstairs office, the Floorwalker has beaten the Manager over the head with the intent of keeping the stolen cash for himself. As the Floorwalker tries to sneak out he comes face to face with the Tramp and both notice the similarity in their appearance. The Floorwalker needs a disguise and the tramp needs a job so they agree to switch clothes. "The change will do us both good," suggests the Floorwalker. The Tramp assumes the identity of the Floorwalker and the Floorwalker assumes the identity of the Tramp. The Floorwalker (as the Tramp) tries to make his escape with the cash but he is accosted and removed by one of the detectives. In the meantime the Manager regains consciousness and is furious. When he finds the Tramp

2.2 Gypsies, Tramps; Tramps and Thieves

(as the Floorwalker) who he thinks is the Floorwalker the Manager throttles him, intending to reclaim the money which is still in the store. The Manager and the Tramp (as the Floorwalker) continue to fight until a detective intervenes and chases the Tramp (as the Floorwalker) when the film ends abruptly—and inconclusively—with the elevator crashing down on the Manager's head.

Like most of Chaplin's output stemming from the Mutual Film Corporation contract there is outright comedy in the form of slapstick and *The Floorwalker*—the first of his Mutual films—is no exception. Beneath the slapstick and Chaplin's predilection for ass kicking there is dramatic conflict—the agony of alterity. The Floorwalker is an overseer of the department store floor, ensuring that all the employees and customers are behaving and that the items for sale are set up accordingly and is presentable. When we first see the titular Floorwalker we are forced to look twice because his appearance—hair and moustache—is strikingly like that of Chaplin's iconic Tramp. And this of course is the point because *The Floorwalker* is a comedy of errors in the tradition of Shakespeare and Plautus before him. One can see something of Dromio in the hapless tramp—"I should kick, being kicked"—an Elizabethan clown transposed into a twentieth century vagrant.[2]

The dramatic conflict arises because of assumed and mistaken identities. Chaplin's Tramp is mistaken for the thieving Floorwalker and the Floorwalker is mistaken for the Tramp. Without the comedy of errors the conflict would still be there but it is all the more comedic, that is to say, dramatic, because violence is doled erroneously. The Floorwalker inevitably would have to deal with the Manager having cheated him, but the switching of identities results in the Tramp being victimized for something he did not do; the Tramp must then use all his scurrilous cunning, which is the basis and substance of the plot. The Tramp (as the Floorwalker) must evade the Floorwalker's pursuers and the Floorwalker (as the Tramp) must evade the Tramp's pursuers. The two opposite characters—Tramp and Floorwalker—are united in conflict through semblance. Semblance is the source of the conflict, which conflict creates the drama, all of which derives from the characters.

The dialectic of alterity, or otherness, is the locus of conflict, resulting in the confusion and comedy that we find so charming in farce. If the resemblance between the Floorwalker and the Tramp were not so close the switching of identities would be impossible and the resulting conflict would be of a different kind and an entirely different narrative would be the outcome. It is because the appearances of the two characters are so similar that this particular narrative is made possible. Narrative is an outgrowth of Character and is specific to the characters. The mistaken identities pit two opposites at variance; opposites that are unified, simultaneously the same and different, both self and other; a unity of opposites: the fundament of conflict. Thus the Tramp-as-Floorwalker and the Floorwalker-as-Tramp bring their own Plot into being.

2.3

Aristos, Scholars and Swans

Vera Dubovskaia
(from *Sumerki Zhenskoi Dushi* / *Twilight of a Woman's Soul*, Russia, 1913)

Vera is a young woman from an aristocratic family. She has wealth, she has leisure and she belongs to high society in pre-revolutionary Russia. But Vera is lonely and visibly dissatisfied with her life. One day her mother, a countess and president of a philanthropic society, takes her to visit the poor to dole out food. One of the peasants Vera meets is Maxim, who has injured his arm. Vera tends to his wounds using her own handkerchief as a bandage. Maxim is smitten by Vera and the kindness she showed to him so—as he is apparently literate—he writes a letter to Vera. In the middle of the night Maxim finds Vera's house, climbs in through the window and leaves his letter on the dresser for Vera to find. When Vera finds the letter she is at first afraid—the very thought of a pauper gaining access to her room is unnerving—but Vera makes the choice to visit Maxim alone (this is the Princess playing with her golden ball by the pond). After Maxim has been fed he attacks Vera and rapes her. Maxim then succumbs to post-coital drowsiness and falls asleep. But as Maxim sleeps Vera stabs him to death. In the meantime Vera's mother has noticed Vera's loneliness and has introduced her to Prince Dol'skii. Dol'skii is handsome, an excellent swordsman and his shooting prowess impresses Vera. Cupid gets to work and it is not long before Dol'skii declares his love for Vera, but Vera is afraid. Whenever she gets close to the prince the face of the dead Maxim appears. Intimacy results in the inimical. Vera is haunted by the terrible past and cannot commit to the future. Dol'skii approaches Vera's Father, who tries to persuade Vera to accept the prince, but she is taken ill and swoons. Vera eventually recovers and when Dol'skii arrives with flowers Vera welcomes him with open

Part Two. Of Character

arms. The wedding is set. Vera feels that she must tell Dol'skii the truth about her and what happened with the peasant Maxim. Several times Vera tries to confess her secret but each time she is prevented. On the eve of the wedding Vera tries once more to confess. She writes a note to her prince and has her liveried maid take the note but Dol'skii is not there; he has been called away to his estate on pressing business. The note is returned to Vera and she burns it. After the wedding, however, Vera reveals her secret to Dol'skii, who is furious. They argue and Vera walks out. For the next two years Dol'skii searches for Vera with the aid of an expensive private detective. All he knows is that Vera is overseas somewhere, leaving him depressed and dismayed. One evening a friend calls on him and takes him to the opera. From his private booth Dol'skii notices the actress playing the role of Violetta during the last act of La Traviata; the fallen consumptive courtesan is his Vera. After the performance Dol'skii is granted access to Vera's dressing room. Dol'skii begs and pleads with Vera to return to him, but like Violetta whom she had just portrayed, Vera now prizes her freedom. She rejects Dol'skii and asks him to leave. Heartbroken, Dol'skii returns to his estate, where he collapses and dies.

Vera belongs to an aristocratic family in pre-revolutionary Russia. Her nights are filled attending soirees and sipping champagne. She never wants for food and wears the finest clothes. She is young and attractive. She is the perfect specimen of Tsarist womanhood; everything that young Russian princes are looking for in a wife. But Vera is listless. She has grown weary of the soirees, she has become dissatisfied with her life, and she is lonely. Loneliness for Vera could be described as the acute sense of absence in the presence of something other. One, it seems, is even lonelier with others than by oneself. The loneliness that gnaws at Vera's being will drive Vera to make a decision that will irrevocably change her and bring her narrative into being. Her listless attitude does not go unnoticed by her Mother, who has words with her. It seems contradictory to have everything one could want and yet still want for something, but that is how we find Vera at the outset. It is Vera's malaise that her Mother seeks to remedy. If having everything makes one depressed, then perhaps it is time to practice giving to those who have nothing. Vera's Mother is the president of the local philanthropic society. One of her roles is to visit the poor and dole out bread and cheese. In an attempt to lift Vera's spirits the Countess takes Vera with her on this occasion. When Vera sees the condition of the poor she can scarcely believe it. Her ivory tower existence is the antithesis of how the majority of people live. But it is this trip to the poverty-stricken slums that brings about the fateful meeting with Maxim, and after Maxim writes his letter to Vera the loneliness she feels forces her character into seeking out Maxim alone even though they are opposite in sex, manners, and social status. Vera's decision leads directly to Vera's rape and Maxim's death. The interpenetration of sex and death—eros and thanatos—is the catalyst of Vera's transformation. Longing for her counterpart (we recall the Aristophanic dialectic) brings Vera into unity with her antithesis and the conflict leads to death. Eros brings thanatos into being.

The encounter with Maxim has brought death into Vera's life. It is a thanatic secret that she must keep secret. But Vera cannot keep such a secret and live the life of a countess' daughter. Her mother tries to set her up with Prince Dol'skii not knowing anything, and Vera does her best to maintain her demeanor and perform all that is expected of her, but the death of Maxim weighs all too heavily on Vera and his image perpetually haunts her. The closeness she experiences with Dol'skii ends in separation and loneliness with the specter of Maxim looming—death impinging on life. What Vera wants more than anything is to be with the prince, to put an end to her perpetual loneliness, but at the same time she cannot be with the prince and must remain alone. The presence of others makes her loath herself and the private agony she suffers takes its toll on her health and renders her bed-bound. When she finally confesses to Dol'skii and speaks the unspeakable secret he rejects her. Rejection ejects Vera into life and she leaves everything to live life. By the time Dol'skii finds Vera, she is not the Vera she was, she is the Vera she is: renewed, accomplished, talented, and no longer lonely by herself—she has transformed. In the luxury of her dressing room she rejects Dol'skii who dies of grief. Whatever was dead in Vera is now alive. Thanatos has become eros.

Andrei Bagrov
(from *Posle Smerti* / *After Death*, Russia, 1915)

> *If I had never lived, that which I love*
> *Had still been living; had I never loved*
> *That which I love would still be beautiful.*
> —Lord Byron

Part Two. Of Character

Andrei Bagrov is a reclusive scholar. He prefers the company of his books, which he studies with assiduity beneath a portrait of his deceased mother, rather than attending the aristocratic soirees that his peers and contemporaries enjoy. Still, Andrei has a friend from university called Tsenin who persuades Andrei to break from his hermitic lifestyle and try socializing. Reluctantly Andrei attends a party brimming with aristocrats aristocratting, liveried servants serving hors d'oeuvres and endless handshakes and introductions. But he also sees a beautiful young woman whose black eyes captivate him. Unnerved by his being captivated, Andrei quickly leaves the soiree. The next morning Tsenin arrives to invite Andrei to another soiree where a beautiful young actress named Zoia will recite poetry. Andrei consents. At the Soiree Andrei takes his seat on the front row awaiting the performance. When the young actress steps on the stage Andrei sees the dazzling black-eyed Zoia. She recites her poetry and Andrei is amazed. She is as much captivated as she is captivating. After Zoia's performance Andrei is invited to go back stage but he stubbornly refuses. The next day he receives an anonymous note to meet a young lady at the park. Andrei attends the rendezvous almost certain that the anonymous woman is Zoia. It is Zoia. When Zoia arrives she confesses her love for him. Andrei is afraid, until now the only woman he had loved was his mother. They argue because he cannot love her and they part acrimoniously. Three months pass and Andrei is perusing the paper while breakfasting. A story in the theatre section grabs his attention. Zoia is dead. Suicide. Unrequited love is rumored to be the motive. Andrei feels the weight of guilt burdening him. He begins to dream of Zoia. Night after night it is the same dream. He is walking in a windswept wheat field where Zoia stands dressed in bright white. Andrei is determined to track down her family. He meets Zoia's mother and sister, who inform him of the tragic details of Zoia's death. She poisoned herself backstage before a performance and died on a chaise longue. When Andrei hears this he confesses that he did love Zoia. But Andrei's erotic confession does nothing to assuage the dreams and visions that plague him. He loses his senses, suffers hallucinations, and collapses. His aunt helps him to his bed but the final vision is too much and Andrei dies.

Andrei is content be alone with his books which he studies beneath the portrait of his mother. As an aristocrat he wants for nothing, he possesses an estate, enough disposable income to purchase books, and has an aunt living with him who cooks and cleans. But Andrei's lived life is so empty so his imaginative life is all the more dangerous. His mother reigns supreme in his imagination. When his friend Tsenin convinces him to attend a soiree Andrei is entering into a world that is familiar and yet at the same time unfamiliar. As an aristocrat the world of salons and soirees ought to be comfortable but Andrei is uncomfortable. He is socially awkward and perturbed by the demands of social life but when he sees Zoia, his antithesis—a young attractive socialite and the doyen of the salon scene—his attraction to her is immediate. The erotic impulse frightens him and he flees. The unity of this meeting of opposites sparks the emergence of eros which continues to grow at the poetry reading the following evening. As Zoia reads there is a mutual attraction between the two who are complete opposites. Andrei is reserved and Zoia assertive, Andrei is hermitic and Zoia sociable. Andrei reads books in solitude and Zoia performs in public (A is the first letter of the alphabet and Z is the last). It is Zoia, unsurprisingly, who makes the first move. Andrei is far too reserved to act upon his feelings and the absent presence of his mother has a powerful trammeling effect. When Andrei meets with Zoia in the park the unity of such opposites can only bring conflict, and this is the key dialectical moment; the point on which the narrative turns. Andrei loves Zoia but is too afraid to offer himself as lover. Zoia loves Andrei but her willingness to offer herself as lover only makes him more afraid. He cannot love her as she ought to be loved thus he should not love her at all. They part in life unaware they will shortly reunite in death.

Suicide is a unity of opposites. It is both the will to be and not to be, as Hamlet so concisely phrased it. Zoia no longer is because she is dead, yet she is all too alive in Andrei. In his grief Andrei realizes that he loves Zoia in death who he could not love in life. Andrei is opened up to eros by means of thanatos. It is the suicide of Zoia that triggers the dialectical process of growth in Andrei. After her death Andrei learns to live. He abandons his studies and travels far to visit the mother and sister of Zoia; he inquires into people rather than books, and he is no longer under the silent scrutiny of his dead mother's gaze. His learning to live is a tremendous growth because he is no longer the seclusive scholar with which we began; he has been transformed, although his transformation comes with a heavy price. His guilt plagues him and nothing he can do can ameliorate it. It is too late for Andrei. His death reveals to him the sadness of his life but rewards him with the rare and elusive happiness of knowing that he did once love even if it was too late. Andrei finally collapses into the loving arms of thanatos.

Gizella
(from *Umirayushchii lebed* / *The Dying Swan*, Russia, 1917)

> The wild swan's death-hymn took the soul
> Of that waste place with joy
> Hidden in sorrow...
> —Alfred Lord Tennyson

Gizella is a young woman who lives with her father. She loves to dance. It is her passion and chief mode of expressing herself because she is mute. Quite by accident Gizella meets a young man called Viktor. They begin a courtship and Gizella has never been happier. Even her father, Cherubino, approves of the courtship. One day Gizella visits Viktor at his home but discovers him kissing another woman. Gizella is heartbroken. She appeals to her father to find her a dancing company so she can leave town and find a distraction from her heartbreak. The director of the dance company is initially reluctant but in the end accepts Gizella. She is asked to perform the The Dying Swan and quickly earns a reputation as a wonderful dancer and interpreter of the piece. It is her role as the dying swan that brings her to the attention of a young aristocratic artist, Count Valerian Glinskii. Glinskii has been trying in vain to capture death in his art. When he sees Gizella's performance as the Dying Swan he knows he has to paint her—the living embodiment of death. Gizella agrees to pose for him despite her father's dislike of the Count. In the meantime, Gizella continues to dance and her reputation as an interpreter of the Swan continues to spread. One day Viktor reads a review of Gizella's performance in a paper and decides to track her down. When Viktor eventually finds Gizella he apologizes and professes his love for her. Gizella reciprocates and when Cherubino shows up, he grants Gizella's hand in marriage to Viktor. Gizella is filled with joy. She is in love and she is a beloved dancer. She has everything she could hope for. In this happy state she returns to Glinskii to pose one last time, but when Glinskii sees her he is devastated because the sadness and death in

2.3 Aristos, Scholars and Swans

her eyes that previously attracted him to her is now gone. There is now a passion for life in her eyes where sorrow used to reside. If Count Glinskii is to finish his painting he must restore death to Gizella's gleaming eyes and so for the sake of art he strangles her as Gizella poses as the dying swan.

Since antiquity swans have been said to be mute until the point of death when they sing once, and once only, their so-called swansong is their final gesture. Among the Greeks Æsop and Aristotle mention it. The Romans Ovid and Pliny (but only in refutation of the legend) also mention the legend of the swan. The legend reappears in Geoffrey Chaucer, Leonardo di Vinci, William Shakespeare and Orlando Gibbons, to name just a few. The swan in its last act of life does something creative. The swansong is the final affirmation of life in the moment when life is negated—by means of death the swan accrues immortality—such uniting of life and death is the very essence of dialectic. This is the background against which Gizella, a mute dancer, makes her appearance.

Gizella meets Viktor who seems nice and has her father's approval but he proves to be unfaithful and breaks Gizella's heart. We have seen already how quickly Cupid works in film and here we see how quickly Cupid flees. Gizella's love soon turns to hate. In an attempt to distract herself from heartache she throws herself into dancing, which is her passion, and her passion soon brings her fame and fulfillment; it also attracts the attention of Count Valerian Glinskii, a mediocre artist whose favorite subject is death. After seeing Gizella perform the "Dying Swan"—the perfect synthesis of living death—he begs her to pose for him as the Dying Swan, to which she agrees. This work is to be Glinskii's masterpiece. He is convinced that this canvas will capture death at its most vivid; Gizella is the living embodiment of death: the perfect model. So the work begins. Glinskii has no idea, however, that Gizella is becoming reconciled with Viktor, or that the heartache of Viktor's infidelity was the source of her sorrowful joy, that the death Gizella is able to bring to life on stage was initially brought into being by love's hate. The reconciliation with Viktor negates her sorrow, takes away death's sting and reduces Gizella to a vapid model useless to Glinskii's art. When she returns to Glinskii for the last time Gizella *is* Gizella but she is *not* Gizella. Her proposed marriage to Viktor has conquered love's opposite, death. Eros has vanquished thanatos.

Part Two. Of Character

If Glinskii is to complete his masterpiece he must find a way to replace the life in Gizella's eyes with death. Gizella emerges as the swan. He points her to the dais where she poses and he steps back toward the easel holding his canvas, peering over his shoulder hoping to see some vestige of death and sorrow where life and joy reside. Gizella folds herself into the posture of the dead swan. "Let us begin!" Glinskii declares. Gizella senses something is wrong and rises, and of course cannot say anything, but Glinskii urges her to take up the posture of the dead swan again. He looks over her. As an artist he is seeking death and had found it. An authentic and true death that only eyes can truly communicate. It is this truth and death Glinskii seeks to capture in his painting but he is all too aware now that the spirit of thanatos itself is dead and eros has taken its place. The work he has begun will never be complete unless he himself can vanquish eros and let the spirit of thanatos take up residence in Gizella's eyes. If he is to create he must first destroy. Such is the aesthetic dialectic. Like a god with the powers of life and death at his behest Glinskii takes his hands and wraps them around Gizella's throat and strangles her to death. He leans over her lifeless body and speaks, "Be still, Gizella, do not move. That is where beauty and peace lie." He returns with vigor to his canvas to finish his creation in the presence of beautiful destruction. In Glinskii the spirit of *thanatos* is *eros*, destruction is the matrix of creation—in Gizella these opposites have their unity.

2.4

Freaks, Tycoons and Contenders

Cleopatra
(from *Freaks*, USA, 1932)

> There is no human horror or fairground freak
> that has not lain in the womb of a loving mother.
> —C. G. Jung

"*We are about to see something unbelievable, a living, breathing monstrosity. What she is no one knows, and how she came to be this way is a mystery. What she was, was beauty beyond compare….*" So our story is introduced. Cleopatra, the "Peacock of the Air," is a trapeze artist in a travelling freak circus. Among her fellow able-bodied performers are Venus the Beauty, Phroso the Clown, and Hercules the Strong Man. Among the freakier performers are Daisy and Violet the Siamese Twins, the stammering Roscoe who is married to Daisy (a non-performer Mr. Rogers is engaged to Violet completing the ménage à quatre.), Johnny Eck the Half Boy, Josephine/Joseph the hermaphrodite, Schlitze, Zip and Pip, the three "Pin Heads" cared for by Madame Tetrallini, the Bearded Lady (who later gives birth to a bearded baby), Rardion the Living Torso, and two German midgets: the wealthy and distinguished Hans and his fiancée Frieda. Cleopatra is often flirting with Hans and Hans is a willing participant even though he knows his fiancée Frieda gets upset. Hans is infatuated by Cleopatra, because of her beauty and height. She is the most beautiful big woman he has ever seen—he tells her. Hans dotes on Cleopatra with gifts of money and jewels, thus it is very easy for Cleopatra to seduce him. When Frieda confronts Hans he confesses to being a coward for not telling Frieda earlier that he was in love with Cleopatra. Frieda, always mild in temper, tells Hans she only wants his happiness and objects to his love for Cleopatra because she knows it will not bring him true and lasting happiness. Frieda next confronts Cleopatra and accidentally reveals that Hans is heir to a vast fortune. Cleopatra knew Hans was wealthy, but with a fortune to inherit she now plans with Hercules to marry Hans, then poison him, becoming sole beneficiary. Hans is already seduced and the marriage is easily arranged. At the marriage feast a drunken Cleopatra and Hercules publicly mock Hans. In her inebriated state Cleopatra cannot prevent her loathing of Hans escaping and her pretense of faux love crumbles. The Freaks perform an initiation rite to bring Cleopatra into the fold as an official "freak." They dance and chant "One of us, one of us! We accept her, we accept her, One of us, one of us!" A large chalice is passed around like a covenantal grail so each freak may takes a ritual sip. Cleopatra finds the occasion repugnant. The idea of drinking from the same cup disgusts her and she tells them so. She curses the freaks belittling them all with insults. The party falls into silence—the code of the Freaks: "Offend One, Offend Them All" has just been transgressed. Cleopatra knows what consequences her words and actions will provoke. Cleopatra and Hercules plan to go ahead with poisoning Hans knowing that her life is in danger. She administers poison but does not know she is being watched. For a week this continues, but Hans is already wise to Cleopatra's plans. On a stormy and rainy night as the circus moves out, Hercules is sent to kill Venus because she knows too much. Phroso intervenes just as the carriage hits a rock and topples over. Cleopatra in her carriage is about to administer another dose of poison but is confronted by Hans and several knife wielding midgets. Cleopatra runs out into the stormy night screaming pursued by a horde of freaks.... We end as we began, with the announcement that we about to see a living, breathing monstrosity, and what is revealed at the bottom of a pit for all the world to see is the mutilated and freakish form of Cleopatra, squawking and flapping, part bird part woman and yet neither.

Cleopatra perhaps belongs to a cabal of female characters notorious in history for their evil. Athaliah, Jezebel, Lucrezia Borgia, Lady Macbeth, the Countess of Bathory, among others. Cleopatra will use her seductive beauty so as to procure wealth. Cleopatra exemplifies the dialectical movement of transition: opposite becoming opposite. She is at the outset a stunning beauty, a talented trapeze performer described as the "Peacock of the Air."

2.4 Freaks, Tycoons and Contenders

But at the end she is malformed, ugly and crippled. We often find this movement in morality tales, superlative justice brings about an equalizing. The rich are made poor, the foolish wise, and in Cleopatra's case, the beautiful are made ugly. Beauty is not made ugly for the sake of it; we are to learn something about the character and ourselves.

Cleopatra would seem to have everything, at least as far as life in a circus goes, but she remains in want of something. This want, or lack, is a dark vacuity inside her; an emptiness that she is compelled to fill, from which her motives spring. Cleopatra is obviously a woman with expensive tastes. Her crimped hair and her dresses belong in an F. Scott Fitzgerald novel not a freak circus; and yet here she is, and it is her being here that drives her to get out. But to get out of the circus she needs money, and to get money she needs Hans. Hans is willingly seduced despite having a fiancée. He lavishes gifts of money and jewelry on Cleopatra which she willingly accepts. Hans is everything that Cleopatra is not. She is normal, beautiful, tall but without her own money. Hans is a midget but independently wealthy. Cleopatra hates Hans but loves his money. Hans, for the most part, is an honorable gentleman, although the callousness with which he deals with Frieda and the ease with which he is seduced is somewhat less than honorable. Cleopatra is dishonorable and callous, merciless in her dealings with Hans and the other performers. When she learns from Frieda that Hans is not just wealthy but is also heir of an immense fortune she plots to marry Hans and flaunts her plan to Frieda.

Cleopatra succeeds in wedding Hans, but the two are such opposites that conflict is inevitable. As hard as Cleopatra might try she cannot quell the loathing she has for Hans. She hates Hans and every other freak in the circus. And as the saying goes, *in vino veritas*, Cleopatra's disgust comes gushing forth as she gets drunk at the wedding feast. Hate surfaces through her professed love. The whole circus is enjoying the festivities and the freaks are more than willing to accept the happy couple. Only Frieda and Venus know the treachery of Cleopatra, and it is too much for Frieda to attend to the post-nuptial party so she leaves when a drunken Cleopatra kisses Hercules as Hans sits in shame. The Freaks wish to bring Cleopatra into the fold and host an initiation of singing and dance. A cup is passed between them all, partaking of which marks one as belonging, initiated into a sacred covenant. The cup is passed and all the freaks like disabled disciples sip until the cup is passed to Cleopatra. But she is repulsed. Even her callousness cannot bring her to fake participation. In her intoxicated state she becomes suddenly becomes alarmed at the otherness of those surrounding her, and of her own self. The difference is so marked and terrifying that she starts cursing and enunciates the ineffable word that only outsiders use—FREAKS! To one another they are not freaks, they are fellow performers, a family, sharing a oneness, of belonging but by calling them freaks as those out in the normal world do Cleopatra reveals that she is not one of them, she announces her own otherness to them. By marrying Hans she was to all outward appearances sharing in sameness with the group, but her intoxication cannot prevent her mouth from speaking her heart's abundance. After she has uttered the "F-word" there can be no taking it back. She has offended one and all, and freak justice will be meted out. There is often nothing crueler than irony. And there is no narrative better than moral fable to deliver it. That which Cleopatra despised she became, that which was different, she was made the same; that which was the other became the self. The beauty became the beast, the grand peacock the butchered duckling.

Charles Foster Kane
(from *Citizen Kane*, USA, 1942)

> *Inside the unfinished palace of Xanadu we find Charles Foster Kane. He is on his death bed and with his last breath he utters a single word: Rosebud.... Understanding the character of Charles Foster Kane rests on the identity of Rosebud. This is the task of Thompson the reporter who interviews the people closest to Kane in an attempt to uncover the mystery of Rosebud and ultimately the character of Kane. Thompson first tracks down Susan Alexander, Kane's second wife, then his old manager Bernstein, his best friend Jed Leland, and accesses the unpublished memoirs of Walter P. Thatcher who became the adoptive guardian of Kane and his fortune. The testimony of these four characters and the intersecting narratives results in a composite image—or quilt work character—of Charles Foster Kane. The first of these characters is Kane's second wife, Susan Alexander Kane. She is discovered by Thompson running a dive bar called El Rancho, in Atlantic City, where she sings twice nightly. Alexander was a starlet that shone so bright she is now all but extinguished like a collapsed star. When Thompson first attempts to*

2.4 Freaks, Tycoons and Contenders

interview Susan she is too drunk to speak with him. She yells at him to get out. Susan is a pitiful picture of ruination—an inverse Cinderella. Thompson returns a few days later. Susan is still gulping down highballs but this time she is a little more willing to talk to Thompson. Susan reveals how she and Kane first met when she had toothache, the evenings spent together when she sang for him, Kane's later political ambition, the breakup of his first marriage to Emily Monroe Norton, the Susan Scandal, political ruin and retirement to Xanadu. Thompson learns much, in particular Susan's operatic aspirations, but does not discover the identity of Rosebud. Thompson's next lead is the late Walter Parks Thatcher. Because Thatcher is dead Thompson must secure access to Thatcher's unpublished memoirs. Inside a highly secured vault Thompson reads the few select pages allowed him. Thatcher records his first encounter with the boy Charles in the year 1871. Charles is a young boy riding his sled in the Colorado snow. Kane's mother had inherited a gold mine and as a result was worth a fortune. This fortune was to be held in trust until Charles came of age when he would inherit everything, in the meantime he would be handed over to the custody of Thatcher and taken to New York. Kane's family in Colorado is never mentioned again. Learning nothing concerning Rosebud Thompson's next interviewee is Kane's longtime general manager and close associate, Mr. Bernstein. Thompson conducts the interview in Bernstein's New York office, the view from which looks out over the entire city. Above the fireplace mantel hangs a portrait of an elderly Kane. Pointing to the portrait Bernstein says, "You take Mr. Kane. It wasn't money he wanted," then Bernstein mysteriously leaves off, but within the elision, in the nothing that is said we sense the answer to everything. Bernstein begins with Kane's first newspaper. "The first day Mr. Kane took over the Inquirer," begins Bernstein. Thompson learns how one small newspaper grew into a media empire but learns nothing of Rosebud. Thompson is directed to his last source, Jed Leland who now resides in a home for the elderly. "I can remember absolutely everything, young man," says Leland to Thompson. "Memory, that's one of the greatest curses ever inflicted on the human race." Leland begins with the New York Inquirer, moves on to Kane's first marriage to Emily Monroe Norton, niece of the United States president, Kane's later political failure and the scandal with Susan, her career as a singer and the enmity that developed between two best friends. Once again, however,

Part Two. Of Character

> *Thompson fails to discover the identity of Rosebud. It is only we the audience to whom the mystery is revealed. Only we with our photographic vantage are allowed in the final frames to watch Rosebud burning.*

Citizen Kane is a "kind of metaphysical detective story," in the words of Borges, "the investigation of a man's inner self, through the works he wrought, the words he spoke, and the many lives he ruined."[1] It is a detective story that has no narrative solution. No character is privy to the answer of the question: who or what is Rosebud? What Rosebud is is less important than what it represents for Kane. In his quest for power and glory he was unconsciously searching for one thing: the innocence of his childhood. Everything that Kane does is motivated by this loss. It is ironic that his meeting with Susan was the one night he might have found Rosebud, but distracted by her quaint naïveté and innocence he forgot his own search for innocence and took the fork in the road that led to vice, corruption, infidelity, dissolution of his marriage and the loss of his own son. His being with Susan will ultimately result in his dying alone.

Susan would like to be a singer. Kane, having lost his family and his political aspirations as a result of his affair with Susan, now embarks on creating a successful Susan that would mirror his own media success. Using his talents and inexhaustible finances coupled with his incorrigible ambition Kane builds an opera house in Susan's honor—a monument to aspiration never achieved—and secures singing instructors so Susan will be the next soprano sensation. But Susan is not a natural opera singer and her attempts to learn from the world's greatest vocal coaches only lead to frustration and animosity. Kane is acutely aware of Susan's inability to sing but he imposes his will on the situation, as Kane is wont to do in every situation. Kane wants Susan to sing, not because Susan wants to sing but because it is Kane's ambition that Susan sings. He must make Susan an opera singer and his ruthless attempts to succeed will drive Susan to suicide and ruin.

In the Chicago opera house built for Susan she takes center stage in a fictional production of Salammbo (after Flaubert's novel). In the audience Bernstein sleeps, Leland drunkenly shreds the libretto, and Kane scowls as he overhears the snickering voices in the audience confirm what he himself already knows. Susan Alexander is dreadful. The performance mercifully ends. There is a faint pathetic applause of sympathy that quickly peters out.

2.4 Freaks, Tycoons and Contenders

Kane alone offers a standing ovation as he claps with gusto. Leland's negative review for Kane's paper the following morning ends the long and close relationship the two men shared. Kane fires Leland and the two men part ways. Kane is one step closer to total isolation. And as for Susan, she must continue to sing. And while her career lasts it appears successful but only if one is reading a Kane syndicated newspaper. Only Susan's suicide attempt is enough to check Kane's ambition. In the end Kane will find himself begging not to be left alone, because Kane's ambition is revealed in all his relationships. The outcome of his pride and ambition will be a mighty crash. We the audience can see it, but Kane himself is blind to his final trajectory: the wealthy tycoon becoming a spiritually impoverished old man.

This species of exuberant pride (which the Greeks called "hubris") can only bring a character into conflict. It is the satanic pride depicted by Milton that would "rather reign in hell than serve in heaven." Kane loses his wife, his only son and heir, the love and trust of the people closest to him, and any possibility of a political career—and we know the thought of one day being president was on Kane's mind—and it all falls apart because of pride. Kane refuses to be told what to do. When Kane is confronted over the "Susan Affair" and forced to choose between Susan (who he does not love) and his family there is only one rational course of action: choose his family—Kane does the opposite. Everything he has built, a family, a relationship with his son, a promising political career, comes crashing down. He is at the same time creator and destroyer of his future. And in the end it was all for nothing because he utterly ruins Susan, morally, financially, and spiritually.

What Kane cherished most of all was with him all the time and yet he never realized it. All the accumulating of wealth and possessions cannot negate the boyhood loss. The dialectic of childhood loss and later acquisition motivates the character of Kane and drives the dramatic narrative from beginning to end. Kane emerges as a mythic being, a composite existence, structured by others and a thousand and one headlines. As we have learned from Plato: what is is not and what is not is. Kane is and is not. There is no such being as Kane who can say "I am." Rather it is tempting to see Kane as a creation of otherness; a fiction of others recreated as a counterpart to their own selves; "let us make Kane in our image."

Charles Foster Kane is not remembered as Charles Foster Kane *was* (that is within the specific narrative universe), but remembered as he *is* through the filter of alterity which is subject to the private hermeneutics of recollection. Charles Foster Kane is the grand sum of the physicality and the metaphysical; the mythos and the logos that synthesize into the mythology that is the man. While there is one true Charles Foster Kane, he, like the famous Rosebud, will never be found. The citizen that is Kane is an accumulation of Charles Foster Kanes, each one a dramatic being wrought by dialectical relations with others. We can never discover the true Kane because the man is a myth. He is forever in the process of becoming and every generation will contribute to his being.

Terry Malloy
(from *On the Waterfront*, USA, 1954)

> *Longshoreman Terry Malloy is sent by union boss Johnny Friendly to call on Joey. Malloy calls out to Joey about having found his racing pigeon. Joey pokes his head out of the window and the two agree to meet on the roof of the tenement building. What Joey does not realize is that this is a ruse. When Joey gets to the roof Johnny Friendly's henchmen throw him off the building killing him. When Edie, Joey's sister, hears about Joey's death, she takes leave from her convent school and with the help of local cleric Father Barry they try to expose corruption on the dock yard and bring Joey's murderers to justice. Father Barry uses the church as a meeting place for those wanting justice but Johnny Friendly has his thugs terrorize the meeting. Malloy who was sent to the church to spy was surprised by the attack and helps Edie escape unharmed. A relationship develops between Malloy and Edie. Malloy is caught between his feelings for Edie, his loyalty to Johnny Friendly and Charley, and he is plagued by his newly emerged conscience over his part in Joey's death. When the Crimes Commission investigating the alleged dock yard corruption summon Malloy to testify he must make a public choice between his feelings for Edie and filial loyalty.*

Terry Malloy is not very intelligent which makes him easy to manipulate, but his lack of intelligence does not preclude him developing a conscience, or sensing what is right and wrong. At the very outset of the narrative the ethical dialectic is discernible in Malloy's character. Johnny Friendly tells Malloy "You take it from here, slugger." What Friendly means

2.4 Freaks, Tycoons and Contenders

is for Malloy to lure his friend Joey into a trap. There is prevarication on his face. He wants to be loyal to Friendly which means being disloyal to his friend, but he also wants to be loyal to his friend Joey which means being disloyal to Friendly. He is torn this way and that, like Medea whom we cited in an earlier part of this work. Malloy's own body language reveals the tension of being so conflicted. Malloy must make a choice—narrative demands it—and Malloy does choose and the consequences of his choice become the narrative of *On the Waterfront*. He must contend (and in this sense he really is a contender) with the dialectical pushing and pulling within the self.

When Edie, Joey's sister, arrives Molloy's choices become more difficult and the consequences of making those choices more dangerous. Joey's death was a ritual death, a thanatic rite for transgressing the code of silence. This is something that Malloy understands and consents to. Molloy's is a simple morality of the docks. Do it to him before he does it to you—a kind of inverse Golden Rule—but when Edie opens up to Malloy a more complicated and selfless morality—do unto others as you would have them do unto you—then Malloy's filial loyalty is put to the greatest test.

Under the auspices of Father Barry and the supposed protection of the church a meeting is called to provide a haven for free speech without the fear of Friendly's unfriendliness and to bring to justice Joey's killers. Malloy is sent to the church by Charley to spy on the meeting. Malloy knows who killed Joey Doyle. And he is acutely aware of his own implication in Joey's death, but he sits as a silent observer. But, when the church is attacked by Friendly's thugs—something which Malloy did not anticipate—he is quick to protect Edie and escort her safely from the building. Only the interpenetrability of eros and thanatos can produce such a narrative irony: Malloy sent the brother up to the roof and to his death while the sister he rescues from the basement and into life. This act of rescue begins a relationship that will continue to grow throughout the narrative. Out of thanatos emerges eros.

After escaping from the church Malloy and Edie make it to the park across the street. Edie immediately asks Malloy a crucial question. "Which side are you with?" and Malloy responds by evasively shrugging his shoulders and slyly grinning "Me, I'm with me"—self serves self and no other. At this point, Malloy's response may not be wholly untrue. Because he hasn't yet chosen a side, he is wavering, vacillating—the Hamletic response to crisis. To reveal Joey's killers or conceal Joey's killers; to be, or not to be, a

Part Two. Of Character

stoolie. But if the fence on which he rests must stand somewhere then it is in the property of Johnny Friendly's union. When Edie's glove falls Malloy picks it up and plays with it. The same hand that once slipped inside a boxing glove that was an implement of pugilistic violence is slipped inside the glove of a convent school girl—the sexual overtones are obvious and need no elucidation. This scene presents us with a unity of opposites—a dialectic of character—Malloy is an unintelligent man and failed boxer who now works as a longshoreman. Edie is an educated woman training to be a teacher. Malloy professes no faith, Edie is a woman of faith. Malloy is a physical man with a brutish demeanor. Edie is a spiritual woman with a delicate frame. Two opposites are brought together in unity—thesis and antithesis—and the process of dialectic will bring Malloy's dramatic being to a final synthesis.

When Edie visits Malloy among the rooftop pigeon coops Malloy reveals his own dialectical *weltanschauung*. He tells Edie that the city is full of hawks who hang around the top of the big hotels and when they spot a pigeon in the park they swoop down on them. For Malloy, the world in which he lives is marked between the hawk-esque (*accipitine*) and pigeon-esque (*columbine*). The hawks kill the pigeons, Johnny Friendly is a hawk, his own brother, Charley the Gent is a hawk and Malloy, is by proxy a hawk; whereas Joey was a pigeon and he died like a pigeon, preyed on by a hawk. Predators and the prey—a natural unity of opposites—and Malloy seems partly conscious that if his brother Charley was not a hawk then he would not be a hawk. Malloy's is a twofold nature. He is both predator and prey—hawk and pigeon.

When Malloy takes Edie for a beer at the saloon he restates his ornithological dialectic. Edie counters with the sentiment "Isn't everybody a part of everybody else?" But the love thy neighbor philosophy runs in stark contrast to the waterfront cynicism of Malloy who subverts the Golden Rule. One is either predator (hawk) or prey (pigeon). Edie is shocked. Such a life and outlook is no better than an animal, to which Malloy retorts "Better a live animal than a ..." omitting the ending "dead man" implying Joey Doyle. Malloy's words echo Solomon's pessimistic aphorism: "Better a live dog than a dead lion." Malloy's is a philosophy of the purely vitative, living in the state of being alive is the be all and end all. Life is a struggle and one must continue to fight if one is to survive a hostile world. And again it harks back the contrast of hawks and pigeons, the dialectic of the accipitine and the columbine, victor and victim, life and death.

2.4 Freaks, Tycoons and Contenders

Edie and Malloy meet once more on the rooftop among the pigeon coops. Edie brings Joey's jacket. The Jacket serves as a ritual symbol like the mantle passed from Elijah to Elisha in Old Testament prophecy. Joey testified to the Crime Commission and died. His jacket is given to Kayo Dugan who testifies to the Crime Commission and died. Edie now brings the jacket to Malloy who must testify to the Crime Commission and must choose to live or die. Thus the jacket becomes a kind of mantle of truth; the wearer of which must bear no false testimony but—and in accordance with the dialectic of sacrifice—losing one's life is to gain one's soul. Edie knows that this might be end of Malloy and so they kiss for the first time. The troubled habitués of the coops are nervous from the ever-present threat of a hawk which is no accident—the king pigeon Malloy is about to enter a nest of hawks. In the labial lock of a kiss Malloy makes his choice. He is no longer torn between his brother and Edie, nor is he torn between the camaraderie of men folk and the delicate touch of a woman, neither is he torn between truth and lies. The kiss brings two opposites together, whose separate mouths form a single point of being, opposites melding into unity, Molloy must choose and chooses.

At the court hearing Malloy testifies against Johnny Friendly. The son has turned against the father. Friendly threatens him and he is given a police escort for protection. But in the world of the dockyard when a "canary" sings no one whistles back. Malloy is alone. In contrast to his situation at the beginning, in the midst of the corrupt union, Malloy must make his stand alone. Malloy finally confronts the father figure like Oedipus at the crossroads with Laius; except Malloy is fully conscious of his act (more conscious than Oedipus): Malloy's parricide is deliberate.

Having chosen to be a pigeon Malloy must confront Friendly the hawk one last time. The final conflict takes place on the docks. Malloy is all but beaten until a sacerdotal lie from Father Barry impels Malloy to get to his feet. Unlike the boxing matches in the past when Malloy had willfully taken a dive at Friendly's orders Malloy now staggers to his feet, picks up his longshoreman's hook and stumbles under his own power. Like Christ dragging himself along Calvary Malloy staggers into work followed by all the longshoremen. Malloy has come of age. Having overthrown his father figure Malloy is now a leader inspiring men by example to do the right thing. He has redeemed himself through sacrifice and his sacrifice offers redemption for others.

2.5

Vaudevillians, Hollywoodians and Magicians

Checco Dal Monte
(from *Luci del varietà / Variety Lights*, Italy, 1950)

Checco Dal Monte is the impresario of a small and financially insecure vaudeville troupe. One night as they perform in a small Italian village one young woman named Liliana is particularly enamored with the performance. Liliana wants to be a performer so after the show ends she looks for Checco but is summarily dismissed. Checco has more important issues—financial problems—there is no money to be paid. When the troupe leave town on a train, Liliana follows. She seeks out Checco and finds him asleep. Liliana wakes him and shows him her portfolio. She tells Checco that she wants to get into show biz and has had that passion since childhood. Checco is attracted to Liliana and cannot help himself and tries to feel Liliana's legs. When they arrive in the new town they have no money for a carriage ride from the station and so the entire troupe must walk into town. After a short while, the carriage they could not afford pulls to a stop. Liliana is on board. She invites everyone one to climb aboard and off they go. At the new venue Liliana expresses the desire to be a dancer but there is consternation among the group. How can they afford to pay a new dancer when there is not enough money or food for the troupe already? Liliana gets her chance to dance. She does her best not knowing any of the dance moves but when her pants fall down the crowd—the majority of which are men—go wild. Liliana is embarrassed and flees but the local contractor drags her back on to the stage without her pants and the crowd once again goes wild. Liliana quickly becomes a sell-out act. Night after night she is sought out by adoring fans. After one performance

2.5 Vaudevillians, Hollywoodians and Magicians

a lawyer called Renzo who loves to sing arias from Le nozzi di Figaro offers to take Liliana to dinner. A large group of performers from the troupe accompany Renzo and Liliana to his villa where they entertain themselves by preparing the food and after which they dine. After dinner everybody joins in singing and dancing. Checco, however, is getting jealous of Liliana and Renzo. He breaks up the party using the excuse that they all have an early start in the morning. When Renzo plays a waltz Liliana asks Checco to dance before they all retire for the night. While Liliana sleeps Renzo enters her room but Checco ensures that any and all coitus is interrupted. Renzo is angry and kicks everybody out of his house. Checco is too absorbed with Liliana on the walk home to help his fiancée, Melina lift the hung-over member of the troupe. Cupid works his magic and very soon after Checco has left Melina and is acting as Liliana's agent with dreams of forming a company together. But Liliana grows tired of having no money and demands instant stardom. Checco is desperate to please Liliana and when he meets Johnny, an American jazz trumpeter, on the streets of Rome, he gathers together a poor vagabond variety act. Checco needs money however. He visits Melina to beg for money which she gives him but asks that she never see him again. Checco is delighted, he has money and his vagrant variety act with Liliana as the star. Checco sets up a grand rehearsal and invites a theatre director to watch. On the day of the rehearsal Liliana tells Checco she has signed a contract with Parmesiano and is off to Milan. She thanks him for everything and says goodbye. After Liliana leaves Checco collapses…. Liliana is adored in her new company and on her way to being a star. Checco returns to Melina and his old company.

"The meaning of the dance," says the Hungarian choreographer, "is a struggle between good and evil." All art is a conflict between opposites. Art is dialectic. So too is the character of Checco. But the character of this mediocre artist is not a conflict as grand and universal as that between good and evil, but the contrary nature of reality and dreams; of believing oneself to be something greater than one is. At the outset Checco believes himself to be a great artist demanding the highest respect, but his talents are meager and the vaudeville troupe to which he belongs can only offer the paltriest of performances at best. Yet Checco dreams of grandeur, the same grandeur that he insists belongs to him.

When the beautiful but talentless Liliana appears on the scene, his belief in great things and his dreams of success begin to obfuscate his view of reality. He encourages Liliana to join and pursue her dream of show business even though she can neither sing nor dance. Although everyone else in the group, including the long-suffering Melina, can see that Liliana is using Checco, he is blinded by his desire for Liliana and dreams of his own success. The dream soon usurps reality and Checco becomes so convinced that he will have success with Liliana that he abandons Melina. Melina had believed that they would soon marry and had been saving money together for a future outside of performing arts.

Checco, with all the skill his mediocrity can muster, works to assemble a group of performers to form his own company and make Liliana a star, but the best that Checco can achieve is to gather vagrant artists from off the streets of Rome. With no money of his own and an increasingly demanding Liliana he is forced to beg money from Melina to finance his operation—pride must be humbled, but Checco is less humble than conniving in securing money from Melina, and one suspects that Melina knows deep down that Checco will return to her. She knows Liliana is using Checco and once he is spent he will have no recourse other than return to Melina. It is a curious kind of eros that will submit temporarily to thanatos. Melina's is an eros of faith. In the end Liliana wants more than Checco can offer and ruthlessly abandons him to perform in Paris and Milan with Parmesiano's company. Checco's dream and Checco's reality are so opposed and he has been so blind to the opposition so long that his realization does violence to his consciousness. Checco collapses. His collapse is a symbolic death. The final synthesis of his struggle. He recovers and returns to his old life. He returns to Melina who takes him, because he was always Melina's and always will be even when he is not.

Norma Desmond
(from *Sunset Blvd.*, USA, 1950)

> *Joseph C. Gillis is a dead screenwriter. Six months earlier he was very much alive but very much in debt. When his car is almost repossessed Gillis begs for money from his friends and his agent without success. As he is driving home the repo men spot him on the road and give chase.*

2.5 Vaudevillians, Hollywoodians and Magicians

One of his tires blows so Gillis pulls into the driveway of a dilapidated mansion. Gillis is invited inside by Max the butler. Gillis is mistaken for an undertaker to oversee the burial of a pet chimpanzee. When Gillis sees the mourning pet owner he recognizes her as Norma Desmond, a famed actress from the era of silent pictures. When Norma discovers that Gillis is a screenwriter she tells him about her own script based on the story of Salomé which she intends to star in. Gillis has nowhere to be and no car to get anywhere so he agrees to read the script late into the night. Gillis is subsequently asked to edit the script for Norma and if he agrees he can stay in a room above the garage. With no money to pay his rent Gillis agrees. When he wakes the next morning he is a little perturbed to find that all his belongings, his books and typewriter have all been fetched for him. Over the next few weeks Gillis works on the script during the day and in the evening he and Norma watch old silent films in which she starred. One night heavy rain falls and water leaks through Gillis' roof so he is moved into the main house, although it means he will lose the only private time and space he has. Gillis notices that there are no handles or locks on any of the doors. When he asks Max why, Max tells him that in moments of melancholy Norma has displayed suicidal behavior and her doctor advises against locks so she cannot harm herself. After a little time Gillis also finds out from Max that the many fan letters that keep Normas's spirits up are in fact written and sent by Max. Things get stranger still when Norma hosts a New Year's party. There is champagne, a live band plays tango, but Norma and Gillis are the only guests. The situation is too strange for Gilles and he and Norma fight. She flees upstairs and Gilles leaves to find a real New Year's party. Gilles hitchhikes into the city and tracks down an old friend hosting a party. He recognizes Betty, a young and attractive script reader who had negatively critiqued a baseball script he had previously pitched to Paramount studios. The two flirt but guilt creeps into Gillis' conscience and he calls Max to find out how Norma is doing. Max tells him that Norma has cut her wrists. Gillis rushes back to Norma. She tells him to leave and threatens to kill herself again. "Happy New Year," he tells her and they kiss. "Happy new year, darling." The two are officially a couple now. One evening Max gets a call from Paramount. Norma is convinced it is Cecil B. DeMille wanting to work on her Salomé script. Several days later Norma visits the studios and asks to see DeMille—who plays himself.

Part Two. Of Character

DeMille pities Norma and agrees to see her. She is offered his director's seat in the studio and everyone rushes to see her. DeMille makes a phone call and discovers that the real reason Paramount called Norma is to rent her antiquated car for a film they are making. Elsewhere Gillis spots Betty, and she tells him that she really does like his baseball script and that they should work on it together. Norma, however, still believing she will be making a film with DeMille, subjects herself to a rigorous beauty regimen and early nights. Every night after Norma has gone to bed Gillis sneaks out to Betty's office where they work through the night on his script. Even though Betty is engaged to Arty she senses she is falling in love with Gillis and Gillis is falling in love with Betty, but—ever the professional—the script must be finished before Gillis will allow himself to get too close to her. One night after Gillis returns from seeing Betty, Max is waiting for him. He knows exactly what Gillis is doing with Betty. Max tells him that he was Norma's first husband, that he first made her a star and that he will not let her be destroyed by anyone, including Gillis. Cupid is difficult to thwart and despite their valiant efforts Gillis and Betty are in love. Betty plans to leave Arty and Gillis plans to leave Norma. Norma, for her part, is not oblivious to what is going on. Norma calls Betty on the telephone and Gillis overhears Norma telling her the truth about Gillis' circumstance. He takes the phone from Norma and tells Betty to come over. Betty arrives to find Norma weeping. Gillis tells Betty the whole story and Betty asks Gillis to leave with her. Gillis, however, lists his belongings and the perks of his relationship with Norma. He walks Betty out and tells her goodbye and sends her on her way to Arty, who is unaware of everything and waiting for her in Arizona. Gillis goes to his room to packs his things. He is leaving Norma, Hollywood and heading back home to Dayton, Ohio. Norma refuses to let him go and shoots him. We return to the beginning. The police are pulling Gillis' body out of the pool. Norma, under arrest, descends the stairs for her final scene as Salomé. The reporters are set up with their cameras and Max directs the action. Norma at the acme of her career utters her most important line: "All right, Mr. DeMille, I'm ready for my close-up."

Norma Desmond is ephemeral like all things in Hollywood. Time spent in the limelight is finite, and one remains interesting only so long as nothing of greater interest arrives. Norma's plight however is her belief in

2.5 Vaudevillians, Hollywoodians and Magicians

the infinite, in her own eternal worth, in the bygone age of silent pictures. Within her dilapidated mansion she has set up a shrine of sorts to the old days keeping at bay the outside world that pushes in at an ever increasing rate. Within her mansion she can live and relive her days as a star of the silver screen. The finite made infinite. And had Joe Gillis not turned up on her doorstep she would have continued to exist as such until her quiet death. But the arrival of Gillis brings novelty to a world that is long past its used-by-date. Gillis by his being present makes stark the contrast between Norma's reality and everyday life. She is shut away inside a dilapidated mansion with her first husband, Max, who now exists as her servant, and protector. For Desmond the only reality is the fictional life of cinema. Not the drab everyday life. The dead that she knew in life are still alive every night on film. The only movies she watches are her own from the glory days of silent film allowing her relive and resurrect the ones she loved. Her existence is a stagnation that has slowly festered and decomposed like the exterior of her house. The only things kept new are the old.

The arrival of Joe Gillis, a penniless screenwriter, tempts Norma into trying something new. She has a script based on the story of Salomé, who in legend was the beautiful daughter of Herod whose sensual dance earned the head of John the Baptist on a platter. Norma takes him in, pays for everything, and falls in love with him while he writes her great cinematic piece. Cecil B. DeMille, with whom she worked in her glory days, will direct. Even when trying something new Norma is in reality trying to resurrect the past. Norma lives in the past, in the time of silent pictures before speech adulterated gesture. "I can say a thousand things with my eyes," says Norma. Her entire mansion and its décor are all situated in the past, just like the old car she keeps in the garage, which is the only interest the modern studios have in Norma. She believes the call from Paramount will initiate her comeback; working with DeMille again, on the Salomé script with a bright future awaiting her. But it is not Norma that Paramount want, but a prop, the value of which is its history. The dialectic between the past and the future and the impossible task of recreating a bygone age is the source of Norma's agony, and the agony is so extreme at times that suicide becomes a possibility.

Norma is finite believing herself to possess some species of infinity. But she is all too conscious of her finitude and at times the torment caused by such consciousness leads to depressive episodes and suicidal behavior and will in the end drive to her to insanity and homicide—and perhaps a

Part Two. Of Character

celebrity she could never otherwise attain. Norma is a relic of Hollywood and in Hollywood relics do not even possess archeological value, they are of no more worth than dust and ash. Norma is old and valueless. Hollywood values only novelty, youth, and profit. Even the veteran director, Cecil De Mille, who had retained value by moving with the times, dismisses her. Norma's deluded sense of her own value when confronted with her valuelessness in the eyes of Hollywood is the source of her inner conflict and eventual madness. Norma's insanity confirms her belief that she belongs to the race of cinematic immortals and so Gillis must die because Norma will not.

Albert Emanuel Vogler
(from *Ansiktet / The Magician*, Sweden, 1958)

> *Albert Emanuel Vogler is chief magician and practicing magnetizer of the Magnetic Health Theatre. One night they are travelling by carriage through the woods when the coach driver stops the carriage at the sound of ghouls and spirits howling. Albert investigates and finds a very sick Johan Spegel—a drunken actor. Vogler returns to the carriage with the drunk. Vogler and Spegel discuss the nature of truth and deception just before Spegel dies. They report the death to the local police, who take them to the house of Consul Egerman, who is interested in spiritualism. Vogler is questioned regarding his activities but Vogler is a mute and cannot answer any questions. Mr. Aman (Vogler's wife, Manda Vogler, in disguise) must answer for him. Vogler's skills and abilities are questioned by the Consul and his companions. His skills are put to the test by the skeptical Doctor Vergerus, the local minister of health. The Chief of Police decides that a private drawing room performance in the morning ought to verify Vogler's alleged abilities. Vogler accepts the challenge. A wager between Egerman, who is a believer, and Doctor Vergerus, a skeptic, is placed—a unity of opposites. The night passes slowly as parlor tricks are performed in the kitchen and among the Consul's servant staff, love potions are sold and sexual encounters are embarked upon. To the surprise of everyone, Spegel—the dead drunken actor—is alive. He surges into the kitchen and helps himself to brandy. Meanwhile, Vogler is sternly preparing for the morning performance when Egerman's wife,*

2.5 Vaudevillians, Hollywoodians and Magicians

Ottilia, visits him, dressed in black and mourning for her stillborn daughter. She believes that Vogler has been sent by God to explain to her why her child died and what God's purpose was. Ottilia asks Vogler to come to her room at 2 a.m. Meanwhile, Vergerus discovers Vogler's wife, Manda, out of her disguise. When questioned by Vergerus she tells him it is all a fraud. It is all pretense; a lie through and through. When Vogler enters and finds Vergerus alone with his wife the two men grapple and Vergerus is forced to leave. Vogler then takes off his disguise and speaks: "I hate them!" The following morning Vogler's theatre performs. Egerman and his companions laugh and jeer at the mostly vaudevillian performances but Vogler is able to make the Police Chief's wife, Henrietta, speak all kinds of embarrassing things and the rather burly stableman Antonssen is inexplicably bound by "invisible chains." Antonssen is so disturbed by his inability to break free that he tries to attack Vogler before running away. The strain of the performance takes its toll on Vogler and he collapses and dies. The Police Chief says there will be no criminal investigation but the body of Vogler will be autopsied by Doctor Vergerus for scientific reasons. Vogler's body is taken up to the attic where Vergerus will work on the autopsy. Alone with Vogler's body Vergerus begins to experience strange happenings. He finds an eyeball in his ink well. His papers fly off the desk. A disembodied hand touches him. He thinks it must be the heat or momentary nausea. When Vergerus tries to leave the attic he finds himself locked in. His eyeglasses are pulled off his face. Vergerus tells himself it is a dream or a sudden onset of madness. He looks for some way to escape but is confronted by the dead Vogler. Vergerus runs from what he thinks is an apparition but falls down the stairs. Vogler leans over Vergerus. He wants to kill him but Manda brings him to his senses. Still, the ever-skeptical Vergerus refuses to believe anything supernatural took place. Vogler has done all he can but it is now time to leave. Just as the theatre group are getting ready to leave a large police escort arrives. Vogler is informed that the King of Sweden requests their presence and they are to be escorted to His Royal Presence.

What appears to be is not necessarily what is. As we have already discovered in Plato, dialectic can play tricks with us: what is is not and what is not is. Vogler appears to have collar length black hair and a beard but

Part Two. Of Character

does not. He appears to be mute, but he is not; his wife, Manda appears to be a man (called Aman) but is not. Vogler appears to have uncanny powers but does not, and at one point Vogler appears to be dead but is not. Appearance and reality are often opposites. Vogler is a grand representative of semblances, a high priest of seeming. Vogler finds his antithesis in the character of Doctor Vergerus, who is a man of science, and as a man of science demands empirical evidence if anything is to be proven beyond what seems or appears to be. An appearance no matter how spectacular is not reality. Vogler is more acutely aware of this than anyone.

The darkness that resides in Vogler, from which his loathing of others shines, is his being acutely aware of his own self as a mere appearance. Vogler's agony stems from that fact he wishes appearances were reality; that his tricks were not tricks but substantial powers under his control. But he knows his preternatural powers are only as natural as his beard. Unrealities are real only to those who gulp down love potions expecting Aphrodite's touch. The apparent becomes real to those who make it real, who are willing to believe the apparent is real, but reality has its own appearance, and a man like Vogler is painfully aware of the distinction. There is great art in quackery but it has nothing to do with reality. Quackery pays the bills for Vogler, but it cannot feed the soul. And as long as there are people willing to believe in the apparent as real there will be a paying audience and Vogler can feed his stomach. Just such a believer swoops in at the end: the King of Sweden himself wants an audience and orders the police commissioner to provide an escort to his royal court where—as everyone knows—appearances matter more than anything else. Vogler does what he does because there is an audience for it but he is himself remains discontent. He spends his day being what he is not thus he has no way of being what he is and his agony is manifest.

2.6

April Lovers, Chanteuses and Writers

April Lovers
(from Aprili / April, Georgia, USSR, 1961)

    Two young lovers are playful and unencumbered as they court one another in poverty. When they marry they move into a newly built apartment. The apartment is small and bare but their love provides them with electricity and running water. Every kiss provides for their essential needs. A hunchbacked little neighbor offers them a chair—a small and unassuming comfort—so they do not have to sit on the floor. They are happy and spend the day in the country and kiss beneath the boughs of a great tree. But slowly they are encouraged by the little Hunchback to acquire one or two more items. Everybody else is busy accumulating things. Slowly the two April Lovers begin to acquire tables and chairs, cabinets and glassware to fill the cabinets. Next they acquire electrical items: vacuum cleaners, oscillating fans, blenders, etc., all running at once so that the hum and din of the electricity makes the hunchbacked neighbor complain of the noise. More and more items are acquired and wood is needed to build these new items so the tree beneath which the April Lovers previously kissed is chopped down. The April Lovers begin to argue and with every argument further belongings are acquired. They argue and acquire, argue and acquire, until the love they once had has disappeared leaving acrimony and the clutter of material possessions to fill the apartment. With so little love left the power runs out. A complete and total blackout puts everyone in darkness. One light remains. A simple trumpet player whose music is able to restore the light long enough for the April Lovers to remember the simplicity of the old days. Only by ridding themselves of materialistic encumbrances can they return to the initial purity of the love they had at first. They throw everything away, the love that was crowded out now has space to flourish and happiness returns. Running water and electricity return with each kiss. Love has returned to the April Lovers.

Aprili was banned by the Soviet authorities for being "too spiritual" and it is not difficult to see why. On the Sermon on the Mount Jesus told his followers:

> The light of the body is the eye: if therefore thine eye be single, thy whole body shall be full of light. But if thine eye be evil, thy whole body shall be full of darkness. If therefore the light that is in thee be darkness, how great is that darkness! No man can serve two masters: for either he will hate the one, and love the other; or else he will hold to the one, and despise the other. Ye cannot serve God and mammon.[1]

At first the April Lovers had a simple, single and focused eye. It was their love. They did not need the accoutrements and material acquisitions that everybody around them seemed to be busying themselves with. They needed each other only. Like the Aristophanic dialectic each counterpart had found the other and in finding each other had found satisfaction. Even the new apartment was no impediment to their love. It was a fresh start. A foundation on which to build the rest of their relationship. The April Lovers loved each other and their life was "full of light." Light literally filled their apartment when love was present. A kiss is enough to illuminate the light bulb, or ignite the gas stove. But temptation lurks in the form of the Hunchback—a minion of Mammon—and the two April Lovers get caught up in the frenzy of acquisition. And it is not the acquisition of necessities but the acquisition of superfluities that endangers their love. Before long material things crowd the apartment. There is neither space to move nor sleep. Love is crowded out leaving space for its opposite, hate to flourish—opposites becoming opposites. The two April Lovers suddenly find themselves in "darkness," and "how great is that darkness!"

When the April Lovers remember the days of old and how simple life was before they were caught up in snares of the Mammonesque hunchback they want to return to how things were. No one can serve two masters. The April Lovers must make a choice. They must choose to serve eros and return to the purity of love or they can serve Mammon and sacrifice love to

2.6 April Lovers, Chanteuses and Writers

thanatos. After the large tree was felled—a Tree of Life symbol—under which they once kissed the two April Lovers appeared to be on an irremediable course toward spiritual death. The great darkness that had shrouded everyone in the building was the enveloping embrace of thanatos. It was almost too late. But one man kept the idea of the simple life alive, the aged trumpet player whose music like Orpheus brought the inanimate to their senses. The April Lovers threw out all that they had accumulated because it was all unnecessary impediments to love. Every piece of newly acquired furniture fashioned from the fallen tree had the flavor of death—the taste of thanatos—and as such had no place among the simple accoutrements of eros. In the decluttered space love began to flourish. The light of eros returned and the darkness of thanatos extinguished.

Florence "Cléo" Victoire
(from *Cléo de 5 à 7 / Cléo from 5 to 7*, France, 1962)

> He hath a daily beauty in his life
> That makes me ugly.
> —Shakespeare

Florence "Cléo" Victoire is a chanteuse living in 1960s Paris. So far she has released three singles but a recent illness threatens her bright future. She is afraid she has cancer and is awaiting the results of tests from her doctor. In an attempt to circumvent the waiting and discover the results Cléo consults a Fortune Teller. The Fortune Teller uses Tarot cards and is able to read that Cléo is sick—that she does have cancer—but the Fortune Teller withholds from Cléo what the cards reveal. To make herself feel better Cléo wants to buy a hat, but she is warned by the superstitious Angèle, her maid and keeper, that it is ill-advised to wear a new hat on Tuesdays or to carry anything new on Tuesdays. The hat is therefore delivered to Cléo's apartment. Cléo returns to her apartment to rehearse with her songwriter and lyricist. They perform a new song, but the lyrics contain the word despair which is too much for Cléo to handle and she breaks down. When she is called a spoiled child, she petulantly leaves so as to be alone effectively ending the rehearsal. Cléo visits a café and plays one of her own songs on the jukebox but nobody cares. She

Part Two. Of Character

leaves the café and visits her friend, Dorothée, who works as a nude model for artists and sculptors, a job Cléo says she could never perform. Later Cléo meets with Raoul, Dorothée's boyfriend, a young film maker. They watch a few minutes of a short film before leaving. Cléo shares a taxi with Dorothée and tells her about her fears, but Dorothée is dismissive of Cléo's superstitions. After dropping Dorothée off Cléo continues to a park. She meets Antoine, a soldier who is due to be deployed to Algeria on the night train. The two talk and when Cléo tells him that she is awaiting a test, Antoine suggests they visit the hospital rather than call the doctor. They take the bus to the hospital and when they catch up with Cléo's doctor she receives her test results.

"Ugliness is a kind of death. As long as I am beautiful I am alive," Cléo says to herself. Few characters offer such an explicit utterance of dialectic. Ugliness is Death. Beauty is Life. Thanatos in conflict with Eros. Cléo is afraid of ugliness and there is no greater form of physical ugliness than disease and there are few diseases more frightening than cancer. Cléo is convinced by her superstitious maid, Angèle, to have her fortune read and when she does the cartomancer tells Cléo: "The illness is upon you," Cléo pulls out the death card—the very image of thanatos. Cléo leaves feeling doomed. She does not know for certain she has cancer but uncertainty often breeds more fear than certainty. When Cléo visits her best friend Dorothée who is posing naked for a sculpting class we find two opposite views of the female body expressed. Cléo tells Dorothée that it would not be possible for her to pose naked.

Cléo sees her body as a concrete thing, a canvas of potential imperfections that, if they were not pointed out by others, she herself would notice. Dorothée, on the contrary, conceives of her own body differently. Her body is not a concrete thing with imperfections but an abstract entity capable of inspiring the artist or the sculptor. Her body is the starting point of great ideas, and when she poses Dorothée is not acutely conscious of herself, as Cléo would be, but enjoys a kind of sleep, a reposing unconsciousness only to become self aware when the job is done. Cléo and Dorothée represent opposites of a corporal dialectic.

When Cléo and Antoine meet the dialogue that takes place in the park returns to the topic of nudity. Antoine tells Cléo that nudity is "like the sun, like birth, and health." But Cléo claims that nudity is "indiscreet like night,

2.6 April Lovers, Chanteuses and Writers

or illness."—a unity of opposites. What Cléo sees as negative is viewed by Antoine as positive; the dialectic of perspective. This scene echoes the idea in Raoul's short film. The situation for the protagonists remains the same. But when the young man puts on his dark glasses everything takes on a negative aspect. His lover's skin turns black and her white dress also changes color to black—what matters is inverted like a photographic negative.

When the young man takes off the dark glasses his world immediately reverts to the way it was. Perspective suddenly shifts from the negative into the positive—from one opposite into the other. Realizing that his lover is safe and the world is bright as it ought to be he disposes of the dark glasses. The film ends when the two young lovers kiss. The conflict—the dialectic—is revealed in a world of white perceived as black. Opposite perceived as opposite. As the conversation with Antoine continues he declares that it is the first day of summer and as such the goddess Flora should be venerated and Cléo will be his Flora for the day. Excitedly he tells Cléo that the summer solstice means, in astrological terms, that Gemini is leaving Cancer. But the word "cancer" perturbs Cléo and she tells him to be quiet. The discussion then turns to love and death—a unity of opposites which we know to be expressions of eros and thanatos—Antoine, who is set to be deployed to Algeria, tells Cléo that he would happily die for a woman but not in a senseless war; for Antoine thanatos is worthwhile only in the service of eros.

Cléo is a unity of opposites, she is the embodiment of beauty united with the ugliness of disease. Just as health and disease are aspects of the same spectrum so too are beauty and ugliness varying degrees of the same thing. Cléo as the embodiment of beauty is that which radiates and also that which degenerates. Her body which affords Cléo her beauty is in revolt, and the very thing that is beautiful is subject to malady and decay. For Cléo's that which is not beautiful is dead. "Ugliness is a kind of death." There is nothing more ugly than cancer. But cancer is erotic. Cancer is that which teems with life, new cells splitting, growing; but the superabundance and superfluity brings with it death. Thus cancer is also thanatic—it consumes that which supplies it with life until there is no more life to consume. Within Cléo a conflict rages between life and death, the beautiful and the ugly; the eternal dance of eros and thanatos.

Part Two. Of Character

Pontus
(from *Svält / Sult / Hunger*, Denmark, Norway, Sweden, 1966)

    Pontus is a starving writer living in Christiana (now Oslo). He struggles to earn enough money to pay his rent and has not eaten properly for many days. His days are spent wandering the streets looking for work and when he can't find work he is forced to pawn his meager belongings for a few pennies. He tries to enlist with the fire brigade but is turned down—twice—because of his emaciated condition. When he meets an artist friend he is invited to dine but eats nothing because he cannot afford food. When he sees a small dog getting scraps he walks out. Pontus spends much time on benches trying to write his masterpiece but is too easily distracted by others. On one occasion Pontus is distracted by two well-dressed ladies. He follows them for half a day, until well after sundown. The younger he follows home and names her Ylajali. Pontus is awakened from a nightmare by a police officer who finds him on a park bench. Pontus returns home to find a note from his landlady evicting him. The visions and hallucinations brought on by starvation become more and more severe. After regaining his senses Pontus writes an article which he believes is a masterpiece. He takes it to a publisher and is told to return at 3 p.m. for the editor's decision. Pontus takes to the streets again, killing time until he can return to the publishers. Pontus encounters a limping beggar whom he follows when the beggar asks for money Pontus pawns his waistcoat and gives the money to the beggar, but when the beggar realizes what has happened and sees the condition of Pontus' shoes the beggar refuses the money. Pontus indignantly refuses to take the money back and leaves abruptly. While still waiting for 3 p.m. Pontus tries to get a job as bookkeeper for Christie's but is turned down because his letter has the date 1848, when it is 1890, an error that Mr. Christie cannot overlook. Pontus returns to the editorial office and is told that he must return the next day at 3 p.m. if he wants to get his article published. With no money and no room Pontus is forced to spend the night under a bridge. The next day Pontus must wander Christiana until 3 p.m. But his mental faculties are rapidly deteriorating. He tells an old homeless man a fantasy tale about Ylajali and him being a "gentleman thief" before cursing the old man for not believing him. Pontus takes a

2.6 April Lovers, Chanteuses and Writers

carriage ride from one place to another on phantom errands looking for imaginary people. On one of the errands Pontus finds a rooming house for tourists where he manages to secure a room for the night on credit. When 3 p.m. finally arrives Pontus speaks with the editor. The Editor likes his article but it needs toning down a little. He will be paid 10 kroner when it is rewritten. If Pontus can finish the piece he will be paid. His room has no candle so Pontus rewrites the article under a streetlamp. But he catches sight of Ylajali. He follows her and they talk. She agrees to meet him the following evening at the same place, kisses him and runs into the night. The next night Pontus meets with Ylajali, who invites him up to her apartment. But her coquettishness becomes coyness when he tries to undress her. Pontus leaves disgusted. He returns to his room to find it has been let to another man and he must finish rewriting his article in a family room with babies crying and children taunting a senile old man who spits. The next morning the postman delivers 10 kroner for Pontus' proposed article but Pontus throws the money at his landlady's face walks to the docks where he boards a boat leaving Christiana behind.

Pontus wants to eat, but more than anything he wants to write. By the end of the narrative Pontus has done neither. Writing like eating belongs to the will to life, the life drive, or the creative principle of eros. Sadly for Pontus the entire narrative as it unfolds is a litany of self-defeating actions and thanatic gestures that distract from his creative endeavors and actively oppose his will to life. In the opening scene he is scribbling away with a pencil. The act of writing is a manifestation of creation and life. But he quickly becomes frustrated puts the paper into his mouth and starts chewing. Writing becomes unwriting. Life succumbs to death. It is a symbolic act by which Pontus tastes the bitterness of his own words. He coughs and spits the wad into the river below where it enters into a living death—the limbo of literature, neither written nor read. It has been said that man cannot live on bread alone, but Pontus lives on neither bread nor his own utterance.

Pontus is perpetually in need but at every turn his necessities are negated by himself. He needs money but when he acquires money he gives it away; when he pawns his belongings he gives the proceeds to a vagrant. He needs food and buys food but cannot stomach it yet will gnaw at raw flesh on scrap bones in a dark alley. Pontus needs to write but cannot. He needs charity but refuses it. He is a walking mass on contrary impulses. His existence is a nightmare of contradictions. When he accidentally receives change from a grocer the shame and indignation that is aroused in him causes him to give the money to a poor widow and then lambast the grocer for his negligence. To keep the money for himself is unthinkable even though he is in desperate need of money. His honesty while noble stems from the same pride that refuses help and is in the end self-defeating. Pontus is persistently pulled one way and another—like Plato's horses—so fierce is the tension that his psyche begins to fragment. Pontus exhibits paranoia, suffers hallucinations and is obsessed with time and its accurate accounting. As his disintegration continues he pretends to be someone other than himself searching for fictitious people. Even the beautiful lady he names Ylajali like a magical incantation—as Nabokov would do with LO.LEE.TA in the following century—is both real and unreal. Hunger feeds his hallucinations while his sanity starves. And all the time Pontus should be writing.

2.7

Ascetics, Asses and Alters

Simón
(from *Simón del desierto* / *Simon of the Desert*, Mexico, 1965)

> *I prayed you for chastity and said: "Grant me chastity and continence, but not yet."*—St. Augustine

Simón is a devout man who has adopted the extreme ascetic life of a stylite. To be closer to God and away from the distractions of human interaction that interfere with spiritual purification he has lived on a small platform at the top of a tall pillar for 6 years 6 weeks 6 days—readers of the Apocalypse cannot but find significance in the number. Simón's basic needs are supplied by pilgrims and devotees who bring him water and lettuce. A wealthy man purchases a new column for Simón to live on. For the occasion of his ascension to the new pillar hundreds of pilgrims arrive for the rare privilege of kissing his feet. Among the faithful throng is his mother but Simón is so devout that he—like Jesus before him—will not suffer his mother's interference. Simón even refuses Holy Orders claiming to be too unworthy a sinner to hold the office of priest. Simón climbs to the top of his new column as the throng below praise him. He conducts a prayer. One woman cries out about her husband's stumps. Her husband had his hands cut off for stealing and if Simón is merciful can he restore them. Simón prays in silence. Then he cries "You are whole" and man's hands are restored—which he uses to slap his child. Simón is alone and meditating when a young girl approaches. Down by the base of the pillar the young girl exposes her thighs and breasts to Simón. Then she is suddenly next to him playing with his beard. She shows Simón her tongue which writhes sensuously before she stabs him. Simón knows this is a temptation of Satan. On another occasion Simón is giving a sermon to the brotherhood of monks. One monk

Part Two. Of Character

finds wine, bread, and cheese in Simón's knapsack, insinuating that he is a fraud. The elderly monks put faith in Simón but the allegation is enough to create consternation among the younger monks. They decide that a prayer will reveal the truth. Their prayer is answered. The monk who accused Simón is revealed to be possessed by the devil. He spits and curses Simón, crying "Death to Jesus Christ" before collapsing from a seizure. The other monks carry him back to the monastery to perform an exorcism. Sometime later Satan appears again as Jesus—although Jesus looks more like a Greek hermaphrodite holding a lamb—"If you would please me stop your penance and taste earthly pleasure until you are nauseated." But Simón knows this is Satan speaking and not his Lord the Christ. The hermaphroditic Jesus attacks Simón with a sling shot and then vanishes. Simón chastises himself for mistaking the wolf for the lamb and vows to stands on only one foot as penance. Later a coffin appears dragging itself across the ground to Simón's column. Inside is the Devil. Satan transports Simón away from his tower into the future. We see airplanes, New York City; inside a modern club we hear rock music, see young people dancing wildly, others are smoking and drinking. Simón is sat at a small table with Satan. "Get thee behind me," he says apathetically. Simón has decided to go home. But Satan tells Simón that he cannot go home. He is stuck here until the end. Someone else has taken his place.

From all outward appearances Simón is the greatest example of purity and penance. Great crowds of monks and peasant regularly visit him with food, to listen to his sermons, and occasionally receive a blessed miracle. When questioned or ridiculed he answers in the mild-tempered manner of Christ claiming that he is only an unworthy sinner trying to do the Lord's will. So when Satan tempts Simón—three times as the Gospels say of Jesus—it is easy to answer "Get behind thee, Satan." Outright opposition is easier to make a stand against. What is more difficult to oppose are his own inner longings. When alone, as he often is, Simón's thoughts are not always of a spiritual nature. Fleshly longing creep in. Simón admits to himself that he would love to run on the ground, to run with young women, and even spend time with his mother whom he had so curtly dismissed in public. For Simón it is not the devil that poses the greatest threat, it is his own self. All the ascetic desire in the world cannot completely eradicate the lingering urges that once thrilled the flesh. He must contend with the same Pauline agony—the wretchedness of one's own inner conflict; consciousness of a war between the flesh and the spirit. Simón is a pious man; a man gifted with powers to heal and preach and teach like Paul and can bravely contend with the temptations of the devil but his own fleshly desires prove to be the source of greatest conflict.

In the third and final temptation Satan arrives and offers to show Simón, not all the kingdoms of the world as he had done with Jesus, but all the pleasures of the world, so Simón may taste and see that the world is good and then renounce his penitent path. Satan transports Simón to modern New York City, whose skies above are filled with airplanes and its streets filled with nightclubs inside which young people jive and dance to rock music, electric guitars and saxophones; whose bodies are filled with nicotine and alcohol and spasm in simulated sexual ecstasy. Simón is seated calmly sipping his drink. Satan is seated beside him. Simón rather half-heartedly bemoans, "Get thee behind me." Satan responds glibly, "Get thee gone." But Satan knows that Simón is trapped here. There is no going back. Simón has tasted the flesh—like Eve who tasted the forbidden fruit and tasted both delight and death—the sacrifice of piety is the ascension of thanatos. Simón is told that there is nothing to go back to. His pillar is occupied already. Simón is nothing special in God's grand scheme, just one more holy man among thousands; one ascetic stylite in an era of many ascetic stylites scattered throughout the Holy Land. God loses nothing with Simón's departure; God is the eternal eros—the ultimate creative principle. The loss is Simón's. From the bosom of Abraham Simón falls into the arms of pleasure and thanatos.

Marie
(from *Au hasard Balthazar*, France, 1966)

> Jacques and Marie are childhood friends who adopt an ass named Balthazar and baptize him. While they are young Jacques and Marie adore Balthazar. But the years pass, Balthazar grows older, and no longer cared for by Jacques or Marie Balthazar becomes a beast of burden. After his carriage crashes Balthazar breaks free but the locals hunt him with pitchforks and dogs. Balthazar escapes and finds his way to a dilapidated estate where he finds himself face to face with Marie, who is

Part Two. Of Character

now a young woman. That night Marie picks wild flowers and decorates the donkey's brow with a floral crown then tenderly kisses its snout. Marie does not realize that she is being watched by Gérard, a choir boy and local trouble-maker, and his gang who snicker at the insinuation that Marie and the ass share a bestial love. After Marie goes inside to bed she watches from her window as Gérard and his gang kick and beat Balthazar mercilessly. In the meantime a feud has developed between Jacques' father and Marie's father over farmland. Most of the village considers the pride and obstinacy of Marie's father as the main problem protracting the case. Jacques visits Marie and they sit on the same bench where Jacques as a child had inscribed his promise of love to Marie. Jacques tells Marie, "I will love only you." To which Marie responds, "I am not sure I love you." Jacques leaves. Balthazar is now in the possession Gérard who uses him to carry bread which Gérard delivers. When Balthazar refuses to move, Gérard sets his tail on fire, sending the donkey bucking. After this maltreatment Balthazar submits to Gérard. Marie is passing in her car and sees an unhappy Balthazar by the roadside. Marie stops for Balthazar but when she returns to her car she finds Gérard in the passenger seat. Gérard makes several sexual advances. Marie's reaction is to weep, then run, but after being caught she allows herself to be taken by Gérard. Balthazar is the only witness. But Balthazar understands maltreatment and submission. Marie now belongs to Gérard just as Balthazar does. Balthazar next passes into the possession of Arnold, a vagabond drunk, who has implicated Gérard and his gang in border smuggling. Balthazar is abused by Arnold and runs away and ends up in a circus performing as a mathematical genius. When Balthazar sees Arnold in the crowd during one of his performances he bucks and brays and is kicked out of the circus. It is not long before Gérard possesses Balthazar once more. But Balthazar gets sick. Gérard is about to have Balthazar killed when Arnold turns up and takes him. One day the police arrive at Arnold's place, not to arrest him, but to inform him that he has inherited a large sum of money in his uncle's will. There is a large party in town and Arnold is paying. Marie's mother finds Marie at the party and tries to persuade her to return home, but Marie runs to Gérard who passes her to a friend. Gérard vandalizes the bistro and smashes all the bottles and mirrors before he and his friends embrace Arnold and mount him on Balthazar, crying "Vive Arnold!" Arnold rides unconscious on Balthazar

2.7 Ascetics, Asses and Alters

until he falls off some distance from town, splitting his head on the road and dying. Balthazar, along with everything else in Arnold's possession, is sold off because Arnold has no heir. Balthazar is forced to turn a wheel under a whip to draw water for a water bottling business. The businessman who now owns Balthazar gets a late night visit from Marie. He tells her to go home to her father whom she has already shamed. Marie tells the old man that she is done with Gérard and his friends and offers herself to the old man. He offers her money in exchange. Maries turns the money down and they have sex. The next day Marie's parents turn up looking for Marie. The old man tells them they can take Balthazar as it will cheer up Marie. Jacques returns. Marie and Jacques sit on the same park bench. Marie has apparently told Jacques everything that has happened and asks him, "You still want to marry me?" "Oui!" replies Jacques. Then Marie turns on Jacques. She tells him that they are not children anymore, that his make-believe world of marriage is not the real world and that he bores her. Later Marie visits an old ruined house looking for Gérard. She is stripped, gang-raped and left naked. It is Jacques and her father who find her and take her home. When Jacques later inquires about Marie he is told by her mother that she is gone and will not be coming back. Marie's father despairs and is bedridden. A priest is called before he dies from despair. Late at night Gérard uses Balthazar as a pack mule to smuggle goods across the border. There is shooting. Gérard flees but Balthazar is wounded. The following day amidst a flock of sheep Balthazar dies.

The ass has a privileged position in Scripture. From the talking ass upon which Balaam rode,[1] to the prophecy of the Messiah and King of the Jews riding into Jerusalem upon an ass, the ass is the most unassuming symbol of the saint.[2] Balthazar in Bresson's film is no less saintly, loved by Marie, scorned by men, and dying ignominiously. But it is not the ass that we are interested in—although Marie and the ass share the same maltreatment—many more capable writers than we have tackled the allegory of an asinine Christ. From a dialectical point of view we are interested in the character of Marie.

Marie and Jacques are close friends as children—in fact they are like virginal lovers—whose love is as pure as it is innocent, but as they grow they separate, and the separation is felt even more because of the ongoing feud between their fathers. But in a small village such as this they will always have opportunity to meet each other. As young adults they meet on the same park bench where Jacques carved their names so many years before. Jacques tells Marie that he still loves her and that she is only one he can love, but Marie cannot say the same to Jacques. "I don't know if I love you," she replies. Marie's equivocation could mean that she genuinely does not know if she loves Jacques or it could mean that she is incapable of saying no she does not love Jacques. As the narrative unfolds it become apparent that the latter is true. Saying no and meaning no are not the same for Marie. This occurs with Gérard for the first time in her car. His sexual advances are met with tears, then she runs away, but after falling she consents to have sex with him—no is not no—after which Marie effectively belongs to Gérard in the same way the mistreated Balthazar does. Again, toward the end of the narrative, the old man with the water bottling business takes Marie in out of the rain. As she eats jam from a spoon his sexual advances are merely slapped away but in the end Marie has sex with him, refusing the money that was offered—what was no is not no.

By the time Jacques and Marie meet again she has evidently told Jacques everything and Jacques—whose moral rectitude is inferior only to the ass Balthazar—remains desirous of marrying Marie. Marie asks Jacques, "Do you still want to marry me?" "Oui!" he replies without hesitation. But this assent is not enough for Marie. If her no is not no then she finds it difficult to accept Jacques' yes. Surely a yes is a not yes—what is is not and what is not is—Marie tells Jacques that they are no longer children. Life is not the same; it is different from before. The time they spent as children was a dream but the present, the here and now, is the opposite of a dream, it is reality; and a harsh reality at that. Dreams and reality are opposites. Jacques represents the dreamer, Marie the realist. It is Marie's flight from dreams into a world that is all too real, all too brutal and beastly among men, that results in her flight from reality and final disappearance. Having rejected Jacques there is no dream, no more innocence. Left with only abject reality Marie abandons all hope and flees into despair and nothingness.

Mr. Okuyama

(from *Tanin no kao* / *Face of Another*, Japan, 1968)

> When an industrial accident leaves Mr. Okuyama with a disfigured face he seeks the help of his Psychiatrist, who offers him a prosthetic

2.7 Ascetics, Asses and Alters

mask. Mr. Okuyama is unsure but agrees to try the prosthesis after his wife rejects his sexual advances. As part of an experiment proposed by his Psychiatrist, Mr. Okuyama agrees to live a double life but he must record everything that takes place and report to his Psychiatrist. Mr. Okuyama first rents an apartment with his bandaged face, and then after the prosthesis has been attached he rents another apartment in the same complex. Nobody can tell the difference except for Yoko, a simple-minded girl—the daughter of the building's superintendent. Yoko appears to recognize Mr. Okuyama whether he is wearing bandages or the prosthesis. Mr. Okuyama is concerned about this. However, the ultimate test of whether the prosthetic face works or not is for Mr. Okuyama to seduce his own Wife. If his Wife cannot tell the mask from the man then no one can. Using the mask he follows his Wife home. He engages her in conversation and asks her if she would like to drink tea. They later enjoy dinner then retire to his apartment where they have sex. Afterward Mr. Okuyama is upset and tells her that he cannot believe she would cheapen herself with adultery and tries to unmask himself, but she stops him. She tells him that she knew it was him all along and that she too wore a mask, a thick layer of make-up—which she would not usually wear—all married people wear masks of some sort after all. But Mr. Okuyama is rapidly becoming unstable and the line where his personality ends and the persona of the mask begins are quickly becoming blurred. One night while walking in an alley he suddenly and without motive assaults a young woman. He is arrested and his Psychiatrist is called to bail him out. In the end Mr. Okuyama is free to go. But still wearing the mask Mr. Okuyama's final act of freedom is to murder his Psychiatrist before disappearing into the night.

To have no face "feels like exile," Mr. Okuyama tells his doctor. That which is hideous belongs in the darkness and only that which is beautiful ought to be granted light. "That is why deep sea fish are ugly," Mr. Okuyama says to his wife, "because they live in the dark." And with the lights turned off—because Mr. Okuyama is now an ugly fish—he attempts to seduce his wife. She throws him off and tries to soften the rejection by telling him that it was more the shock and suddenness of his moves and not his ugliness that repelled her. When Mr. Okuyama next visits his psychiatrist he is angry; he wants to burn his wife's face so she would not be so prejudiced against

Part Two. Of Character

ugliness—how could something made hideous reject something hideous—reasons Mr. Okuyama. Mr. Okuyama's psychiatrist is sympathetic to his patient's pain, but rather than resort to criminal behavior he offers an alternative solution—adopt a mask—although the psychiatrist admits that this will raise certain ethical and moral problems. This dialectic between the wearer and the mask—the person and the persona—is central to the narrative.

As an exile Mr. Okuyama is estranged from work, not because he is held accountable for the accident but because of his appearance. Without an occupation, a sense of doing; he quickly fears for his sense of being. He is becoming a stranger to himself. He no longer recognizes the face in the mirror and each time he undresses the bandages he must reacquaint himself with himself. Most painful of all is his wife rejecting him, treating him like a stranger—it is ironic that his wife will later accept him and offer herself to him as a stranger. As the narrative progresses the mask exerts its influence and Mr. Okuyama begins to feel like someone that is both the same and different. Thus we have the development of the dialectic of identity—or sameness and difference. The word "another" in the film title corresponds with the word "tannin" in the original Japanese title and refers to someone that is not just someone perceived by others as a stranger but differentiated from the *self*, the "I" or the *ego*. This is Mr. Okuyama's agony. He possesses a sense of self, although the accident has made such a sense of self precarious, but when he adopts the mask or the prosthetic face of an Other, the mask brings with it its own sense of being, a self, and the two selves—the I and the Other—begin to merge. But this merger is not mutual but unilateral. War is father of all, we recall from Heraclitus, and so one—Mr. Okuyama or the Other—must be become dominant at the expense of the other. In Mr. Okuyama's case the other self-desires the play of reality but can only do so at the expense of Mr. Okuyama's original self. Such is the dialectic of Mr. Okuyama's character.

The face is the surface; what people first see. "The face is the door to mind," says Mr. Okuyama; it opens up the gateway into the consciousness of the other. But only if the face is interesting or alluring do we want to open it up and peer beyond. Should the face we see appear ugly, deformed or damaged, we are reluctant to look beyond; to delve beneath the surface for fear that what lies beneath is even more hideous. A man may be considered a beautiful soul but united in body with an ugly face. Conflict burns

2.7 Ascetics, Asses and Alters

within Mr. Okuyama and is manifest without. Mr. Okuyama knows himself to be both beautiful and ugly, but feels the spurning rejection of the world whose preoccupation seems to be that of appearances. As a result he grows to hate the world in which he lives and to hate himself for participating in it. The mask consoles the burning anger, and any subsequent rejection is deflected from the ugliness beneath to the mask—the persona becomes the buttress of the self. After killing his psychiatrist Mr. Okuyama will walk away free. But his freedom is at the same time a condemnation. He remains conflicted; divided between the man and the mask, the person and the persona.

2.8

Politicos, Cabbies and Jedis

Anna
(from *Ucho / The Ear*, Czechoslovakia, 1970)

Deputy Minister Ludvik and his tipsy wife, Anna, return home from a diplomatic party at Prague Castle. Ludvik notices that a black car has followed them home and has parked across the street with the headlights turned off. Ludvik soon realizes that their villa has been entered. The spare keys are missing, the power has been cut off and the phone line is dead. They first suspect that their teenage son, Ludek, might be to blame but it later occurs to Ludvik that they are being listened to by "The Ear," the surveillance arm of the Communist Party. Ludvik thinks back to the party and the various conversations he had for any indication that he is under suspicion. Ludvik recalls that the chief minister of construction, Kosara, was called to Moscow and has since disappeared, along with several others involved in the brickworks program. Ludvik searches the house for any documents that link him with Kosara and burns them but at the same time Anna, who is upset because today is the their tenth wedding anniversary—which Ludvik has forgotten—follows him from one room to another screaming abuse at him and making snide comments about his sexual inadequacies. As Ludvik's paranoia increases the animosity between Ludvik and Anna intensifies. Argument after argument reveals just how deep their marital crisis runs. When Ludvik and Anna discover multiple listening devices planted throughout the house Ludvik's fears are confirmed and he believes the Party will come and make him disappear too. He locks himself in a room but Anna, fearing Ludvik will shoot himself, climbs out on to the window ledge to plead with him not to commit suicide. She finds Ludvik on the floor—the Party has already taken his pistol. The telephone rings. Ludvik answers. He is Kosara's replacement.

2.8 Politicos, Cabbies and Jedis

Banned for twenty years and first seen at Cannes in 1990 following the Velvet Revolution in 1989, Karel Kachyňa's *Ucho* remains a damning indictment of totalitarian control and at the same time a fascinating examination of marital discord. The film portrays the intense paranoia and fear of being presumed guilty by the State, the same kind of "guilt that is never to be doubted" that one finds in Kafka. As this book concerns itself with the dialectical nature of character we will focus our attention on Anna; a shrew as shrewish as Shakespeare's Katharina.

The story begins when Ludvik a deputy minister in Czechoslovakia's Communist Party and his wife Anna return home from a State held reception. They notice keys missing, the power is turned off, and the phone line dead. They assume it was their son Ludek up to mischief, but Ludvik sees strangers in trench coats in his garden and wonders if he is under suspicion by the Party. As he wanders around their house with only a candelabra to light his way he suddenly flashes back to the State reception from which they just arrived and tries to recall the many conversations and the thinly veiled surprise on his comrades' faces at his own attendance—what at first seemed innocuous suddenly seems replete with menace.

Throughout the night Anna harangues Ludvik constantly about his disinterest in her, both emotionally and sexually. "We ought to have sex at least once a week even if it is bleak," she scorns. And as Ludvik's fears intensify so the domestic jousting becomes more violent as the couple move from room to room, closing doors, screaming one moment then whispering the next, knowing "The Ear" is always listening. Fuelled by more and more alcohol Anna's caustic jibes reveal the innermost secrets of their private life. At one point Anna confesses to having had an affair with a curly haired driver for twenty days while Ludvik was in Moscow. Ludvik seems apathetic and simply retorts that it must have cost a lot of money for twenty days of sex. Ludvik's apathy and disinterest fuels Anna's drinking. She is often left alone and must fill the void she feels somehow with other men or anesthetize the pain with vodka straight from the bottle.

In between the jousts there are small glimmers of affection. When the gate bell is rung and Anna fears Ludvik is about to be taken away, Anna follows him down the path with an overnight bag containing cleans socks and underwear so his incarceration will be more comfortable, it is a small, negligible, but honest and caring gesture. But the depth of Anna's feelings is revealed at the very end of the film. On the following morning after the sun has risen, Anna fears that Ludvik will commit suicide. She scrambles out of one window, shuffles across a ledge, only to break into another window in order to save Ludvik whom she finds on the floor. He is alive as the Party has already taken his gun. In despair Anna weeps on his chest—the closest we come to seeing the couple expressing love. When we first meet with Anna she is a scathing shrew, unhappy, and not without cause—the wedding anniversary had been forgotten, after all—but by the end of the story we are sure that the tenderness Anna shows is genuine. As an inebriated Xanthippe she is protecting herself. No doubt Ludvik's neglect has contributed much to her being scornful but we witness a transformation when the threat of Ludvik dying is real. The lashes of her tongue are evidence of her love; in fact, if she loved Ludvik any less her ferocity would be softened. The thought of Ludvik's death—the ever-present threat of thanatos—is all it takes to reveal Anna's eros hidden by disdain.

Travis Bickle

(from *Taxi Driver*, USA, 1976)

> *I fired four more shots deliberately, point-blank, and in cold blood, at my victim.*
>
> —Albert Camus

New York is a nocturnal wasteland. Its denizens commute throughout the dystopian environment in taxi cabs. Dazzling lights reflect from the rain soaked ground and the noxious evaporations from the sewers rise like perverted incense. Within this milieu we find Travis Bickle. He is a twenty-six-year-old veteran of the Vietnam War, having toured twice before honorable discharge from the Marines. An inveterate insomniac, he decides to earn a little extra cash by driving a taxi cab at night. Travis does not care when or where he drives: "Anytime, anywhere," he says, "Anytime, anywhere." One day he parks his cab outside the fundraising headquarters for a future presidential candidate. But it is not the platform or policies of Senator Palantine that catches his interest but the young blonde woman working inside the building. Travis enters and introduces himself to the beautiful young woman. Her name is Betsy, she tells him. Travis feels there is a connection between them—she is lonely and he can feel it—which

2.8 Politicos, Cabbies and Jedis

gave him the right to introduce himself. He asks her out on a date. Just coffee and pie. She agrees and tells him to meet her at 4 later that afternoon. Travis and Betsy meet for date. They eat coffee and pie as suggested. Travis expounds on his peculiar philosophy in his own idiolect. "I have never met anyone like you," says Betsy. "You're like that Kris Kristofferson song, 'a walking contradiction, partly truth and partly fiction.'" Betsy agrees to go see a movie with Travis but he takes her to see a pornographic film from Sweden. She sits uncomfortably for a short while before walking out in disgust. Travis is apologetic but didn't realize that she would be offended by such a movie. He tries to console Betsy but to no avail. His relationship with Betsy is over. Soon after Travis meets a twelve-year-old prostitute called Iris. Travis is not aware but his relationship with Iris will result in bloody violence. Travis quits drinking and stops taking amphetamines. He trains his body and purchases a large selection of firearms. Travis is going to clean up the streets of New York. His first target is the Senator Palantine. Palantine arrives to deliver a speech. Secret Service men scan the crowds vigilantly. Travis approaches but he is unable to draw his gun. He is detected and flees. He runs all the way home, dejected. After the failed assassination attempt he returns to the plight of Iris. At first Travis tries to talk her out of prostitution and tells her to return home to her parents. He takes her out for ice cream. When this does not work he adopts the dangerous ploy of paying for her services so he can dissuade her from prostitution. This too also fails. When Travis returns to Iris he does so with profound violence. He first shoots her pimp then enters into the building where Iris entertains her clients. He shoots the timekeeper but Travis is shot in the neck. He continues through the building in a whirlwind of blood and gunshots forcing his way into Iris' room, where he collapses. By the time the police arrive all but Travis and Iris are dead. Travis is proclaimed a savior. Iris returns home to her ever-thankful parents. Travis meanwhile returns to his job of taxi driver.

Travis Bickle is the cinematic avatar of Shakespeare's Hamlet, Kierkegaard's angst, Baudelaire's *ennui*, and Jean-Paul Sartre's *nausée*. He is young man but has been deranged by war. He returns to civilian life incapable of being civil—taking Betsy to a pornographic film on a first date is proof of that—he wants to clean up the streets of New York but feels powerless to do anything about it. He is listless and lacks purpose. After his obsession with Betsy ends in disaster he discovers Iris, a twelve-year-old prostitute and becomes obsessed with saving her. At the same time he has decided to take matters into his own hands and assassinate Senator Palantine—perhaps as a way to hurt Betsy or to strike at the politicians who sanction action in Vietnam—whatever the case, Travis has a moment that is Hamletic. He has trained himself, quit drinking and taking amphetamines, and armed himself as an assassin. But when he approaches Palantine he vacillates. He does not shoot soon enough and is detected by the Secret Service. Travis wants to shoot but does not shoot. It is a moment of profound conflict. Everything he has been planning and working toward was for this moment to strike but it is Travis that is struck by inaction. He hesitates. His hesitation forces him to flee. But that drive to kill has not been extinguished. Thanatos is not easily thwarted and in the end, accompanied by eros, will create carnage; like Hamlet the finale is a bloodbath. Dead bodies everywhere.

As Jesus freed Mary Magdalene from demonic possession and prostitution so too will Travis free Iris from Matthew's possession and prostitution. "I came not to bring peace, but a sword." Travis brings a Magnum. Like Jesus, Travis submits to self-sacrificing crucifixion that leaves him pierced by bullets, and after resurrecting from the deathlike state of being comatose he emerges a savior and hero. Thanatos emerges as eros. United in the one mind and body is the saint and the sinner. Travis is the giver of life and the purveyor of death. When Betsy remarks that Travis reminds her of the Kris Kristofferson lyric, it is no coincidence. This is an expression of dialectic. Betsy refers to Travis as "a walking contradiction." Contradiction is dialectical and was considered by Hegel to be the motive force of existence. In Travis contradiction is the motive force of his character and the character of Travis brings his narrative into being. The contradictions of character are the outworking of plot. Hence the trajectory of Travis' character from *ennui* and aimlessness at the outset to saintly vigilante at the end. Sometimes self-sacrifice appears to be contradictory; but as we have examined previously contradiction is only another guise of dialectic.

Luke Skywalker
(from *Star Wars IV: A New Hope*, USA, 1976)

> *For every force there is a counterforce.*—Lao Tzu

2.8 Politicos, Cabbies and Jedis

The infamous rolling credits inform us that we are in a galaxy far, far away and the universe is torn by a conflict between the Empire and the Rebel forces. A key figure in the rebellion is Princess Leia, who is attacked at the beginning. Before she is captured she secretes a hologram message into an R2 droid unit. The R2 unit and its companion C3PO are jettisoned from an embassy ship before the Imperial forces led by Darth Vader can prevent any escape attempts. The jettisoned droids land on the planet Tatooine, where they are captured by a dwarfish scavenger tribe called Jawas. The Jawas sell the droids to young farm boy and wanna-be-pilot Luke Skywalker who lives with his aunt and uncle. Having the chore of cleaning the droids before putting them to work Luke accidentally activates a small portion of the hologram message, a message that is intended for Obi Wan Kenobi, an old hermit and Jedi knight who is known to Luke as Ben Kenobi. Luke sets off in search of old Ben Kenobi with his droids and after being rescued by Ben Kenobi from Sand People Kenobi tells Luke a little of his father, the best star pilot and most cunning Jedi warrior, who was betrayed and killed by a young Jedi called Vader. Vader succumbed to the dark side of the force—the force being a spiritual energy that infiltrates all living things. Luke then receives his father's light saber from Obi Wan. The message for Obi Wan is a request from the Princess to get an important message to her father on the planet Alderaan. Obi Wan recruits Luke and says he must learn the ways of the Force but Luke insists that he must stay at the farm and help his uncle. When Luke discovers that the Jawas he bought the droids from have been killed Obi Wan assures him that the Imperial forces must have slaughtered the Jawas. Luke fears for his aunt and uncle. He speeds home but when he gets there he finds a smoldering corpse and his home burned to the ground. With nothing left Luke chooses to learn the ways of the Force and accompany Obi Wan to Alderaan. They look for a pilot to take them to Alderaan so head to Mos Eisley, a "wretched hive of scum and villainy" is how Obi Wan describes it. Here they find the pilot Han Solo and his co-pilot Chewbacca, who fly the Millennium Falcon. Han Solo agrees to fly them because he needs money to pay off his debts. When the Millennium Falcon arrives where Alderaan should be there is nothing but planetary debris. They realize that the entire planet of Alderaan has been destroyed. An Imperial fighter surprises them and they give chase but the Millennium Falcon

Part Two. Of Character

gets caught in the tractor beam of the Death Star—a planet-like battle station—and is forced to dock. They hide during a search of the vessel and kill a pair of storm troopers. Han Solo and Luke then disguise themselves as storm troopers. Obi Wan tries to disable the tractor beam but runs across Darth Vader. Darth Vader and Obi Wan fight and Obi Wan is killed (in the only way an immortal soul can be killed). Han Solo and Luke search for the Princess. With the help of R2D2 and C3PO they locate her detention cell and free her. But as soon as the Princess is free they come under attack. The only way to escape is to jump down a garbage shoot that leads to a squalid trash compactor. When the trash compactor is activated, only R2D2 can save them by plugging into the system and shutting it down just in time. Han, Luke, Chewbacca and the Princess return to the make their way back to the Millennium Falcon where they witness the "death" of Obi Wan. The Millennium Falcon is able to escape from the Death Star and they make their way to the rebel base on Yavin 4. But the Death Star has tracked the Millennium Falcon to the rebel base and in thirty minutes will have a clear line of sight. One strike will destroy the rebel alliance completely. The rebel plan of attack is to fire proton torpedoes into a small vent that leads to the Death Star's power source that will start a chain reaction destroying it. A squadron of X-Wing fighters is deployed to attack the Death Star. One by one they close in on their target but are destroyed. Luke takes his turn. (The disembodied voice of Obi Wan encourages him to use the Force.) Luke uses the Force to aim but is closely pursued by Darth Vader. Luke is in Vader's sights when the Millennium Falcon suddenly appears, disrupting Vader's pursuit. Luke takes the shot, which hits the target, destroying the Death Star. Luke becomes the hero of the rebellion.

Luke Skywalker belongs to a trilogy (the number three being the sacred number of parable and fairy tale) comprising the *Empire Strikes Back* (1980) and *Return of the Jedi* (1983) all of which comprise one long space saga (the prequel sequels are of no merit and not worth considering). We need only cite this one film because it sets up the principal dialectic: the Imperial forces in conflict with the Rebel alliance and Luke Skywalker in conflict his father, Darth Vader.

The transition principle of dialectic compels change; opposites become opposites. Life becomes death for example. We witness life becoming death in the scene where Obi Wan Kenobi fights Darth Vader. Obi Wan sees that Luke is watching him and sacrifices his life. By allowing Vader to kill him Obi Wan enters into thanatos, but out of thanatos emerges an immortal eros. Luke does not realize that a Jedi's death is ephemeral, because death is eternal life—the Jedi believe in an immortal soul as Plato did—it is the everlasting voice of Obi Wan that ministers to Luke at the end: "Use the Force, Luke." This thanatic voice is the source of wisdom that brings life to Luke and enables him to save the rebel base. This exhortation from out of death convinces Luke to believe in his own interpenetration with the Force.

Luke himself transforms. At the beginning of the narrative he is a naïve farm boy with dreams of becoming a pilot. He performs chores for his uncle and tends to droids. By the end of the narrative Luke is the hero of the rebellion, celebrated and medallioned, by the Princess. Farm boy to rebel hero; the one could not be more opposite from the other—but by means of dialectic Luke's character is able to grow. Luke has transformed from a state of youthful immaturity to virtue and maturity; from self-absorbed to self-sacrificing. More important is Luke's spiritual transition; from living a mundane and secular existence to embracing the great spiritual energy that is the Force.

2.9

Arias and Angels

Brian Sweeney Fitzgerald
(from *Fitzcarraldo*, Germany, 1982)

    Brian Sweeney Fitzgerald, or Fitzcarraldo, as the South American natives call him, is passionate about opera and especially the tenor Enrico Caruso. When Caruso and the opera visit the Amazon, Fitzgerald and his lover, Molly, try desperately to attend. They are late but even though it is a gala performance the usher takes pity on them and allows them to enter quietly and stand by the back wall. As Caruso sings Fitzgerald is transported by the performance. It is as if Caruso is speaking to Fitzgerald. His dream will become reality. Fitzgerald will build an opera house in the jungle village of Iquitos and Caruso will sing at the premier performance. Fitzgerald needs money for his operation. His ice-making chemistry is not enough to attract investors—as ice needs not patent or trademark. Fitzgerald learns from Don Aquilino about an unexploited stretch of forest that is difficult to access because of rapids and head-hunting natives known as the Jivaros. Fitzgerald wants to claim the land and use the profits from the rubber trees to finance his dream of building an opera house in the Amazon and to fulfill the promise he made to his pet pig regarding its own velvet chair. Don Aquilino will not invest any money himself, as he has a bet going on how soon Fitzgerald will bankrupt himself, but Aquilino agrees to sell him a steamboat. Fitzgerald asks Molly, who is the madam of a very busy bordello, to provide the money for the boat and the rights to exploitation of the land; to which she agrees excitedly. In honor of Molly and his love of opera Fitzgerald names the steamboat the Molly-Aida. Fitzgerald secures a captain, "Orinoco" Paul, whose eyes are not so good but he can taste the difference in river water; Huerequeque, a perpetually drunken

2.9 Arias and Angels

cook; and Cholo, the chief engineer and Aquilino's own man. Fitzgerald and his crew set off upstream along the Amazon River, which baffles everyone on shore. They first stop at the defunct TransAndean railway stop to pick up rail tracks, then they set off upstream along the Pachitea River towards a mission. Farther up the river they hear drumming and chanting from the forest. Some of the crew are scared and want to turn back. They fear their heads will be shrunken by the Jivaros. Huerequeque, who knows a little of the Jivaros language, tells Fitzgerald about their belief in a white god who sails a great white vessel that will transport their people to a world without death or sorrow. When Fitzgerald wakes in the morning he finds that the crew has abandoned ship, that only he, "Orinoco" Paul, and Cholo are left. They must continue. So they do, playing the opera from the rooftop gramophone as they go. They notice that they are being followed by the Jivaros, who are cutting down trees to prevent the steamboat from turning around. That night the Jivaros' Chief boards the boat. After inspection the Chief does not think that Fitzgerald is a god but his boat is very impressive (when compared to their canoes). After a drunken Huerequeque appears (having slept through the desertion) Fitzgerald continues with tall Jivaros on board. Fitzgerald has a cunning plan. Fitzgerald and his crew find the point along the river he has been looking for. It is the point closest to where two bends in parallel rivers meet. He will build a track so that his boat will cross over a mountain and eliminate the need for following miles of river. Using (or rather exploiting) the Jivaros to fell trees, dig out rock and build ramps, Fitzgerald builds an ingenious system of pulleys. They put the winch system to work and the boat starts moving. Everyone is excited, but when the Jivaros stop pulling the boat slides backward, crushing two Jivaros to death. Work ceases for several days as the Jivaros disappear to mourn. When they return Huerequeque has the idea of using the steam power of the engine and attaching Fitzgerald's winch to the anchor system so the boat will pull itself up under its own steam. The plan goes ahead and with the assistance of the Jivaros the boat climbs closer and closer to the summit of the hill. When they get the boat down the other side there is a big party, dancing, pan pipes, bonfires and gallons of saliva-fermented yucca on which the natives get as drunk as Huerequeque. But while everyone sleeps, the Jivaros' Chief has the ties cut and the Molly-Aida begins to drift with all the natives and crew on

Part Two. Of Character

board. By the time Fitzgerald is woken by the crashing and jolting it is too late. The steam boat is heading into the Pongo—the deadly rapids. Fitzgerald's dream is over. He is told that the Chief had to put the boat through the rapids in order to appease the evil spirits. The chief was aware that Fitzgerald was circumventing the rapids when he dragged the boat over the mountain, but the for the sake of his people the spirits must be appeased. Fitzgerald returns to Iquitos and Aquilino, who buys back the damaged boat but before Fitzgerald hands it over he has a promise to keep to a pig. He learns that a European opera company is in a nearby village performing Bellini's *I Puritani* so he hires them to play on top of the Molly-Aida as "Orinoco" Paul sails it along the banks of the Amazon.

The Padre at the mission tells Fitzgerald, "Life is an illusion behind which is the reality of dreams." This contrary way of viewing life is exactly what Fitzgerald is interested in. For him there is no better way of living than living a dream; and no better artistic expression can be found than the opera. "Opera gives expression to our deepest feelings," he tells Aquilino as he pitches the idea of opera in the jungle to him. But Fitzgerald's dream falls on deaf ears. Fitzgerald is passionate but his passion is so consuming that it borders on frenzy—even insanity. At one point Fitzgerald barricades himself inside a church, effectively holding the church ransom, and he will stay there until his opera house is built in Iquitos. He is an aesthete in a mercantile world of capitalist exploitation. Still his ambition is more admirable than his success, and it is his ambition that drives him and his crew upstream along several jungle rivers, into the territory of feared "savages," only to perform the most Sisyphean task of hauling a steamboat up and over a mountain. If Fitzgerald had believed only in reality he would never have gone so far, but his belief in dreams transcends reality—in spite of all the setbacks and danger—his rejection of reality fuels his ambition.

Damiel
(from *Der Himmel über Berlin* / *Wings of Desire*, Germany, 1987)

> The sons of God saw the daughters of men that they were fair; and they took them wives of all which they chose.
> —Book of Genesis

2.9 Arias and Angels

Damiel is an angel. His function is to document the actions of humans in a particular section of Berlin. The job is simple. Damiel has no difficulty in performing his task, but like his angelic brothers aforetime his curiosity with humans develops into fascination and such fascination cannot remain satisfied without experience—tangible experience. Damiel visits a circus where the trapeze artist Marion performs. Damiel becomes enamored of her and longs to be human. The erotic impulse swells within him. When he meets with actor Peter Falk and discovers that Peter Falk is a materialized angel, Damiel renounces his angelic existence and becomes human. He tracks down Marion and they unite as if they were meant to be together, drawn somehow by an ineffable force.

As an angel he is immaterial, and as a dramatic being, he desires materiality, and this conflict between what he is and what he is not; being immaterial and being material, is the central dialectic of Damiel. The blissful condition of being in the very presence of God should be replete with joys, but an angel is precluded from ever being anything but an angel. He can never be God. An angel can never rule. It must minister and serve. Angels do not get promoted to cherub or seraph, there is no such promotion of angels. An angel is what it is because it was created so. There is no such concept as promotion in heaven. One must serve and observe and if a change in status is desired then there is only the downward path. If an angel is to rule it must do so like Milton's Satan, someplace beneath heaven. Like Milton's Satan, all angels must make a choice: to reign freely in hell or subject oneself to servitude in heaven. Such is the angelic dialectic.

Damiel is an angel who watches, reports, files, notates, a celestial bureaucrat observing mankind's deeds and notes them in an angelic notebook. We may suggest that his place within the angelic hierarchy is of the messenger type, a lesser angel. Along with his friend Cassiel, Damiel reports on a small section of Berlin. But Damiel is growing tired of eternity of always being on the outside looking in on life, he wants to participate in life even if it means lifting an apple or staining his fingers with ink from a newspaper he had read. He confides his anxiety and desire to his friend Cassiel who is sympathetic but knows where he belongs as a rank and file angel and even if he had the desire would not pursue it. At the same time a film is being made starring the actor Peter Falk (playing himself). Damiel is intrigued

Part Two. Of Character

by Falk, who senses whenever Damiel is there. Falk tells Damiel how the little joys of being human make it all worthwhile, like smoking a cigarette or sipping hot black coffee on a cold night. Falk should know—he used to be an angel. Falk's description of humanity combined with Damiel's attraction to Marion influences Damiel's decision to sacrifice his angelic immortality for life as a flesh and blood creature. With the help of Cassiel he sloughs off his angelic immortality and seeks out what it means to love in human terms. The angel dies so that the man may live. Eros emerging from thanatos.

The conflict that Damiel experiences is an inversion of the traditional Pauline dialectic that plagues the Christian, in which flesh must pummel itself so as to aspire to the spirit. Damiel is a spirit that longs to be flesh in all its imperfection. There is no indication of how long this conflict has existed within Damiel, but we can be sure that this crisis point brings his narrative into being. "War is father of all" announced Heraclitus. War is conflict. Conflict erupts at the juncture of opposite forces. Damiel the spirit wants to be made flesh. This conflict of opposites is the ordnance of becoming, and from this conflict Damiel becomes a new being, his character is born, created; endowed with a new ontology. His dramatic being is born from dialectic. Cassiel is not unsympathetic but he is more pragmatic. It is possible that Cassiel has like so many of his angelic brothers contemplated forsaking the spirit in favor of the flesh. He no doubt has wondered like Damiel about the little and seemingly insignificant joys of being human, but he has made his choice not to rebel or forsake his duty, because it is his duty he has chosen to maintain his position. It was a choice: a free choice to obey. Cassiel tells Damiel "Do no more than look, gather, testify, verify, preserve ... remain spirit." Cassiel while gathering, testifying, verifying and preserving may wonder what it is like to be flesh but he has adopted a policy of looking only: no touching. He does not want to get involved with human affairs for fear of being drawn irrevocably into them. Damiel however has reached the point of *ennui*. Damiel's tolerance for eternity is finite.

After following Marion to her trailer Damiel looks at the photographs. Something strange occurs, in longing for Marion he is able to pick up a rock from her collection, a rock that he keeps and which will reappear later when he divests himself of his spiritual nature. The rock is two-tone. The bottom half is dark, the top half is light; like the yin and yang duality. The rock is a visible symbol of dialectic: the unity of opposites that so often conflict, not just in humanity's existence but also that of the angels. The longing of flesh

2.9 Arias and Angels

for spirit and spirit for flesh, the ultimate goal being to find a balance between the two without irredeemably sacrificing one altogether.

To be, or not to be, a spirit is the question Damiel must answer. Damiel wants to belong to history not a passive observer. He wants to create his own story "I want to transform what my timeless downward look has taught me," he tells Cassiel. "I've been on the outside long enough." "I want to enter into the History of the World." There is no history for angels. They have always been, and will continue to be, but man has history because of his finitude. Damiel whose horizon is that of timelessness wants to enter into the horizon of man, the horizon of time.

Before Marion leaves her trailer for the last night of the circus she contemplates as Damiel looks on through the glass darkly. She says to herself, "I would like to know." In contrast Damiel would like to not know. He would for once just like to guess, to be uncertain, rather than always knowing. The spirit that knows longs to be one with the flesh that knows not. But at the same time the flesh that Damiel wishes to be wants to know because the flesh tires of never truly knowing. Knowing and not knowing, the aversion to know, and the desire to not know; this unity of opposites an epistemological tension that remains unresolved, belongs to Damiel's dramatic being. At one point Marion tells her friend, "Just to be able to say 'I am happy' to have a story." These are also the sentiments of Damiel, who wants to partake of history, to merge his own infinite horizon with that of the finite. He knows there is a cost, or a price to pay, but he is ready—to die in one sense and live in another—thanatos becoming eros.

2.10

Edward and Max

Edward
(from *Edward Scissorhands*, USA, 1990)

> *I know always that I am an outsider; a stranger in this century and among those who are still men.*—H.P. Lovecraft

Our narrative is framed by an elderly grandmother telling a bedtime story. The tale is about an old inventor—a Geppetto of robotics—who lived in the strange mansion overlooking her street. The inventor made a boy—a robotic Pinocchio—with scissors for hands because he wasn't yet finished ... and so, once upon a time.... Peggy is an Avon representative who frequently solicits her neighbors to purchase her products. After a long and disappointing day Peggy is about to give up but notices that there is one place she hasn't yet called on. It is a large dark mansion that towers over Peggy's garish suburb the way a Transylvanian castle towers over a rustic village. Peggy, who works on commission, has little choice but to try to make a sale. When Peggy first arrives at the mansion she is struck by the beauty of the garden. The privet bushes have been manicured into the finest topiary sculptures: mythological beasts, dinosaurs, even a human hand is prominent. Peggy enters with "Avon calling!" She climbs the winding staircase all the way to the dilapidated attic, the roof of which has evidently been in ruin for some time. She hears the sound of scissors clipping and catches a glimpse of someone (or something) hiding in the corner. She manages to coax the strange person out and finds a wild-haired young man with scissor-hands. Peggy asks his name and he tells her in his softly spoken voice "Edward." Ever the sales lady, Peggy notices the scars on Edward's face and applies astringent before taking Edward home. Peggy shows Edward photographs of her family and Edward is quite taken by her daughter Kim. In a small suburban neigh-

2.10 Edward and Max

borhood news travels quickly that Peggy has a new male friend and the neighborhood women begin flocking with excitement—all except Esmeralda, a Moonie, who denounces Edward as demonic and a temptation from Satan—but the pious Esmeralda is largely dismissed by the undersexed women. One day Edward watches as Peggy's husband, Bill, clips the privet bushes. Instinctively Edward starts clipping away and when he is done a topiary dinosaur stands in the yard. Bill is astounded. Because of the interest aroused in the neighborhood women the responsibility of hosting a barbecue is foisted on Peggy and Bill where Edward is formally introduced to the neighbors. His topiary art is popular and soon all the suburban gardens have Edward's handiwork adorning them. Edward does not stop at privet bushes. Edward's scissoring prowess is applied to pet grooming and after the seductress Joyce insists Edward cuts her hair all the neighborhood women have to have Edward original hair-dos. Edward is a hero of the neighborhood. One night Kim, Peggy's daughter, returns early from a camping trip with her boyfriend, Jim, and their friends. She sneaks into her room but is terrified to find Edward in her bed. Her screams wake the whole house, but Peggy tells Kim not to be afraid because Edward is now part of the family. Edward's first look at Kim was a photograph and it is obvious he falls in love. Now he sees Kim in person Cupid works his wonder. One day when Helen takes Edward to the mall to get his blades sharpened Edward sees Jim and Kim together—something approaching jealousy stirs within him. Jealousy is a godly attribute and being made in God's image men are jealous. Edward, being made in a man's image, is jealous also. Jealousy is what makes Edward human. Because of his popularity Edward appears on a tacky TV talk show. He is asked a series of questions by the audience. He is asked if he could have normal hands would he? And he replies yes. When someone remarks that he would be normal like everyone else, Edwards replies that he knows. That's what he wants. Then Edward is asked if he has a girlfriend... it takes a while for Edward to respond. It is obvious that he is thinking of Kim and Kim who is watching on TV at home knows—unconsciously perhaps—that Edward is thinking of her. But before Edward can answer he accidentally (or accidentally on purpose) shocks himself on live TV. In the meantime Joyce has proposed a business plan to Edward. They will open a beauty salon together where Edward can utilize his scissoring prowess. While showing Edward the

Part Two. Of Character

property, Joyce—in the tradition of Mrs. Potiphar—seizes the opportunity to seduce Edward in the back room but Edward—like Joseph before him—flees. Jim, meanwhile, has a plan of his own to make some money. He will use Edward to break into his father's house and steal expensive equipment for quick sale so he can buy a van for himself and Kim. Edward agrees but the alarm is tripped and Jim flees with Kim leaving Edward behind to face the police. Edward is arrested and the only thing preventing him from being shot is the neighborhood women pleading for the police not to shoot him. Edward's arrest, however, begins the turning of the tide—opposites becoming opposites. Rumors start and Esmeralda tells the neighborhood women that she knew he was demonic from the start. Joyce's seduction of Edward becomes Edward's attempted rape of Joyce and soon Peggy's entire family has been alienated. Kim apologizes to Edward for getting him into trouble. Edward tells her he knew what he was doing; he did it because Kim asked him to. At Christmas Edward is carving ice blocks into sculptures—the debris falling like snowflakes—Kim gets closer as she is fascinated but Edward accidentally cuts Kim's hand. Jim takes this opportunity to attack Edward but when Kim breaks up with Jim and tells him to go, Jim is determined to destroy Edward. An angry and drunken Jim forces his drunken friend to drive to Kim's house. Nearing the house the van would have hit an unsuspecting Kevin, Kim's little brother, had Edward not rescued him, but his rescue inflicts some cuts and gashes. The whole suburb—like angry villagers—is out looking for Edward and Edward has no choice but to flee. Kim tells him to run; so he runs back to the towering mansion. Jim and Kim follow where Jim and Edward fight in the dilapidated attic. Edward kills Jim protecting Kim—because he loves her—and Kim tells Edward that she loves him but kisses Edward goodbye—because she loves him....

Edward is a fabulous creature like Frankenstein's creation and Pinocchio to whom he is similar. Like all fables the story of Edward conceals a moral. God made Adam, Doctor Frankenstein made his man, and Geppetto made Pinocchio; our old inventor fabricates a son. The son, however, is markedly different and is incomplete. Had the inventor not died he would have finished Edward, but the death of the inventor left Edward with scissors for hands. If we continue with the analogy of God, then the incompleteness of Edward has its correlative with Adamic sin and the inevitable and irreconcilable dialectic of God's perfection and man's imperfection: a dialectic worthy of Saint Augustine. But the lesson—or fabulous moral—to be learned from the character of Edward is that it is not specific parts of the body that enable us to share in identity as human; it is heart: the heart completes humanity and Edward's self-sacrificing love for Kim completes his humanity in a way that hands could never achieve. It is self-sacrifice that allows Edward to pass from a state of incompletion and inhumanity to completeness and humanity. It was never about the hands or the scissors but the heart and learning to love and love's greatest and most complete gesture is sacrifice. When Edward—like all martyrs to eros—sacrifices himself by removing himself from all that he has come to love he enters into humanity in the most complete way, he undergoes apotheosis, he becomes legend and myth and thus finds his place in the heart of humanity itself; more importantly he secures a place in the heart of Kim. Edward was a stranger but became a beloved brother. He was monster but found human, he was a celebrated hero but soon became a villain. Opposites becoming opposites. And in the end, in order to find peace, he had to die in order to live—thanatos becomes eros.

Maximilian Cohen
(from *Pi*, USA, 1998)

> *And all things that can be known contain number;*
> *without this nothing could be thought or known.*
> —Philolaus of Croton

Maximilian Cohen is a mathematical savant who has built a super computer in his tiny apartment called EUCLID. With EUCLID Max hopes to unlock the secrets of nature and the stock market based on numerical patterns associated with Pi. But Max suffers from seizures and self-medicates. He is also paranoid and reclusive. His one friend is another mathematician, Sol. Sol used to be Max's teacher and searched for the same patterns associated with Pi before suffering a stroke. After much effort EUCLID churns out a 216 digit number. But creating the number causes EUCLID to become conscious of itself as a machine but self-consciousness of its being causes EUCLID to meltdown and the system dies. This number, which is the key to unlocking the secret of the universe,

Part Two. Of Character

is now stored only in Max's memory; and the 216 digit number is not as secret as Max would like. A group of Hasidic Jews is interested in Max's work as well as a powerful Wall Street firm, Lancet-Percy, represented by Marcy. Torn between the spiritual and the material interest of his secret, Max drills into his own head, erasing his memory of the number.

The name Maximilian in multiple languages means "the greatest" and the surname Cohen derives from the Hebrew Kohen meaning "priest"— first used in the Torah at Genesis 14:18 regarding Melchizedek, king and priest of Salem, associated by some with Deluge survivor Shem—so put together we have in the name Maximilian Cohen the greatest priest, or High Priest. Every priest is in some manner a mediator (the original meaning of the Hebrew Kohen) between man and the worshipped deity. Such a being is a bridge that serves to unify opposite natures. The pure with the impure, the holy with the unholy, the divine with the human. The role that Max serves, despite his own opposition, is that of a secular synthesizer. For max the deity is number. But Max is at first fixated on the materialistic world of Wall Street. Searching for patterns on the Financial Times Stock Exchange index and the Dow Jones, he comes to the attention of the Lancet-Percy group. It is only when he is approached by Lenny Meyer, a Hasidic Jew, that the concept of numbers takes on a religious significance. Lenny demonstrates the kabalistic significance of Hebrew lettering and shows Max how the original Hebrew phrase for the tree of knowledge conforms to the Fibonacci pattern. Like the ancient Pythagoras, who was a famed mathematician and a priest of sorts, Max is a post-modern Pythagoras. But Max is a secular priest at best. He has no real interest in God or religion. Mathematics is a science.

But Max is at the center of a conflict between the Wall Street materialists who would use the secret number to procure wealth and the Hasidic sect who want the number because it is the lost name of God. The conflict of Max's character is manifested in dizzying hallucinations, paranoia, and violent seizures. He is torn, like all characters before him, between two ways of being: he can be the scientific mathematician or the priestly mathematician. Unlike the great Pythagoras who was a balanced synthesis of priest and scientist, Max is unable to achieve balance, and the age in which Max lives makes any such attempt at synthesis difficult, perhaps impossible. He has no recourse other than to kill that which is causing the conflict and literally drill the number out of his head.

2.11

Lions, Lightyears and Llamas

Simba
(from *The Lion King*, USA, 1994)

> Hamlet: My uncle?—Shakespeare

Mufasa is the king lion of his pride but his brother Scar is envious of his position. When Simba is born and becomes heir to the kingship, Scar plots to have Mufasa killed. Mufasa is told that Simba is endangered by a stampede and when Mufasa is killed by Scar the young Simba is told by uncle Scar that he is at fault and his guilt demands that he should go into exile as a cub. Wandering as an exile Simba is adopted by a warthog named Pumbaa and a meerkat named Timon, who teach the trouble-free philosophy of Hakuna Matata, or No Worries. Under the guardianship of Timon and Pumbaa, Simba grows into an insectivorous maned young lion. One day a lioness attacks Timon and Pumbaa, but Simba protects them. Simba and the lioness fight until they recognize each other as cub friends from the pride. The lioness is Simba's old playmate Nala. Nala tells Simba what has happened to the pride. Scar has taken over and made an alliance with the kingdom of hyenas, but the food and water is gone and the pride is threatened with extinction unless Simba returns to reclaim his rightful place as the lion king. When Simba returns he sees firsthand the plight of the lions. Simba overthrows Scar—whose trust in the treacherous hyenas is misplaced—and Scar is exiled by Simba who claims his rightful place as the lion king.

The *Lion King* is obviously inspired by Shakespeare (Scar is a shadow of Macbeth and uncle Claudius, Simba of Hamlet, Timon and Pumbaa are poor odes to Rosencrantz and Guildenstern, and Mufasa the Ghost of Hamlet's father with a hint of Darth Vader) yet *The Lion King* is an example of

Part Two. Of Character

high spectacle and negative drama—what is seen negates what is told. Despite twenty-seven hands involved in the writing of the story (proving that a room full of monkeys will never write Hamlet even when working from Hamlet) the characters are stereotypes cut and pasted from elsewhere and the basic plot of a son replacing the father is as old as the oldest narratives.

Even in a narrative that offers little satisfaction, the dialectical process is still at work. Simba begins as a lion cub and will transform into the king of beasts, a process that is dialectical. At the beginning Simba is the one sent into exile by Scar and at the end Scar is sent into exile by Simba—opposites becoming opposites. The exiled becomes the exiler. During his life with Timon and Pumbaa Simba is taught the trouble free philosophy of Hakuna Matata—no worries. Such a philosophy is the negation of responsibility. Unlike Hamlet, who was too full of worry, Simba as heir apparent must possess an opposite philosophy. Simba is Simba and not–Simba; he is a king but he is not a King. Hamlet fell into suicidal despair when he learned that his uncle had killed his father. Simba fell into indifference. At the insistence of Nala, Simba is reminded of his responsibility, not only to himself as a kingly not-king, but his responsibility to his dead father, the pride, and his mother. Simba returns to reclaim the throne and set matters right. If nothing else Simba learns the responsibility of responsibility. The irresponsible philosophy of Hakuna Matata might be the responsible philosophy of a warthog but it is certainly not the philosophy of a lion king. When Simba finally roars at the end this signals that the transformation from cub to king is complete.

Buzz Lightyear
(from *Toy Story*, USA, 1995)

> Woody is the leader of a group of sentient toys and is their designated leader all of whom belong to Andy. Woody's leadership skills are needed especially as Andy's family is moving house and organization of the toys is uttermost so that no toy gets left behind. Because of the move Andy's birthday is brought forward by a week—birthdays being a time of great anxiety for toys because there is always some new toy delivered. This year Andy receives the most sought-after toy on the market—a Buzz

2.11 Lions, Lightyears and Llamas

Lightyear space ranger complete with space craft. It does not take long for Buzz to usurp Woody's prized spot of favorite toy. All the cowboy imagery disappears and is replaced by Lightyear bedding, wallpaper and posters. Woody becomes increasingly jealous of Buzz, especially when the other toys take to him as well, and what is more infuriating is Lighyear's obliviousness to his being a toy. When Andy's mother offers to take him for pizza Andy is told that he can bring one toy—only one— and Andy wants Buzz. Woody decides to do away with Buzz by getting him stuck behind a dresser, but the plan goes awry and Buzz falls out of the window. Andy searches for Buzz but cannot find him and settles for Woody instead, rescuing him just in time from the other toys who know what Woody did and were about to defenestrate Woody. Woody realizes that he has to find Buzz but when Buzz refuses to be rescued—because he is, after all, a "real" space ranger—Woody and Buzz fight and both toys are lost. Buzz, who is still convinced that he is a real space ranger, must get to star command. When Woody spots a delivery car from the pizza chain called Pizza Planet—the pizzeria where Andy and his mother will be—that has a rocket on the roof, he uses Lightyear's belief in his being a space ranger to hitch a ride. Once inside Woody only wants to return to Andy, but once again Lightyear's insistence on completing his mission gets them into trouble. Woody must sacrifice his only opportunity to return to Andy in order to rescue Buzz. The rescue suddenly turns extremely dangerous when they end up in the clutches of vicious Sid. Sid takes his two new toys home and devises unspeakable forms of mutilation. While attempting to escape, Buzz sees a television commercial advertising the Buzz Lightyear toy—he realizes at this moment that Woody was right all along—Buzz Lightyear is a toy, he is a toy and has always been a toy. In a last-ditch attempt to repudiate his fear he attempts flight but falls and crashes like Icarus, losing all sense of himself. Woody tries desperately to rescue Buzz and tries to get the help from Andy's other toys, but they still consider him a traitor and Woody is abandoned by them. Woody must save Buzz on his own. And this means working together. Sid receives a large rocket in the mail and fastens Buzz to it; he is prevented from detonating it immediately because of the rain. He goes to bed exited that he will explode the rocket tomorrow. Woody and Buzz have only the night to save themselves. But they are too late. Morning arrives. The alarm wakes Sid and he rushes out

Part Two. Of Character

with the rocket. The only thing that can save Buzz now is for Woody to break the cardinal rule of all toys—he must reveals himself as a sentient being. With the help of Sid's menagerie of mutilated toys they attack Sid, who panics and runs away in terror. Buzz is free but Andy and his family are already moving with the truck. After several attempts both Buzz and Woody are reunited with Andy, but more important, Woody and Buzz are united in friendship.

When Buzz Lightyear arrives there is more than just rivalry between toys. There is a vast gulf, a cultural dialectic. Woody is a cowboy and belongs to the old frontier—the only era in American history that has any claim to Romanticism—and Buzz, his opposite, is an astronaut who belongs to a new romanticism of space travel, the final frontier, of *Star Wars* and *Star Trek*. It is not just his place as favorite toy that Woody is in danger of losing but his entire being, which is rooted in the old. His existence as a representative of a bygone age is threatened with nothingness by the being of Buzz Lightyear and the forward-looking and adventurous species of toy he represents. Woody is a pull-string toy whereas Buzz is garnished with lights, buttons, and wings powered by batteries and a trigger mechanism. The fear of Buzz becoming the favorite is bigger than the fate of a single toy; it is the locus of cultural change, of opposite generations clashing. The other toys accept Buzz, warming to him almost from the start, but Woody cannot, precisely because of the cultural baggage he carries. Piggy banks and Slinky toys do not really have much cultural inheritance, hence they do not have much to lose, either consciously or unconsciously (we are, after all, discussing sentient toys). Woody, on the other hand, has much to lose and must oppose Buzz because he is an existential threat. Woody's being in the presence of Buzz is threatened with nothingness.

Buzz on the other hand is convinced of his reality, of being, not a toy but, a bona fide space ranger, and his unwavering belief in his being more than a toy infuriates Woody, who knows both are just toys. As gifted with awareness as they both are, their existence is solely for the crepundian pleasure of Andy their owner. Nevertheless, and despite Woody's objections, Buzz must carry out his assignment from star command and his insistence on this brings him into conflict over and over again with Woody and in the end into the clutches of the vicious Sid. It is here in Sid's room, a kind of Hades full of shadows and monstrosities, that Buzz comes to the realization

2.11 Lions, Lightyears and Llamas

that he is just a toy. His belief in any kind of transcendent being is crushed and he must admit that Woody was right all along. His ego is shattered and in a half-hoping half-desperate gesture that could be considered a flight from life into death, Buzz leaps into the air only to crash like Icarus and for a short time afterwards is rendered senseless. Buzz, however, survives the journey into hell, the symbolic death, and the madness that followed and emerges transformed, not in form itself but transfigured in consciousness. He accepts his being as it always was; that he was, is, and always will be a toy, and surviving this realization he is renewed and reinvigorated—it is a resurrection of sorts—out of thanatos eros emerges. Buzz passes throughout the narrative from opposite to opposite, and one that is now united with Woody his initial opponent. Like Gilgamesh for the Gerber generation the clash of cultural opposites finds unity in conflict.

Kuzco
(from *The Emperor's New Groove*, USA, 2000)

> The kingdom is departed from thee. And they shall drive thee from men, and thy dwelling shall be with the beasts of the field: they shall make thee to eat grass as oxen.
> —Book of Daniel

Kuzco is an egotistical Incan Emperor. He is so haughty and self-absorbed that he capriciously orders the execution of villagers, fires Yzma his imperial advisor, and has one old peasant thrown from a high window for throwing off his "groove." He has plans to build a swimming resort called Kuzcotopia as a birthday gift to himself but before he settles on a location he invites the village chief, Pacha, to inquire into the amount of sunlight Pacha's hill gets. When Pacha confirms that the sunlight at dawn makes the hillside sing Kuzco dismisses Pacha, telling him his village is to be demolished. Pacha is sent home dejected. In the meantime Yzma and her hulking half-witted man-servant Kronk are planning to kill Kuzco. They attempt to poison him at dinner but Kronk administers the wrong poison, which transforms Kuzco into a llama instead. Kronk is told to dispose of the llama but his conscience gets the better of him and instead of killing the llama he ends up losing possession of it to

Part Two. Of Character

the disheartened Pacha when it falls on the back of his cart. When Pacha returns home he finds that he is in possession of a talking llama that he recognizes to be the emperor Kuzco. Pacha agrees to help the llama get back home if the emperor reconsiders his proposed swimming resort. Kuzco arrogantly refuses and enters into the jungle alone. He very quickly finds himself about to be eaten by a horde of black jaguars when he is rescued from their claws by a vine-swinging Pacha. Again Pacha requests Kuzco change his mind about Kuzcotopia but the stubborn llama refuses. After a cold night and Pacha's kind gesture of warming Kuzco, Kuzco relents. He agrees to reconsider Kuzcotopia if Pacha helps him get back home. Pacha, a simple man of his word, is willing to believe Kuzco on the strength of a handshake. But we know the llama is lying. And when they are about to cross a wooden bridge Pacha falls. Kuzco reveals his selfish nature and lets Pacha fall. Only his gloating brings him back to Pacha, which causes him to fall too. Only by working together can they extricate themselves from alligator-infested waters. With newfound respect between them, Pacha and Kuzco the llama set out together back to the imperial palace. Yzma and Kronk, however, have tracked them down to a diner. Pacha overhears their conversation and informs Kuzco who they are. Kuzco, still not cured of his imperial arrogance, is excited because he believes Yzma and Kronk worship him. Kuzco says goodbye to Pacha but he overhears Yzma and Kronk's plans to assassinate him a second time. He quickly returns to Pacha, but Pacha is gone. Kuzco is alone. He must spend a long rainy night in the jungle. Hair matted and cold—the antithesis of imperial luxury. But Pacha is a good man and is not willing to abandon the llama. He gave his word and shook hands so Pacha keeps his promise to return Kuzco to the palace. When they get there they search for the potion to return Kuzco back to his human form, but once again Yzma and Kronk prevent him returning with ease. After a fight with Yzma over the potion and after Kuzco undergoes a rapid series of metamorphoses, Pacha is left hanging. Kuzco could save him but the potion is also within reach. Kuzco must make a choice: save himself or save Pacha—Kuzco saves Pacha and by saving Pacha he saves himself turning Yzma into a kitten in the process. Kuzco is restored to his throne and Kuzcotopia is situated on a nearby hill where Pacha's family enjoy playtime with the emperor on the waterslides.

2.11 Lions, Lightyears and Llamas

Pride, says the proverb, comes before a fall. And "O how the mighty fallen," sang Moses as the haughty Pharaoh and his armies perished in the crashing waters of the Red Sea. Kuzco belongs to a tradition of haughty kings whose prideful ways are punished in the most severe and publicly humiliating form. Kuzco will throw an old peasant from a window for interfering with his "groove" and he will callously demolish a village for a water park built to honor his own birthday; his pride is as abundant as his selfishness. But at the outset of the narrative Kuzco soon feels the full weight of humiliation when—like the arrogant king Nebuchadnezzar of Babylon who was transformed into a beast of the field—Kuzco is metamorphosed into the pitiable form of a llama. He has become the opposite of a regal prince and is now a craven camelid. Even the physical transformation is not enough to make Kuzco question his attitudes. He still must learn selflessness and unlearn selfishness, and it is through the various trials with Pacha that he slowly learns what it is like to be human. Only in the form of an animal can he fully comprehend what caring and kindness is. It is only in the cold loneliness of a rainy night and all alone that the lesson begins to take effect.

Kuzco cannot remain an animal forever. At some point Kuzco must transform back into his imperial self, and so he does at the end when he makes the selfless gesture to save Pacha's life rather than instantly transform himself. The transformation is there, deep within, and is far more important and precious than the physical metamorphosis that will take place. Kuzco has undergone a transformation of essence. The soul first becomes human and the body follows. Trapped in the shape of a beast, like Jonah trapped in the belly of the fish, Kuzco has undergone a species of death locked in the arms of thanatos, and it is under the aegis of death in the crucible of dialectic that he begins to transcend his old way of being. Like Nebuchadnezzar returning to his throne after seven years of bestial madness or Jonah vomited up onto the shore, Kuzco is metamorphosed into life, into his new self under the governorship of eros, into a selfless self. He has learned the very hard but vital lesson that pride will be punished, that hubris will meet with nemesis. Kuzco has experienced fully the dialectical nature of existence—opposites becoming opposites conflicted and in unity—falling from a princely perch into a state of abject animality. In the final scene the aged peasant who was so unceremoniously defenestrated at the start receives an apology from the young emperor and we find that Kuzco's character is almost unrecognizable

Part Two. Of Character

from the first. If we had not witnessed the transformation, which is the narrative, we would scarcely believe them to be the same person. Kuzco's qualitative transformation in character is the emperor's "new groove" mentioned in the title. This transformation, from the old to the new, like Kuzco's transformation from haughty to humble, is the outworking of dialectic.

2.12

Male Models, Machinists and Matrimony

Derek Zoolander
(from *Zoolander*, USA, 2001)

In Malaysia the new president is to put a stop to child slave labor and sweatshops, on which the Western fashion industry is dependent. Jacobim Mugatu is ordered by a secret cabal of fashion designers to assassinate the president of Malaysia. Mugatu needs a stupid male model for a patsy (because all major political assassinations from Abraham Lincoln to JFK were carried out by male models) and Mugatu finds the perfect patsy in Derek Zoolander. Derek is a dim-witted male model whose look "Blue Steel" made him a star on the masculine catwalk. When Derek is challenged by upstart new age model Hansel, Derek decides to retire from the world of male modeling. Mugatu needs Zoolander to be active in order to assassinate the Malaysian president and is desperate to bring Derek back into the fashion world. Mugatu creates a new line with Derek in mind—Derelicte. Derek finally returns to the runway after a misguided attempt to find his roots in the coal mines of New Jersey. But when Derek returns he is subjected to an intensive mind-control procedure and Pavlovian response techniques—which he believes is a day spa—turning him into a Manchurian candidate. The trigger is "Relax" by Frankie Goes to Hollywood. In the interim Derek and Hansel have made their peace and it is Hansel who assists Derek. With Hansel's help and his new look, "Magnum," a look that can stop throwing stars—Derek saves the Malaysian president.

Beyond the satire and farce there is in the character of Derek Zoolander a species of conflict, a minor but recognizable agony. Beneath the looks and

Part Two. Of Character

the face that is really, really, ridiculously good-looking, there is an ugliness, a non-beauty, the vanity of beauty and the vacuity of beauty. The key moment of crisis when Derek is conflicted is when he retires from the fashion industry and returns home to his father and brothers. "Who am I?" he inquires of his reflection like an imbecilic Narcissus. When he returns to the small coal mining town to see his father it is the antithesis of his current existence. Here are rough, work-hewn men, sweat-soaked and covered in coal dirt and dust, pouring beer into dentally ill mouths, as opposed to the chiseled featured, pampered and moisturized men of the male modeling world. Here among the working class miners Derek is not a star as he is in the modeling milieu, he is a clown and an embarrassment, someone who prances about in ludicrous clothes and swims around on TV in a mermaid (merman) costume. Derek realizes that he is not of this world. When his father tells him "You are dead to me, boy"—an utterance of thanatos—Derek realizes that his life belongs to modeling. Derek is a Zoolander; he has the characteristic hedgehog hair of a Zoolander but he is not a Zoolander, he is not a manual laborer, nor is he made of the same stuff as his brothers and father, and he is not—his father assures him—what his dead mother would have approved. He is paternally negated by his father who considers him as dead though living.

This instance of conflict and rejection by his father (which is one of the few serious dramatic moments in *Zoolander*) thrusts Derek into his narrative. Derek returns to modeling under the specious aegis of his agent Ballstein by taking up the offer of Mugatu to be the face of Derelicte. All the action that follows: the fellowship with Hansel, the winning of a woman previously unwinnable, the finale in which Derek is pushed and pulled as the trigger music is turned off and on is an outgrowth from the critical moment in New Jersey with his father. The desire to be accepted by his father and the painful awareness that he has been rejected is the conflict that drives Derek the man and *Zoolander* the narrative. Derek is a son bereft of sonship, a brother made brotherless, forsaken for the sake of a family name, a family name which he has made famous; but famous only in a world antithetical to his family and so Derek cannot be accepted as part of the family. Strip away the farce and satire, the punning and outrageous costumes and what we find is the timeless dialectic of father and son. In the final moments his father finds pride. We must imagine Derek returning home at some point to the mines of New Jersey triumphant, this time into the erotic embrace of his father.

2.12 Male Models, Machinists and Matrimonia

Trevor Reznik
(from *The Machinist*, 2004)

> I've prayed sometimes, prayed and kept
> thinking about my great guilt before him.
> And so it's turned out to be true.
>
> —Dostoyevsky

Trevor Reznik is a lonely man. He is shockingly emaciated; a skeletal figure resembling a Concentrationnaire. He also suffers from debilitating insomnia. His closest relationship is with Stevie, a prostitute whom he solicits regularly, but Trevor seeks out Stevie more for companionship and conversation than the coital contract. At the outset Stevie is really the only friend Trevor has. Reznik works as a machine operator where he is tolerated but not really liked by his colleagues. Because of his appearance Reznik is asked to provide a urine sample by the bosses. When he goes outside he meets Ivan (a good Dostoyevskian name). Ivan tells him he is taking over from Reynolds because Reynolds is being investigated by the FBI. Reznik does not think too much about it, but the next time he does see Ivan, Ivan makes a slitting throat gesture from the welding pit that causes Reznik to accidentally activate a machine which rips off Miller's arm. After the accident there is an investigation and Reznik admits his concentration was broken by Ivan—but Ivan does not exist. When his own arm is caught in a machine and almost severed he accuses everyone at work of colluding with Miller for vengeance; he attacks his boss Tucker and is fired. From this point Reznik's disintegration is rapid. He follows Ivan, whose red car keeps appearing, to find out who this mysterious person is; he even lets himself get run over so he can report a hit and run and have the police trace Ivan's license plate, but when the police tell Reznik the license number belongs to him (because Ivan is him) Reznik runs and has to escape through the city sewer system. Fragment by fragment the memory of what really happened is recalled. The only way for Reznik to get sleep is to confess to the truth, the truth that he has been running from for over a year.

Like the typical Dostoyevskian character, of which Reznik is both an avatar and legitimate offspring, he is worthless in the arms of anyone who

Part Two. Of Character

is not also the embodiment of repudiation and scorn. Reznik works as a machinist in a machine shop, hence the title, and his nights are spent sipping coffee and eating pie at an airport café in the early hours where he innocently flirts with the attractive waitress. His spare time at home is spent assiduously cleaning with bleach both the surfaces of his apartment and his own hands. Reznik even tries to read Dostoyevsky's novel *The Idiot*—a less than subtle hint from the director—such is the existence of Reznik when we first encounter him.

Ivan is the opposite of Reznik because Ivan is Reznik—what is is not and what is not is—Ivan is buff and bald whereas Reznik is lank and emaciated. Ivan is imposing with a resonating voice whereas Reznik is quiet and softly spoken. It is the conflict between these two characters—which is to say Reznik's conflict with himself—that will provide the source of the narrative because out of the Character issues Plot. "A little guilt can go a long way," says Trevor to Maria, the cafeteria waitress at the airport. Guilt drives everything Reznik does and says. Maria tells Reznik that she is planning to use a maternal guilt-trip against her son in return for a few moments of consideration on Mother's Day, but Reznik is unaware that his own repressed guilt will turn his life upside down; or the fact that Maria is the person to whom he owes guilt. Maria is both real and not real. It was her son he killed and it is it his own consciousness trying to bury consciousness of that fact that reduces Reznik's being to the point of nothingness.

The Machinist is an exploration of a dialectical state of mind; the violent conflict between consciousness of guilt and a suppressed consciousness of guilt. This dialectic is perhaps nowhere more symbolically expressed than in the fairground scene. Reznik takes the young boy and on a scary ride. Here we see the carnage of a car crash, the strewn bodies, the blood and the sound of sirens. This is the reality from which Reznik flees. It is all too real and all too nightmarish for Reznik to accept and so he has repressed it, but within him the violence and the guilt of causing such carnage seethes in his consciousness. The guilty Reznik and the guiltless Reznik cannot coexist without disaster.

One of the earliest indicators that Reznik is troubled is seen when we witness him cleaning his hands with powdered bleach. The bleaching of his hands does not belong to the same species of behavior as the compulsive or the phobic; rather it is an extreme form of Pilate's gesture—washing one's hands of guilt that is historically inerasable. It is the indelibility of guilt that motivates Reznik's extreme bleaching of his hands. The guilty Macbeth suffered the same thing when he said that all Neptune's oceans could not wash the blood from his hands: All the waters of Noah's flood, let alone all the bleach in Walmart, can wash the blood-guilt from Reznik's hands. What is done cannot be undone. Time cannot be reversed only traversed in the precarious and haphazard halls of memory, and more often than not only as a form of infernal repetition and self-recrimination. All the stress that Reznik suffers is rooted in guilt and the futile attempts to abrogate that guilt. Until Reznik accepts his guilt it will not be assuaged, he will continue to waste away until he is nothing but a corpse and after he has become a corpse he will rot to nothingness.

Nader & Simin

(from *Jodaeiye Nader az Simin* / *A Separation*, 2011)

> Either take them back on equitable terms or part with them on equitable terms.—Al-Qur'an

Simin wants to leave Iran and take her daughter Termeh so she might have a better future. Nader, the husband and father, does not want to leave but lives with his father, who has Alzheimer's disease. Leaving the country would mean leaving his father behind. Simin has secured travel visas but they will expire shortly and no final decision has been made. Simin petitions for divorce so she can take her daughter and moves in with her mother temporarily. With Simin gone and Nader working during the day he must hire someone to care for the house and his father. He hires Razieh, who finds the work too much to handle—she is both pregnant and very devout so cleaning the father after he has soiled himself leaves her feeling sinful. One day Nader arrives home from work. Razieh is not there to let him in. When Nader uses an extra set of keys to get into the house he finds his father tied to the bed and barely conscious. Razieh is nowhere to be seen. She turns up later and Nader is furious. He fires her and accuses her of stealing money which is now missing. When Razieh refuses to leave without being paid for at least one day's work Nader pushes her out the door, but she falls on the steps. Razieh is later taken to hospital where the doctors tell her she has had a miscar-

Part Two. Of Character

riage. Razieh and her hot-tempered husband, Hojjat, file a complaint against Nader, who is charged with the murder of the unborn child. Simin raises the money to bail Nader out and keep him from spending time in jail, and Nader has little choice but to file a countersuit charging the Razieh with criminal negligence for tying his sick father to the bed and leaving him to die. Termeh, Nader and Simin's daughter, is caught up in the scandal. Termeh wants her mother to come home and asks her father to ask Simin to come home, but he cannot do it. Simin tries to arrange that blood money be paid for the miscarried child so the law courts can be satisfied and drop the case but when Simin suggests this to Nader he refuses to pay on the grounds that to pay blood money means that he is guilty. Simin wants Nader to accept the terms and will move back in with him if he accepts, but he refuses and Simin leaves angrily. What Simin really wants to be asked to come home, but she herself will not ask if she can come home. It is the daughter Termeh who tells her father that if he had accepted his wife's terms Simin would return. Her bags were ready in the car. Simin was ready to move back. Sometime later, and in confidence, Razieh confesses to Simin that she thinks the baby was already dead inside her before she slipped. She was in fact hit by a car trying to retrieve the old man and later that night suffered abdominal pain. She is afraid that she will be punished if she accepts the blood money unjustly. Simin swears not to mention this to anyone, including Nader. Nader, however, having been made aware of Simin's intentions from Termeh, has agreed to pay the blood money and the two families sit for tea, along with Hojjat's creditors who have been hounding him. Nader wants one final assurance of his guilt and requests that Razieh swear on the Qur'an that her child died because he pushed her. Razieh cannot do it. She cannot swear on the Qur'an to a lie and Hojjat is furious. In the end Nader and Simin continue their separation. One question remains: Who will Termeh choose to live with?

Pride comes before a fall. It is not the first time we have come across this proverb in this book, the reason is because it beautifully and poetically embodies the ethic of dialectic. The angel who became Satan (or Iblis in Islam) became so because he succumbed to pride and his pride precipitated his fall from heaven. In ancient Thebes pride was the cause of Oedipus losing his crown, his father, mother and his eyes, and in modern Tehran pride

2.12 Male Models, Machinists and Matrimonia

threatens to tear apart Nader and Simin. Both parents are prideful and their pride becomes a kind of petulance that even their adolescent daughter has outgrown.

Simin, as a mother, wants only the best for her daughter and she feels the best for her is to grow and continue her education outside of Iran. Nader on the other hand has a filial obligation to his father, who has Alzheimer's disease. Of course he wants the best for his daughter but he cannot abandon his father. Simin moves out because of pride. She doesn't want a divorce, and she says so, she wants her husband with her, but she wants to be gone from Iran. Stubbornly she moves out to prove a point and this sets off a series of events that throw Nader and their daughter into much trouble. With Simin gone, a housekeeper is needed; when the housekeeper has a miscarriage her husband gets involved, the courts get involved, and teachers get involved, which gets their daughter Termeh involved.

With all the stress that Nader is going through he could ask Simin to come home, and Termeh even asks him to do so, but he cannot, and it is pride that prevents him from asking. Even if Simin does not return to him, she will at least be there for his father and their daughter; but pride and stubbornness prevent this. Simin also only has to ask if she can come home but she will not ask; Simin does not want to ask she wants to be asked. At one point she has her bags gathered and waiting in her car if only Nader would set aside his pride, but an argument erupts and Simin leaves angrily. Neither Nader nor Simin will ask because pride prevents them. If only one of them were to set aside their pride and ask the other then they would be one step closer to an equitable reconciliation. Sadly, like Buridan's ass that starved to death because it could not choose which food to eat, Nader and Simin—asses that they are—cannot commit to choice and their love starves.

Conclusion: Towards a Cinema of Agony

We have suggested a dialectical approach to understanding cinematic characters and have demonstrated through numerous and diverse examples that all such characters are governed by the force of dialectic. Dialectic like gravity is impartial. Martian or earthling, prince or pauper, lion or Muslim, all are subject to gravitational force, so too are all dramatic beings subject to the force of dialectic, whether they emerge from Hollywood or the far flung regions of world cinema; a tramp or a guilt-plagued machinist is equal when weighed in the balance on dialectic.

In John Milton's dramatic poem *Samson Agonistes*, Samson, the blind and humiliated Hebrew hero, cries out:

> O dark, dark, dark, amid the blaze of noon,
> Irrecoverably dark, total eclipse,
> Without all hope of day![1]

What we hear is the cry of a character of agony enduring agony, that is to say, conflict; and dramatic conflict always consists of the unity of opposites—for Milton's fallen hero Samson, the opposition lies in the darkness of being blind contrasted with the full blaze of a Palestinian noon—the despair of knowing sight is irrecoverable. This is the source of Samson's agony. In the preceding pages we attempted a modest analysis of a small number of cinematic characters through which we introduced the idea of a dialectical character. Some are more well-known, some are more likable, and others more apt to be analyzed; but we hope at least to have taken the first step in promoting the dialectical nature of character; that narratives unfold as part of a natural dialectical process; that Character by undergoing the dialectical process creates Plot, or to phrase it another way, Plot emerges from Character: Character brings Plot into being. In contrast to the prevailing Aristotelian model we express the dialectical model this way: *ethos is mythos, mythos ethos*.

Conclusion

Tramps become involved in conflict because they are alone and find their opposite, either in wealthy heiresses or alters who usurp their identity. Aristocrats get involved with their opposites—the proletarians—and as a result, in Vera's case, ultimately discover who they really are. Gizella becomes associated with the brooding Count Glinskii, who is obsessed with death and kills her because the spirit of eros drives him toward thanatos. In contrast the character of Charles Foster Kane begins with immense wealth but in the end all he wants is an old sled from his childhood. He possesses more material wealth than men can dream of, but in the end he dies alone spiritually bankrupt. Terry Molloy begins as a loyal minion of his brother and father figure Johnny Friendly but learns what possessing a conscience means, and in the end he is transformed, from a follower of men into a leader of men. Cléo's obsession with beauty and ugliness reveals the inextricability of opposites. Pontus is a writer who does everything but write. Mr. Okuyama is torn between himself and his mask. Travis Bickle, a disenchanted soldier from Vietnam, whose life is meaningless and lacks purpose, ends up saving a young prostitute and becomes a hero. Damiel is an angel who gives up immortality in heaven for mortality on an earth. Edward Scissorhands, who is incomplete and searching for something that will complete him, must return to his isolation knowing he can never—unlike Pinocchio—become a real boy. Trevor Reznik is plagued by guilt and only his admission of guilt in the end will save him and let him get a good night's sleep.

Conflict is dramatic, and what is opposed to the dramatic is the spectacular. The fashionable adulation of the spectacle derives from the common (mis)interpretation of Aristotle, in his *Poetics*, who stated that "the first essential, the life and the soul, so to speak, of Tragedy is the Plot; and that the Characters come second." Action has, in Hollywood, taken on more importance than character. Particularly in the last decade with advances in technology and Computer Generated Imagery (CGI), the focus has shifted from the characters in conflict—which has always been the essence of drama dating to the first Greek tragedians—to the invention of spectacle and wizardry of the computers. The special effects used in films like *Titanic* (1997) and *Avatar* (2009) are praised for their spectacular quality, in the same way that the earliest moving pictures inspired childlike wonder in their audiences, but what of their characters?

The earliest movies, to our postmodern vision, are no longer wonderful—in that they no longer create a sense of wonder—because we have

Conclusion

been sophisticated by technology. The imageless exploits of Odysseus, of Don Quixote, of Falstaff, Hamlet, Sherlock Holmes, and others continue to elicit wonder because they are tridimensional dramatic beings and wholly dialectical (can anyone remember the characters' names in *Avatar*?). Image alone is not sustenance enough. The image must be supplemented with tridimensional Character. Whenever we participate in cinema we ought to ask are these dramatic beings tridimensional beings from which the plot emerges or are they Aristotelian puppets, "included for the sake of the action," stock characters in a cinematic version of *la pièce bien faite* or well-made-play?

The Greeks, who bequeathed to us our Western theatrical tradition, made use of the word "agon" (αγον) in the sense of a combatant, or competitor, particularly in athletic games. The Greek word "agon" is still present in words used today to describe dramatic beings, i.e., *protagonist* and *antagonist*. The word protagonist literally means the "first combatant," or the first to step on to the tragic stage. Today the protagonist is almost always associated with the "hero" or the "good guy," and the antagonist, which means "opponent of the combatant," is now associated with the "bad guy" or "the villain." These *agonic* words pertain to conflict and struggle—they determine a dialectical relationship between characters that is necessary for dramatic narrative to exist.

We can see such agony reflected in the Empedoclean conception of Love and Strife, two cyclical forces of integration and disintegration that shape and maintain the cosmos—out of such cosmic agony all things come to be and cease to be. We have also mentioned the conflict between the spiritual man and the secular man rendered by early Christian evangelist Paul, who wrote of his wretchedness, or agony, but it is only by enduring such agony that the Christian proves his faith and receives salvation. The concept of "agon" also emerges in the discontent that Sigmund Freud observed in civilization, the balance of which shifts constantly between the death and life instincts—eros and thanatos—such is cultural agony.

What is needed is a cinema of agony, that is, a cinema peopled by dramatic beings whose internal torment reflects that of the Empedoclean cosmic agony, or the Pauline agony. For this we do not need grand and elaborate stories, but simple tridimensional characters possessing a depth that allows room for mythos to take root and develop out of the character. What are needed are characters in which a unity of opposites conflict: characters who are conceived dialectically whose ontology is comprised of irreconcilable opposites in unity. Such conflict is little present in the popular movies of spectacle. We must have a cinema of agony because a cinema of agony is a cinema of existence.

Drama when governed by dialectic reveals insight into the human condition and contains universal relevance. When this occurs we properly term such dramatic conflict as agonic. We want to see a cinema of agony: that is a cinema replete with conflict, replete with dialectic, replete with characters in agony. The cinema of action and spectacle is an Aristotelian cinema. Conflict is not found in explosions and car chases, multimillion-dollar CGI effects, kung fu fighting or a teenage werewolf / vampire *ménages à trois*: these are spectacles and spectacle is not dramatic. Such spectacles are mere distractions, like the parlor magician's sleight of hand distracting the gaze and attention of his audience. Audiences deserve better than banality. And all of this apparent visual magic exists for the purpose of distracting the audience from a lack of Character, the lack of conflict—the absence of agony.

For true dialectical conflict to exist within any dramatic narrative there must be a unity of opposites and these opposites must be equal in strength, like the Love and Strife of Empedocles, both of which alternating and twisting helically between dominion and servitude. They must be as balanced as the immortality of mortals and the mortality of immortals suggested by Heraclitus. The agony that arises from such conflicts becomes the supreme quality of narrative: from this emerges true conflict—characters in agony creating a *cinema of agony*.

Filmography

Ansiktet /The Magician (1958). Screenplay: Ingmar Bergman. Director: Ingmar Bergman. Running time: 107 mins. Color type: B&W. Country: Sweden. Language: Swedish. Distributed by the Criterion Collection, http://www.criterion.com.

Aprili/April (1961). Screenplay: Erlom Akhvlediani and Otar Iosseliani. Director: Otar Iosseliani. Running time: 46 mins. Color type: B&W. Country: Georgia. Language: Georgian. Distributed by Facets Multimedia, http://www.facetsmovies.com.

Au hasard Balthazar (1966). Screenplay: Robert Bresson. Director: Robert Bresson. Running time: 95 mins. Color type: B&W. Country: France. Language: French. Distributed by the Criterion Collection, http://www.criterion.com.

Citizen Kane (1941). Screenplay: Herman J. Mankiewicz and Orson Welles. Director: Orson Welles. Running time: 119 min. Color type: B&W. Country: USA. Language: English. Distributed by Warner Home Video, http://www.wbshop.com.

Cléo de 5 à 7/Cleo from 5 to 7 (1962). Screenplay: Agnès Varda. Director: Agnès Varda. Running time: 90 mins. Color type: B&W/Color. Country: France. Language: French. Distributed by the Criterion Collection, http://www.criterion.com.

Edward Scissorhands (1990). Screenplay: Caroline Thompson. Director: Tim Burton. Running time: 105 mins. Color type: Color. Country: USA. Language: English. Distributed by 20th Century Fox Home Entertainment, http://www.foxconnect.com.

The Emperor's New Groove (2000). Screenplay: David Reynolds. Director: Mark Dindal. Running time: 78 mins. Color type: Color. Country: USA. Language: English. Distributed by Walt Disney Pictures, http://disney.com.

Fitzcarraldo (1982). Screenplay: Werner Herzog. Director: Werner Herzog. Running time: 158 mins. Color type: Color. Country: West Germany. Language: German. Distributed by Artificial Eye, http://www.artificial-eye.com.

The Floorwalker (1916). Screenplay: Charles Chaplin. Director: Charles Chaplin (uncredited). Running time: 24 mins. Color type: B&W. Country: USA. Language: Silent (English intertitles). Distributed by Image Entertainment Inc., http://www.image-entertainment.com/.

Filmography

Freaks (1932). Screenplay: Clarence Aaron "Tod" Robbins. Director: Tod Browning. Running time: 64 mins. Color type: B&W. Country: USA. Language: English. Distributed by Warner Home Video, http://www.wbshop.com.

Der Himmel über Berlin/Wings of Desire (1987). Screenplay: Wim Wenders and Peter Handke. Director: Wim Wenders. Running time: 128 mins. Color type: B&W/Color. Country: West Germany, France. Language: German, French, English (English subtitles). Distributed by the Criterion Collection, http://www.criterion.com/.

Jodaeiye Nader az Simin/A Separation (2011). Screenplay: Asghar Farhadi. Director: Asghar Farhadi. Running time: 123 mins. Color type: Color. Country: Iran. Language: Farsi. Distributed by Sony Pictures Classics, http://www.sonyclassics.com.

Kárhozat/Damnation (1988). Screenplay: Lazlo Krasznahorkai and Béla Tarr. Director: Béla Tarr. Running time: 120 mins. Color type: B&W. Country: Hungary. Language: Hungarian. Distributed by Artificial Eye, http://www.artificial-eye.com.

The Lion King (1994). Screenplay: Irene Mecchi, Jonathan Roberts and Linda Woolverton. Directors: Roger Allers and Rob Minkoff. Running time: 89 mins. Color type: Color. Country: USA. Language: English. Distributed by Walt Disney Pictures, http://disney.com.

Luci del varietà / Variety Lights (1950). Screenplay: Federico Fellini, Alberto Lattuada and Tullio Pinelli. Directors: Federico Fellini and Albert Lattuada. Running time: 97 mins. Color type: B&W. Country: Italy. Language: Italian. Distributed by the Criterion Collection, http://www.criterion.com.

El maquinista/The Machinist (2004). Screenplay: Scott Kosar. Director: Brad Anderson. Running time: 101 mins. Color type: Color. Country: Spain. Language: English. Distributed by Tartan Video, http://www.palisadestartan.com.

On the Waterfront (1954). Screenplay: Budd Schulberg. Director: Elia Kazan. Running time: 108 mins. Color type: B&W. Country: USA. Language: English. Distributed by Sony Pictures Home Entertainment, http://www.sonypictures.com/.

Pi (1998). Screenplay: Darren Aronofsky. Director: Darren Aronofsky. Running time: 84 mins. Color type: B&W. Country: USA. Language: English. Distributed by Pathé/Live Entertainment, http://www.pathe.co.uk.

Polse Smerti / After Death (1915). Screenplay: Evgeni Bauer. Director: Evgeni Bauer. Running time: 46 mins. Color type: B&W. Country: Russia. Language: Silent. Distributed by Image Entertainment Inc./Milestone Films, http://www.image-entertainment.com, http://www.milestonefilms.com/.

Filmography

Simón del desierto/Simon of the Desert (1965). Screenplay: Luis Buñuel and Julio Alejandro. Director: Luis Bunuel. Running time: 43 mins. Color type: B&W. Country: Mexico. Language: Spanish. Distributed by the Criterion Collection, http://www.criterion.com.

Star Wars: Episode IV—A New Hope (1977). Screenplay: George Lucas. Director: George Lucas. Running time: 121 mins. Color type: Color. Country: USA. Language: English. Distributed by 20th Century Fox Home Entertainment, http://www.foxconnect.com.

Sumerki zhenskoi dushi / Twilight of a Woman's Soul (1913). Screenplay: V. Demert. Director: Evgeni Bauer. Running time: 48 mins. Color type: B&W. Country: Russia. Language: Silent. Distributed by Image Entertainment Inc./Milestone Films, http://www.image-entertainment.com, http://www.milestonefilms.com/.

Sunset Blvd. (1950). Screenplay: Charles Brackett, Billy Wilder and D.M. Marshman Jr. Director: Billy Wilder. Running time: 110 mins. Color type: B&W. Country: USA. Language: English. Distributed by Paramount Pictures, http://www.paramountmovies.com.

Svält/Sult/Hunger (1966). Screenplay: Peter Seeberg and Henning Carlsen. Director: Henning Carlsen. Running time: 112 mins. Color type: B&W. Country: Denmark, Norway, Sweden. Language: Danish, Norwegian, Swedish. Distributed by Project X Distribution, http://www.projectxdistribution.com.

Tanin no kao/The Face of Another (1966). Screenplay: Kobo Abe. Director: Hiroshi Teshigahara. Running time: 124 mins. Color type: B&W. Country: Japan. Language: Japanese. Distributed by the Criterion Collection, http://www.criterion.com.

Taxi Driver (1976). Screenplay: Paul Schrader. Director: Martin Scorsese. Running time: 113 mins. Color type: Color. Country: USA. Language: English. Distributed by Columbia TriStar Home Video, http://www.sonypictures.com.

Toy Story (1995). Screenplay: Joss Whedon, Andrew Stanton, et al. Director: John Lasseter. Running time: 81 mins. Color type: Color. Country: USA. Language: English. Distributed by Disney/Pixar, http://www.pixar.com.

Ucho/The Ear (1970). Screenplay: Jan Procházka and Karel Kachyňa. Director: Karel Kachyňa. Running time: 94 mins. Color type: B&W. Country: Czechoslovakia. Language: Czech. Distributed by Second Run DVD, http://secondrundvd.com.

Umirayushchii lebed /The Dying Swan (1917). Screenplay: Zoya Barantsevich. Director: Evgeni Bauer. Running time: 49 mins. Color type: B&W. Country: Russia.

Filmography

Language: Silent. Distributed by Image Entertainment Inc./Milestone Films, http://www.image-entertainment.com, http://www.milestonefilms.com/.

The Vagabond (1916). Screenplay: Charles Chaplin. Director: Charles Chaplin (uncredited). Running time: 26 mins. Color type: B&W. Country: USA. Language: Silent (English intertitles). Distributed by Image Entertainment Inc., http://www.image-entertainment.com/.

Zoolander (2001). Screenplay: Drake Sather, Ben Stiller and John Hamburg. Director: Ben Stiller. Running time: 89 mins. Color type: Color. Country: USA. Language: English. Distributed by Paramount Pictures, http://www.paramount.com.

Chapter Notes

Preface

1. Lucius, in Thomas Taylor's translation of Apuleius' asinine adventure, is transformed into a "complete ass" in book III of *The Metamorphosis* (Second Century A.D.). "But I, though I was a complete ass, and, instead of Lucius, a labouring beast, yet retained human sense." Apuleius, *The Metamorphosis, or Golden Ass*, trans. Thomas Taylor (London: Triphook & Rodd, 1893), p. 48.
2. Blake Synder, *Save The Cat! The Last Book on Screenwriting You'll Ever Need* (Studio City, CA: Michael Wiese, 2005), p. 122.
3. Linda Seger, *Creating Unforgettable Characters: A Practical Guide to Character Development* (New York: Henry Holt, 1990), p. 170.
4. Herbert Marcuse, *The Aesthetic Dimension: Toward a Critique of Marxist Aesthetics*, trans. Herbert Marcuse and Erica Sherover (Boston: Beacon, 1978), p. 16.

Introduction

1. John Donne, *The Variorum Edition of the Poetry of John Donne*, vol. 7, eds. Gary A. Stringer and Paul A. Parish (Bloomington: Indiana University Press, 2005), p. 20.
2. William Shakespeare, "Richard II" in *Shakespeare: The Complete Works*, ed. W.J. Craig (London: Oxford University Press, 1966), p. 398.
3. John Neville Figgis, *The Divine Right of Kings* (Cambridge: Cambridge University Press, 1922), p. 67.
4. Sigmund Freud, *Civilization and Its Discontents*, trans. David McLintock (London: Penguin, 2004), p. 100.

1.1

1. Plato, "Republic, Bk. VII, 534e" in *Complete Works*, eds. John M. Cooper and D.S. Hutchinson (Indianapolis: Hackett, 1997), p. 1150.
2. See *The Bhagavad Gita*, which contains countless expression of dialectic, opposites in unity that conflict with standard logic: "For all things born in truth must die, and out of death in truth comes life" and "Prepare for war with peace in thy soul." *The Bhagavad Gita*, trans. Juan Mascaró (London: Penguin, 2003), p. 12. Similarly the Upaniṣads contain such dialectical expressions as, "The unreal is death, and the real is immortality," and "In the beginning this world was simply what is non-existing; and what is existing was that." *Upaniṣads*, trans. Patrick Olivelle (Oxford: Oxford University Press, 1998), pp. 13, 127. In the *Tao Te Ching*, we find these expressions: "Being and Not-being grow out of one another; Difficult and easy complete one another," and "the Sage relies on actionless activity." *Tao Te Ching*, trans. Arthur Waley (Hertfordshire: Wordsworth, 1997), p. 2.
3. Plato, *Complete Works*, "Republic, 440e," p. 1071.
4. Ibid., 440b.
5. Ovid, *Metamorphoses*, Bk. VII, trans. Nahum Tate, ed. Sir Samuel Garth (Hertfordshire: Wordsworth, 1998), p. 203.
6. Ovid, *Metamorphoses*, Bk. VII, trans. Horace Gregory (New York: New American Library, 1960), p. 187.
7. Romans 7: 14–25.
8. Matthew 26: 41. See also Mark 14: 38.
9. Shakespeare, *Complete Works*, p. 886.
10. Freud, *Discontents*, p. 100.

Chapter Notes

1.2

1. Joseph Campbell, *The Masks of God: Primitive Mythology* (Harmondsworth: Penguin, 1987), p. 147.
2. Ibid., p. 146. We might add that the word copulation itself can be understood etymologically as an example of dialectic. It derives from the Latin *copulare* meaning to "fasten together," "join," "couple," and in a figurative sense to "unite opposing elements." Thus the sacred copulation of a king and queen is both ritually and symbolically dialectical.
3. The word sublation was coined to translate the German Aufheben, which can mean "to cancel" as well as "to preserve." The double meaning of the word was used by G.W.F. Hegel to describe the dialectical process of negation of negation that leads to synthesis.
4. David A. Leemings, introduction to *Creation Myths of the World: An Encyclopaedia*, 2d ed. (Santa Barbara, CA: ABC-CLIO, 2010), p. xviii.
5. Carl Gustav Jung, *The Essential Jung: Selected Writings*, ed. Anthony Storr (London: HarperCollins, 1998), p. 70.
6. Henri Frankfort, et al. *Before Philosophy: The Intellectual Adventure of Ancient Man* (New York: Penguin, 1974), p. 15.
7. Ibid., p. 13. The dialectical philosophy of I and Thou was developed by Austrian philosopher Martin Buber in his book *Ich und Du* (1923), translated from German into English as *I and Thou* (1937).
8. Ibid., p. 54.
9. Ibid., pp. 184–186.
10. Ibid., pp. 192–195.
11. *Epic of Gilgamesh*, trans. Andrew George (Harmondsworth: Penguin, 1999), p. 87.

1.3

1. John Burnet, *Early Greek Philosophy*, 3d ed. (London: A&C Black, 1920), p. 7.
2. Aristotle, "Metaphysics" 983b, in *The Basic Works of Aristotle*, ed. Richard McKeon, trans. W.D. Ross (New York: Modern Library, 2001), p. 694.
3. G.S Kirk and J.E. Raven, *The Presocratic Philosophers: A Critical History with a Selection of Texts* (Cambridge: Cambridge University Press, 1982), p. 119.
4. Aristotle, "Physics" 239b—240a in *Basic Works*, pp. 335, 336.
5. Burnet, *Early Greek Philosophy*, p. 100.
6. Ibid., pp. 99—105.
7. Kirk and Raven, *Presocratic Philosophers*, p. 326.
8. Ibid., p. 327.
9. Aristotle, "Metaphysics" 985b in *Basic Works*, p. 697.
10. Victor J. Stenger, *God and the Atom—From Democritus to the Higgs Boson* (Amherst, NY: Prometheus, 2013), p. 17.

1.4

1. Plato, *Complete Works*, "Republic" VII, 534e, p. 1150.
2. Ibid., "Phaedo" 59b, p. 51.
3. Ibid., 60b, p. 52.
4. Ibid., 60c, p. 52.
5. Ibid., "Sophist" 250e, p. 273.
6. Ibid., 241d, p. 262.
7. Ibid., "Symposium" 191b, p. 474. *Ff.*
8. Ibid., 193a, p. 476.

1.5

1. Romans 7: 14—24.
2. Galatians 5: 17.
3. Matthew Henry, *An Exposition of the Old and New Testaments*, vol. III. (London: Joseph Ogle Robinson, 1828), p. 1114.
4. 2 Corinthians 10: 3,4.
5. Romans 8: 6, 7.
6. Ibid., vss. 10–16.
7. 1 Peter 3: 18.
8. Ibid., 4: 6.

1.6

1. *The Gospel of Philip*, trans. R. McL. Wilson (London: A.R. Mowbray, 1962), p. 29.
2. Arthur G. Mackey, *The Symbolism of Freemasonry: Illustrating and Explaining Its Science and Philosophy, Its Legends, Myths and Symbols* (1882), pp. 84–87.

1.7

1. Philip Schaff, *Ante-Nicene Fathers, Vol. I: The Apostolic Fathers with Justin Martyr and*

Chapter Notes

Irenaeus, trans. Philip Schaff, eds. Rev. Alexander Roberts and James Donaldson (Grand Rapids, MI: Christian Classics Ethereal Library, 2010), p. 314.

2. Philip Schaff, *Ante-Nicene Fathers, Vol. II: Fathers of the Second Century: Hermias to Clement of Alexandria*, trans. Philip Schaff, eds. Rev. Alexander Roberts and James Donaldson (Grand Rapids, MI: Christian Classics Ethereal Library, 2010), p.182.

3. Matthew 10: 39.

4. Schaff, *Ante-Nicene Fathers, Vol. II.*, p. 601.

5. Philip Schaff, *Ante-Nicene Fathers, Vol. III: Latin Christianity: Its Founder, Tertullian by Tertullian*, trans. Philip Schaff, ed. Allan Menzies (Grand Rapids, MI: Christian Classics Ethereal Library, 2006), pp. 79, 80.

6. Ibid., p. 459.

7. Philip Schaff, *Ante-Nicene Fathers Vol. IV: Fathers of the Third Century: Tertullian Part Fourth; Minucius Felix; Commodianus; Origen, Parts First and Second*, trans. Philip Schaff (Grand Rapids, MI: Christian Classics Ethereal Library, 2006), p. 1014.

8. Ibid., pp. 424, 425.

9. Philip Schaff, *Ante-Nicene Fathers Vol. V: Fathers of the Third Century: Hippolytus; Cyprian; Caius; Novatian*, trans. Philip Schaff, eds. Rev. Alexander Roberts and James Donaldson (Grand Rapids, MI: Christian Classics Ethereal Library, 2004), pp. 1073, 1074.

1.8

1. Saint Augustine, *The City of God*, trans. Marcus Dods (New York: Modern Library, 1950), p. 362.

2. Ibid., p. 361.

3. Ibid., p. 677.

4. Ibid., p. 709.

5. Bertrand Russell, "Introduction" to *History of Western Philosophy* (London: Routledge, 1991), p. 16.

6. See Acts 5: 29.

7. For the curious reader who wishes to inquire into Mediaeval dialectic we suggest Johannes Scotus (c. 815—c. 877), who wrote *De Divisione Naturæ*, in which he posited that Nature is the totality of all things *which are* and all things *which are not*—thus Scotus postulated reality as a dialectical unity of opposites, the existing and the non-existing. Remigius of Auxerre (c. 841—908), famously stated "homo est multorum hominum substantialis unitas," which means "Man is the substantial unity of many men." This dialectical expression combines the opposites of universal and particular—Man (with a capital M) and man. Remigius believed that the substance of the one universal man, Adam, is the substance of every individual man comprising the entire human race. Remigius was a Benedictine monk and believed that Adam was the first man and father of all men, and so in Adam we are all united and connected to the universal aspect of the Adamic. After Remigius appeared Berengarius (999—1088) who stated, "Recourse to dialectic is recourse to reason." And Pierre Abelard (1079—1142), wrote, "I preferred the weapons of dialectic to all other philosophies," and later wrote a philosophical work of dialectic, *Sic et non*, which means *Yes and No*—a unity of opposites.

1.9

1. René Descartes, *Meditations on First Philosophy: With Selections from the Objections and Replies*, trans. Michael Moriarty (Oxford: Oxford University Press, 2008), p. 60.

2. Ibid., p. 61.

3. Ibid., p. 11.

4. Ibid., pp. 32, 33.

5. René Descartes, *Key Philosophical Writings*, trans. Elizabeth S. Haldane and G.R.T. Ross, ed. Enrique Chávez-Arvizo (Hertfordshire: Wordsworth, 1997), p. 279.

1.10

1. Blaise Pascal, *Pensées*, trans. A.J. Krailsheimer (Harmondsworth: Penguin, 1966), p. 151.

2. Ibid., p. 146.

3. Ibid., p. 36.

4. Ibid., p. 235.

5. Ibid., p. 81.

6. Ibid., p. 65. This idea of man's "dual condition" is glorified in the stories of Dr. Frankenstein and his created *outer* monster, and again with Dr. Jekyll and his *inner* monster Hyde; and notably in the writings of E.T.A. Hoffmann and Fyodor Dostoyevsky.

1.11

1. Immanuel Kant, *Critique of Pure Reason*, trans. J.M.D. Meiklejohn (London: J.M. Dent & Sons, 1945), p. 25.
2. Ibid., p. 26.
3. Ibid., p. 260. Compare to the O.E.D. definition of antinomy, "a contradiction between two beliefs or conclusions that are in themselves reasonable; a paradox." In other words, dialectic.
4. Ibid., pp. 264—281.
5. Ibid., p. 257.

1.12

1. G.W.F. Hegel, *Phenomenology of Spirit*, trans. A.V. Miller (Oxford: Oxford University Press, 1977), p. 115.
2. G.W.F. Hegel, *The Encyclopaedia Logic (with the Zusätze)*, trans. Théodore F. Geraets, et al. (Indianapolis: Hackett, 1991), p. 35.
3. Thomas Hobbes wrote something similar under the heading of "Deliberation" in the *Leviathan*, 1651: "In the mind of man, appetites, and aversions, hopes, and fears, concerning one and the same thing, arise alternately ... that we call DELIBERATION."
4. Hegel, *Logic*, p. 129.
5. Ibid.
6. Ibid., p. 130.
7. Ibid.
8. Ibid.
9. G.W.F. Hegel, *The Science of Logic*, trans. George di Giovanni (Cambridge: Cambridge University Press, 2010), pp. 81, 82. In a similar way the English word cleave can mean to sever or separate (like a meat cleaver or cleavage) and at the same time it can mean to cling to, hold on tight (like to cleave to one's lover or an idea, etc.).
10. G.W.F. Hegel, "Introduction" to *The Philosophical Propaedeutic*, trans. A.V. Miller (Oxford: Basil Blackwell, 1986), pp. xxv, xxvi.

1.13

1. Karl Marx and Frederick Engels, *Manifesto of the Communist Party*, ed. Frederick Engels (New York: International, 2007), p. 9.
2. Ibid.
3. Ibid.
4. Frederick Engels, "Dialectics of Nature" in *Karl Marx and Frederick Engels: Collected Works*, vol. 25 (New York: International, 1987), p. 356.
5. Zachariah Rush, *Beyond the Screenplay: A Dialectical Approach to Dramaturgy* (Jefferson, NC: McFarland, 2012), pp. 74—76.

1.14

1. Nietzsche, *Basic Writings*, p. 33.

1.15

1. Sigmund Freud, "The Origin and Development of Psychoanalysis—The Clark Lectures" in *Varieties of Personality Theory*, ed. Hendrik M. Ruitenbeek (New York: E.P. Dutton, 1964), p. 12.
2. Ibid., pp. 17, 18.
3. Ibid., p. 39.
4. Sigmund Freud, *Beyond the Pleasure Principle*, trans. and ed. James Strachey (New York: W.W. Norton, 1961), p.32.

1.16

1. C.G. Jung, *Aion: Researches into the Phenomenology of the Self*, trans. R.F.C. Hull (New York: Pantheon, 1959), p. 14.
2. Ibid., p. 17.
3. Ferdinand de Saussure, *Course in General Linguistics*, trans. Wade Baskin, eds. Charles Bally and Albert Reidlinger (New York: Philosophical Library, 1959), p. 67.
4. Simone de Beauvoir, *The Ethics of Ambiguity*, trans. Bernard Frechtman (New York: Citadel, 1976), p. 7. The translations from Latin are my own.
5. Ibid., p. 103.
6. Ibid., p. 105.
7. Simone de Beauvoir, *The Second Sex*, trans. H.M. Parshley (London: Picador, 1988), p. 223.
8. Ibid.
9. Bertell Ollman and Tony Smith, "Introduction" to *Dialectics for the New Century* (New York: Palgrave Macmillan, 2008), p. 4.
10. Ibid., p. 26.

11. Ibid., p. 87.
12. Ibid.

2.1

1. Aristotle, "Poetics" 1450a, in *Basic Works*, p. 1461.
2. See Rush, *Beyond the Screenplay*, pp. 93–98.
3. Asher Garfinkel, *Screenplay Story Analysis: The Art and Business* (New York: Allworth, 2007), p. 23.
4. Ibid., 24.
5. Joseph Campbell, *The Hero With a Thousand Faces* (Princeton: Princeton University Press, 2004), p. 28.
6. Ibid., pp. 45—47.
7. Ibid., p. 37.

2.2

1. Matthew 16: 25.
2. Shakespeare, *Complete Works*, p. 106.

2.4

1. Jorge Luis Borges, *The Total Library: Non-Fiction 1922—1986*, ed. Eliot Weinberger (London: Penguin, 1999), p. 259.

2.6

1. Matthew 6:22—24.

2.7

1. Numbers 22: 20—31.
2. Zachariah 9:9 and Matthew 21: 1–9.

Conclusion

1. John Milton, *The Annotated Milton*, ed. Burton Raffel (New York: Bantam, 1999), p. 753.

Bibliography

Apuleius. *The Metamorphosis, or Golden Ass.* Translated by Thomas Taylor. London: Triphook & Rodd, 1893.

Aristotle. *The Basic Works of Aristotle.* Edited by Richard McKeon. New York: Modern Library, 2001.

Augustine, Saint. *The City of God.* Translated by Marcus Dods. New York: Modern Library, 1950.

Beauvoir, Simone de. *The Ethics of Ambiguity.* Translated by Bernard Frechtman. New York: Citadel, 1976.

_____. *The Second Sex.* Translated by H.M. Parshley. London: Picador, 1988.

Borges, Jorge Luis. *The Total Library: Non-Fiction 1922–1986.* Edited by Eliot Weinberger. London: Penguin, 1999.

Burnet, John. *Early Greek Philosophy*, 3d ed. London: A&C Black, 1920.

Campbell, Joseph. *The Masks of God: Primitive Mythology.* Harmondsworth: Penguin, 1987.

Descartes, René. *Key Philosophical Writings.* Translated by Elizabeth S. Haldane and G.R.T. Ross. Edited by Enrique Chávez-Arvizo. Hertfordshire: Wordsworth, 1997.

_____. *Meditations on First Philosophy: With Selections from the Objections and Replies.* Translated by Michael Moriarty. Oxford: Oxford University Press, 2008.

Donne, John. *The Variorum Edition of the Poetry of John Donne*, vol. 7. Edited by Gary A. Stringer and Paul A. Parish. Bloomington: Indiana University Press, 2005.

Epic of Gilgamesh. Translated by Andrew George. Harmondsworth: Penguin, 1999.

Figgis, J. N. *The Divine Right of Kings.* Cambridge: Cambridge University Press, 1922.

Frankfort, Henri, et al. *Before Philosophy: The Intellectual Adventure of Ancient Man.* New York: Penguin, 1974.

Freud, Sigmund. *Beyond the Pleasure Principle.* Translated and edited by James Strachey. New York: W.W. Norton, 1961.

_____. *Civilization and Its Discontents.* Translated by David McLintock. London: Penguin, 2004.

Garfinkel, Asher. *Screenplay Story Analysis: The Art and Business.* New York: Allworth, 2007.

The Gospel of Philip. Translated by R. McL. Wilson. London: A.R. Mowbray, 1962.

Hegel, G.W.F. *The Encyclopaedia Logic (with the Zusätze).* Translated by Théodore F. Geraets, et al. Indianapolis: Hackett, 1991.

_____. *Phenomenology of Spirit.* Translated by A.V. Miller. Oxford: Oxford University Press, 1977.

_____. *The Philosophical Propaedeutic.* Translated by A.V. Miller. Oxford: Basil Blackwell, 1986.

_____. *The Science of Logic.* Translated by George di Giovanni. Cambridge: Cambridge University Press, 2010.

Henry, Matthew. *An Exposition of the Old and New Testaments*, vol. III. London: Joseph Ogle Robinson, 1828.

Jung, C.G. *Aion: Researches into the Phenomenology of the Self.* Translated by R.F.C. Hull. New York: Pantheon, 1959.

_____. *The Essential Jung: Selected Writings.* Edited by Anthony Storr. London: HarperCollins, 1998.

Kant, Immanuel. *Critique of Pure Reason.* Translated by J.M.D. Meiklejohn. London: J.M. Dent & Sons, 1945.

Kirk, G.S., and J.E. Raven. *The Presocratic Philosophers: A Critical History with a Selec-*

Bibliography

tion of Texts. Cambridge: Cambridge University Press, 1982.

Leemings, David A. *Creation Myths of the World: An Encyclopaedia*, 2d ed. Santa Barbara: ABC-CLIO, 2010.

Marcuse, Herbert. *The Aesthetic Dimension: Toward a Critique of Marxist Aesthetics*. Translated by Herbert Marcuse and Erica Sherover. Boston: Beacon, 1978.

Marx, Karl, and Frederick Engels. *Collected Works*, vol. 25. New York: International, 1987.

_____ and _____. *Manifesto of the Communist Party*. Edited by Frederick Engels. New York: International, 2007.

Nietzsche, Friedrich. *Basic Writings of Nietzsche*. Translated by Walter Kaufmann. New York: Modern Library, 2000.

Ollman, Bertell, and Tony Smith. *Dialectics for the New Century*. Edited by Bertell Ollman and Toby Smith. New York: Palgrave Macmillan, 2008.

Ovid. *Metamorphoses*. Translated by John Dryden, et al. Edited by Sir Samuel Garth. Hertfordshire: Wordsworth, 1998.

_____. *Metamorphoses*. Translated by Horace Gregory. New York: New American Library, 1960.

Pascal, Blaise. *Pensées*. Translated by A.J. Krailsheimer. Harmondsworth: Penguin, 1966.

Plato. *Complete Works*. Edited by John M. Cooper and D.S. Hutchinson. Indianapolis: Hackett, 1997.

Rush, Zachariah. *Beyond the Screenplay: A Dialectical Approach to Dramaturgy*. Jefferson, NC: McFarland, 2012.

Russell, Bertrand. *History of Western Philosophy*. London: Routledge, 1991.

Saussure, Ferdinand de. *Course in General Linguistics*. Translated by Wade Baskin. Edited by Charles Bally and Albert Reidlinger. New York: Philosophical Library, 1959.

Schaff, Philip. *Ante-Nicene Fathers, Vol. I: The Apostolic Fathers with Justin Martyr and Irenaeus*. Translated by Philip Schaff. Edited by Alexander Roberts and James Donaldson. Grand Rapids, MI: Christian Classics Ethereal Library, 2010.

_____. *Ante-Nicene Fathers, Vol. II: Fathers of the Second Century: Hermias to Clement of Alexandria*. Translated by Philip Schaff. Edited by Alexander Roberts and James Donaldson. Grand Rapids, MI: Christian Classics Ethereal Library, 2010.

_____. *Ante-Nicene Fathers, Vol. III: Latin Christianity: Its Founder, Tertullian by Tertullian*. Translated by Philip Schaff. Edited by Allan Menzies. Grand Rapids, MI: Christian Classics Ethereal Library, 2006.

_____. *Ante-Nicene Fathers, Vol. IV: Fathers of the Third Century: Tertullian, Part Fourth; Minucius Felix; Commodianus; Origen, Parts First and Second*. Translated by Philip Schaff. Grand Rapids, MI: Christian Classics Ethereal Library, 2006.

_____. *Ante-Nicene Fathers, Vol. V: Fathers of the Third Century: Hippolytus; Cyprian; Caius; Novatian*. Translated by Philip Schaff. Edited by Alexander Roberts and James Donaldson. Grand Rapids, MI: Christian Classics Ethereal Library, 2004.

Seger, Linda. *Creating Unforgettable Characters: A Practical Guide to Character Development*. New York: Henry Holt, 1990.

Shakespeare, William. *Shakespeare: The Complete Works*. Edited by W.J. Craig. London: Oxford University Press, 1966.

Snyder, Blake. *Save the Cat! The Last Book on Screenwriting You'll Ever Need*. Studio City, CA: Michael Wiese, 2005.

Stenger, Victor, J. *God and the Atom: From Democritus to the Higgs Boson*. Amherst, NY: Prometheus, 2013.

Varieties of Personality Theory. Edited by Hendrik M. Ruitenbeek. New York: E.P. Dutton, 1964.

Index

a posteriori/a priori 65, 66; *see also* unity of opposites
Absolute 25, 71; *see also* Hegel
accipitine/columbine 118; *see also* unity of opposites
Adamic sin: dialectic of 162, 163
aera 27
Aeschylus 75
Aesop 107
An Affair to Remember (1957) 39
After Death (1915) 103–106
agony 5, 13, 15, 16, 53, 56, 57, 90, 99, 103, 125, 128, 139, 144, 173, 182, 183; cinema of 180–183
Albert Emmanuel Vogler (character) 93, 126–128
alterity 99, 115
Anaxagoras 24
Anaximander 11, 24–27, 55
Anaximenes 27
Andersen, Hans Christian 14
Andrei Bagrov (character) 103–106
angst 149
anima/animus 81; *see also* unity of opposites
animate/inanimate 51; *see also* unity of opposites
Anna (character) 146–148
antagonist/protagonist 73, 75, 78, 182
Antigone (character) 58
Antinomies 66, 68; *see also* Kant, Immanuel
antithesis/thesis 25, 56, 61, 66, 67, 80, 82, 97, 103, 105, 118, 128, 170, 174; *see also* synthesis
Anunnaki 22
apeiron 26, 27, 34
Apollonian/Dionysian 75–78
appearance/reality 53, 128; *see also* unity of opposites
April (1961) 129–131

April Lovers (characters) 129–131
arche 25
Aristophanes 38, 39; (dialectic of) 103, 130
Aristotle 1, 25–35, 40, 71, 89–91, 107, 181; *Physics* 28, 29; *Poetics* 91, 82, 181
atom/void 32, 34, 85; *see also* unity of opposites
atomists 32–34, 51
Au hasard Balthazar (1966) 139–142
aufheben 69–74; *see also* sublation
Avatar (2009) 181

Baudelaire, Charles 149
Bauer, Evgeni 93
beauty/ugliness 111, 132, 133, 143–145, 174, 181; *see also* unity of opposites
Beauvoir, Simone de 82, 83; *La Deuxième sexe* 83; *The Ethics of Ambiguity* 82
being/non-being (nothingness) 27, 32, 37, 39, 168, 176; *see also* unity of opposites
black/white 46, 73, 94, 133; *see also* unity of opposites
body/mind 59–61; *see also* unity of opposites
bondsman/lord 67, 72; *see also* Hegel; master/slave
Borges, Jorge Luis 114
Breakfast at Tiffany's (1961) 39
Brian Sweeny Fitzgerald (character) 154–156
Buridan's Ass 179
Burnet, John 24, 25; *Early Greek Philosophy* 24
Buzz Lightyear (character) 166–169

Campbell, Joseph 19, 91–93; *The Hero with a Thousand Faces* 91, 92
Chaplin, Charles 93, 96, 99
Character: Aristotle's treatment 89, 90, 181; definition 89; dialectic 1, 2, 4, 7, 20,

Index

52, 79, 84, 85, 90, 91, 92, 94, 180; as ethos 91; as tridimensional 89, 182; *see also* dramatic being
character arc 91
Charles Foster Kane (character) 112–116, 181
Checco Dal Monte (character) 120–122
Christ 41–43, 49, 119, 138, 141; *see also* Jesus
Christianity (dialectic of) 16, 40, 44, 48–58
Church Fathers 48–50
Cinderella (character) 14, 83, 113
Citizen Kane (1942) 112–116
Clement of Alexandria 50, 52; *Stromata* 50
Cléo (character) 131–133, 181
Cléo from 5 to 7 (1962) 131–133, 181
Cleopatra (character) 109–112
collective unconscious 20, 66, 81; *see also* Jung, Carl Gustav
conflict: as dialectic 3–5, 14, 16, 19, 21, 22, 37, 39, 43, 45, 47, 52, 62, 63, 72–78, 82, 90, 99, 133, 171, 183; as drama 90, 96, 99, 180, 181, 183
conscious/unconscious 77, 78, 92, 132, 168; *see also* unity of opposites
contradiction 12, 29, 35, 63, 66, 67, 136, 150
cosmogony (dialectical) 18, 21, 46
cosmology (dialectical) 26, 31

Damiel (character) 93, 156–159, 181
darkness/light 21, 44–47, 51, 60, 61, 128, 130, 131, 143, 158, 180; *see also* unity of opposites
death instinct 79
death/life 16, 21, 22, 26, 37, 38, 82, 90, 105, 107, 108, 118, 132, 133, 135, 150, 153, 158, 163, 169, 171, 182; *see also* unity of opposites
DeMille, Cecil B. 123–126
Democritus 32, 33, 51
Derek Zoolander (character) 173, 174
Descartes, René 59–62; *Meditations on First Philosophy* 59, 60; *Principles of Philosophy* 61
dialectical materialism 71
Dialectics for a New Century 83
different/same 29, 37, 39, 93, 100, 112, 142, 144; *see also* unity of opposites
Diogenes Lærtius 25, 30
Donne, John 3, 4, 16, 42, 60
Dostoyevsky 175, 176; *The Idiot* 176

dramatic being 1, 4, 5, 11, 13, 89, 90, 93, 116, 118, 157–159, 180–182; *see also* character
dreams/reality 121, 122, 142, 156
The Dying Swan (1917) 106–108

The Ear (1970) 146–148
Edward (character) 160–162, 181
Edward Scissorhands (1990) 160–162
Empedocles 30–34, 37, 53, 54, 56, 63, 67, 71, 78, 79, 81, 82, 90, 182, 183; *see also* love/strife
The Emperor's New Groove (2000) 93, 169–172
Engels, Friedrich 50, 63, 71–73; *Communist Manifesto* 71; *Dialectics of Nature* 72
ennui 149, 150 158
Enuma elish 21, 22
Epic of Gilgamesh 22
eros/thanatos (*death*) 2, 16, 31, 78, 79, 82, 90, 93, 103, 105, 107, 108, 117, 122, 131, 132, 133, 139, 148, 150, 153, 158, 159, 163, 169, 171, 181, 182; *see also* unity of opposites
ethos: dialectic of 89, 90, 91, 180; *see also* character
evil/good 41–48, 50, 53, 56, 63, 121

Face of Another (1968) 142–145
Falk, Peter 157, 158
father/son 119, 152, 166, 174
Fichte, Johann Gottlieb 67
Figgis, John Neville 5
finite/infinite 28, 60, 61, 82, 125, 159
Finnegan's Wake 92
Fitzcarraldo (1982) 154–156
flesh/spirit 40, 41, 43, 57, 58, 61, 78, 138, 139, 158, 159, 182
The Floorwalker (1916) 98–100
Frankfort, H. 20
Frankfort, H.A. 20
Freaks (1932) 109–112
Freud, Sigmund 16, 31, 77–82, 92, 182; *Beyond the Pleasure Principle* 78, 79; *Civilization and Its Discontents* 16, 78, 79; *Psychopathology of Everyday Life* 92

Genesis (Bible) 18, 21, 164
Gibbons, Orlando 107
Gilgamesh (character) 4, 22, 169
Gizella (character) 106–108
Gnosticism 44–47
Gospel of Philip 44
Gregory, Horace 15

198

Index

Grimm Brothers 14, 92; *The Frog King* 92; *The Magic Mirror* 14

Hamlet (character) 16, 89, 105, 117, 149, 150, 165, 166, 182
Hegel, G.W.F. 11, 25, 37, 50, 55, 67–72, 79, 81, 150; *Logic of the Encyclopedia* 67; *Phenomenology of the Spirit* 67; *The Philosophical Propaedeutic* 70; *The Science of Logic* 69
Henry, Matthew 41, 42
Heraclitus 29–32, 34, 44, 48, 50, 64, 71, 79, 82, 83, 90, 91, 144, 158, 183
Hesiod 24, 26, 27
Hollywood 2, 6, 39, 93, 124, 126, 180, 181
Homer 3, 4, 24, 27
hubris 23, 115, 171
Hunger (1966) 134–136

Icarus 23, 167, 169
immaterial/material 12, 18, 26, 59, 61, 157

Jason 14, 15
Jaws (1975) 37
Jesus 16, 37, 42, 130, 137, 138, 139, 150
Jonah 171
Joyce, James 4, 92
Jung, Carl Gustav 2, 20, 80, 81; *Aion: Researches Into the Phenomenology of the Self* 81
Jurassic Park (1993) 37
Justin Martyr 48, 49, 53; *First Apology* 48

Kant, Immanuel 28, 65, 66, 67, 68, 82; *Critique of Pure Reason* 65, 66
Kierkegaard, Søren 149
Kristofferson, Kris 149, 150
Kuzco 169–172

Laing, R.D. 83; *Self and Others* 83
Latin Vulgate 18
Leeming, David A. 19
Leontius (character) 12–16, 93
Leucippus 31, 32, 51
Levins, Richard 84; *Dialectics and System Theory* 84
The Lion King (1994) 93, 165, 166
logos 23, 116; *see also* mythos
love/hate 14, 78, 81, 90, 91, 107, 111, 130
love/strife 30, 31, 32, 34, 37, 53, 56, 63, 67, 71, 72, 78, 82, 90, 182, 183; *see also* unity of opposites
Luke Skywalker (character) 150–153

Macbeth (character) 165, 177
The Machinist (2004) 175–177
Mackey, Albert G. 45
The Magician (1958) 126–128
Marie (character) 139–142
Marx, Karl 20, 50, 58, 63, 70–72; *Communist Manifesto* 71
master/slave 61, 81; *see also* bondsman/lord
Maximilian "Max" Cohen (character) 163, 164
Medea 14, 15, 16, 41, 63, 117
Miller, A.V. 70
Milton, John 115, 157, 180; *Samson Agonistes* 180
Mr. Okuyama (character) 142–145, 181
monomyth 92, 93
Moses 21, 171
motion/rest (immotion) 28, 29, 35, 60, 61, 66
mythos 15, 20, 23, 24, 89, 90, 116, 180, 182; *see also* plot

Nader & Simin (characters) 177–179
nauseé 149
negation 27, 37, 49, 50, 60, 61, 69, 73, 74
Newton, Sir Isaac 23
Nietzsche, Friedrich 29, 75–79; *The Birth of Tragedy* 75
Norma Desmond (character) 122–126
Novatian 53

Oedipus (character) 73, 119, 178
On the Waterfront (1954) 116–119
ontology (of character) 89, 158, 183
opposites becoming opposites 49, 61, 68–70, 72, 83, 91, 110, 130, 133, 152, 153, 158, 163, 166, 169; *see also* unity of opposites
Origen 48, 52, 53; *Contra Celsum* 52; *De Principiius* 52
Ovid 14, 15, 107; *The Metamorphoses* 14

pain/pleasure 35, 36, 39, 69; *see also* unity of opposites
Pascal, Blaise 62–64; *Pensées* 62, 64
Paul (apostle) 40–43, 48, 52, 55, 57, 139, 182
Paul of Tarsus 16; *see also* Paul (apostle)
Perrault, Charles 14, 89
Peter (apostle) 43, 58
Pi (1998) 163, 164
Plato 11, 12, 13, 17, 28, 34–39, 49, 55, 61,

199

Index

68, 70, 71, 115, 127, 136, 153; *Phaedo* 35, 36, 39; *Republic* 12, 13 *Sophist* 36–38, 49; *Symposium* 38, 39
plot 20, 21, 23, 89–92, 99, 100, 150, 166, 176, 180, 181; *see also* mythos
Pontus (character) 93, 134–136, 181
presocratic philosophers 24, 25, 29–34, 45, 51, 53, 79, 81
psychoanalysis: as dialectical 16, 77, 79
Pythagoras 24, 46, 164

qualis/quantus 73, 90
qualitative change (of character) 26, 27, 52, 72, 90, 91, 98, 172
quantitative change (of character) 44, 72, 73, 97

Richard II (character) 4, 5
right/wrong 15, 16, 53, 116; *see also* unity of opposites

sacrifice (as dialectic) 36, 91, 97, 98, 119, 130, 139, 150, 153, 158, 163, 167
Saint Augustine 48, 55–58, 61, 63, 163; *Confession* 55, 57; *De Civitate Dei* 55–57
St. Jerome 18
Samson (character) 180
Sartre, Jean-Paul 83, 149; *Being and Nothingness* 83
Saussure, Ferdinand de 81, 82; *Cours de linguistique générale* 81
Seger, Linda 1
self/other 19, 21, 39, 67, 100, 112, 117, 144; *see also* unity of opposites
A Separation (2011) 177–179
Seve, Lucien 84; *Dialectics of Emergence* 84
sexual dialectic 19, 39, 83
Shakespeare, William 4–6, 16, 59, 78, 99, 107, 147, 149, 165; *King Richard II* 4, 5
signified/signifier 81, 82
Simba (character) 165, 166
Simón (character) 137–139
Simon of the Desert (1965) 137–139
Snyder, Blake 1
Socrates 12, 13, 24, 31, 34–39, 44
Sophocles 58, 73, 75, 91
spectacle (*contra* agonic cinema) 66, 181, 183

Star Wars IV: A New Hope (1976) 150–153
Stenger, Victor J. 32
sublation 19, 22, 50, 69, 70, 72, 74, 75
Sunset Blvd. (1950) 122–126
The Symbolism of Freemasonry 45
synthesis 15, 19, 22, 23, 25, 33, 39, 49, 61, 67, 71–75, 97, 107, 118, 122, 164

Tate, Nahum 14
Taxi Driver (1976) 148–150
Terry Malloy 93, 116–119, 181
Tertullian 50–52, 54
Thales 24–27
Theophilus of Antioch 49
Titanic (1997) 181
to be/not to be 16, 105, 117, 159; *see also* unity of opposites
Toy Story (1995) 93, 166–169
The Tramp (character) 93, 95–98, 181
transition 31, 49, 52, 82, 91, 98, 110, 152, 153; *see also* qualitative change
Travis Bickle 93, 148–150, 181
Trevor Reznik (character) 175–177, 181
Twilight of a Woman's Soul (1913) 101–103

unity of opposites (as dialectic) 4, 13, 14, 16, 18–23, 26, 29, 32, 33, 37, 39, 42, 44, 47, 49, 53, 59–62, 65, 71, 73, 78–84, 91, 93, 100, 105, 118, 126, 133, 158, 159, 180–183

The Vagabond (1916) 95–98
Variety Lights (1950) 120–122
Vera Dubovskaia (character) 101–103, 181

what is/what is not 27, 38, 115, 127, 142, 176; *see also* unity of opposites
Wings of Desire (1987) 156–159

Xenophanes 27, 28, 65

Yin/Yang 21, 81, 158
You've Got Mail (1998) 39

Zeno of Elea 28, 29, 35, 36, 49, 60, 66
Ziegfeld Girl (1941) 39
Zoolander (2001) 173, 174

www.ingramcontent.com/pod-product-compliance
Lightning Source LLC
Chambersburg PA
CBHW032059300426
44116CB00007B/805